Baseball's Offensive Greats of the Deadball Era

ALSO BY ROBERT E. KELLY
AND FROM MCFARLAND

*The National Debt of the United States,
1941 to 2008*, 2d. ed. (2008)

*Baseball for the Hot Stove League:
Fifteen Essays* (1989)

*Baseball's Best: Hall of Fame
Pretenders Active in the Eighties* (1988)

Baseball's Offensive Greats of the Deadball Era

Best Producers Rated by Position, 1901–1919

ROBERT E. KELLY

with a Foreword by Leonard Levin

McFarland & Company, Inc., Publishers
Jefferson, North Carolina, and London

LIBRARY OF CONGRESS CATALOGUING-IN-PUBLICATION DATA

Kelly, Robert E.
Baseball's offensive greats of the deadball era : best producers rated by position, 1901–1919 / Robert E. Kelly ; with a foreword by Leonard Levin.
p.   cm.

Includes bibliographical references and index.

ISBN 978-0-7864-4125-9
softcover : 50# alkaline paper ∞

1. Baseball players—United States—Biography.
2. Baseball players—Rating of—United States.
3. Baseball—Records—United States.
4. Baseball—Offense—United States—History.
I. Title.

GV865.A1K468   2009   796.357092—dc22 [B]   2009003852

British Library cataloguing data are available

©2009 Robert E. Kelly. All rights reserved

No part of this book may be reproduced or transmitted in any form or by any means, electronic or mechanical, including photocopying or recording, or by any information storage and retrieval system, without permission in writing from the publisher.

On the cover: Ty Cobb and Joe Jackson, Library of Congress; background ©2009 Shutterstock.

Manufactured in the United States of America

*McFarland & Company, Inc., Publishers
Box 611, Jefferson, North Carolina 28640
www.mcfarlandpub.com*

To Margaret, wife and soul mate.
And to the memory
of Bud Vidito, Red Zarnota and Dick Mills,
infield teammates of long ago,
and brother Jim, who put a ball in my hands.

Acknowledgments

This book could not have been produced without the editing assistance of my wife, Margaret Rodden Kelly, and the reams of information previously published about baseball players and baseball history.

And thanks to the computer, without which baseball historians would be crippled.

Table of Contents

Acknowledgments	vii
Foreword by Leonard Levin	1
Introduction	5
The World Beyond the Ballpark, 1901–1919	13
The World Within the Ballpark, 1901–1919	15
First Basemen — Analysis, 1901–1919	17
First Basemen — Summary in Domination Point (DP) Sequence	40
Catchers — Analysis, 1901–1919	42
Catchers — Summary in Domination Point (DP) Sequence	62
Infielders — Analysis, 1901–1919	64
Infielders — Summary in Domination Point (DP) Sequence	129
Outfielders — Analysis, 1901–1919	132
Outfielders — Summary in Domination Point (DP) Sequence	200
Summary, 1901–1919	203
Bibliography	207
Index	209

Foreword by Leonard Levin

If ever there was a match made in heaven, it's the marriage of baseball and statistics and, as in all happy marriages, each partner contributes its most valuable assets:

- Baseball, its sheer visual beauty, joy of competition, the thrill of bat meeting ball, ball meeting glove, pregnant pauses that culminate in seconds of excitement and agony. As the eminent philosopher–baseball fan Morris R. Cohen put it, an "extraordinarily rich multiplicity of movements."
- Statistics and their pliability as an analytical tool. Through the manipulation of them, we can tell who are the premier performers in this game that so enchants us with its speed, powerful grace and symmetry.

Like some marriages, this is a May-December affair. Baseball's pedigree goes back to prehistory. Adults and children probably have been whacking round objects with sticks since they could stand erect. But compared to the game itself, the science of wielding statistics to measure the achievements of baseball players is a relative newborn.

Back when organized baseball itself was an infant, the statistics were confined largely to scores of games and the league standings. Henry Chadwick, the pioneer twentieth-century sportswriter and Hall of Fame member, could write a five-hundred-word newspaper article about a Brooklyn Atlantics game without using any numbers other than the final score and the approximate attendance. A.G. Spalding's baseball guides, ghostwritten by Chadwick, usually disposed of the National League's batting and fielding averages quickly — seven pages of the 162-page Spalding Guide for 1886 were considered sufficient to summarize the previous season's individual statistics.

In those simpler pencil-and-paper days, and into the first half of the twentieth century, record-keeping in baseball was hit-or-miss, as any researcher of the game in the pre–1920s era will tell you. It was a simple matter of what was considered important. In the deadball era, for example, runs didn't come in great batches aided by fence-clearing blasts. They had to be "manufactured," from such things as singles and stolen bases and errors and sacrifice hits. So in the assessment of a player's ability, his runs scored was as much valued as the achievement of the player who drove him home. (So highly rated was the achievement of the player who scored the run that runs-batted-in statistics weren't kept until 1920; those you see today for periods before that were compiled retroactively.)

Then came Babe Ruth and the live-ball era with its emphasis on big numbers: hits, home runs, RBIs. Gradually the ability of statistics to determine the best performers at our national game came to be recognized.

And later came the computer. Now, almost four decades into that revolution, statistics mavens crunch numbers with the vigor of rookies in spring training. Like home-run power, the computer's calculating power transformed all parts of our lives in the second half of the twentieth century, including a facet that's probably important to you if you're reading this book: the way we judge the performance of baseball players.

Of all sports, baseball is the easiest to quantify. You can learn more about last night's baseball game by looking at a box score than you can learn about last Sunday's football game by studying the newspaper summary. The subtleties of the batter against pitcher, fielder against batter,

batter against ballpark, have the uncanny ability to expose themselves to your view in that collection of numbers squeezed into a daily sports page column. And over the long haul, the computer can translate that diamond action into numbers that can be manipulated, placed side by side, examined in almost limitless contexts, all with the aim of determining who are the best batters, pitchers, fielders, who are the most valuable players of today, of yesterday, of all time.

But the road to baseball Valhalla can be filled with potholes. Computers speak in many languages that don't always agree on how we should judge which players and which teams are the best. Computer professionals and amateurs who love the diamond game have taken the statistics beyond batting, pitching, and fielding averages and have developed countless formulas by which to judge the accomplishments of baseball players.

Many members of the Society for American Baseball Research, known popularly as sabermetricians, specialize in statistical analysis. Their work fills bookstore sports shelves, as well as the SABR Research Library.

As custodian of the Research Library, I have in my files articles analyzing player and team performance from just about every angle possible: "A New, Normalized Measure of Offensive Production: The Offensive Quotient (OQ)"; "How to Design a Maximum-Runs Batting Order Using Markov Chain Models"; "Park-Adjusted Batting Statistics Made Simple"; "Apples and Apples: Comparing Players with Their Contemporaries"; "The Effect of Relief Pitchers on Aggregate Batting Averages, 1901–1984." Apparently, no part of baseball is so esoteric that it can't be reduced to a mathematical formula.

Don't presume that the crunching of baseball numbers is entirely an avocation of amateurs. Organized baseball, after the strike of 1981, adopted a formula to evaluate players for purposes of free-agent compensation. Known as the "Grebey procedure," after Ray Grebey (then the club owners' contract negotiator), the formula was based on various combinations of players' on-field statistics, among them plate appearances, batting averages, home runs, on-base percentages, runs batted in, fielding percentages, fielding chances, pitching victories, saves, pitchers' strikeouts, and earned run averages. Results were used to label potential free agents as Grade A and Grade B, in order to determine how many players and/or draft choices a team losing a free agent should get in return.

Is the Grebey formula valid in ranking players? Most sabermetricians doubt it. Then how can we determine who are the best over the years? With this book in your hands, you're on the road to answering that question.

You don't have to have a Cal Tech Ph.D. to know that, at bottom, a statistical analysis is valid only if its terms, or criteria, are valid. Wrong data, wrong conclusions. And of the Babel of criteria competing to be recognized as the true source of baseball wisdom, many can be dismissed as arcane, too labored, too contorted, too complicated, too far out of the mainstream, too much a product of feverish imagination.

Robert E. Kelly's analysis falls into none of those benighted categories. He has chosen exactly the correct criteria, set them in the correct framework, manipulated them with the skill of a bat-control artist, extrapolated to exactly the right degree, and come up with a set of rankings of offensive production that should have sabermetricians around the nation scratching their heads and asking themselves, "Why didn't I think of that?"

To find out why Bob Kelly did think of that, be sure to read the Introduction to this book.

If you're familiar with two previous books by Kelly, *Baseball's Best* and *Baseball for the Hot Stove League* (McFarland & Company, Inc.) you've sampled the technique he brings to full flower in this volume. Simply stated (Bob does it in the Introduction at greater length, in more depth, and with grace and clarity), this book compares players against each other, by position (first basemen, catcher, infielder, outfielder) within two-decade eras; a player's offensive statistics are measured and rated against the norm for the position during the era.

No big deal, you say; it's been done before. It may have, but I've never seen it done on such a scale, nor have I ever seen the statistics refined as Bob has done it. For starters, he's stripped home run statistics from both runs scored and runs batted in. Letting HRs stand on their own removes the undue triple emphasis they get in conventional batting statistics (on their own and as part of both runs scored and runs batted in), a practice that skews individual batting statistics and penalizes a player like Hall-of-Famer Charlie Gehringer, who scored a lot of runs and drove in a lot but never hit more than 20 home runs in a single major-league season. (In the Tigers' pennant-winning year of 1934, he had 214 hits, scored 134 runs, and drove in 127, all with only 11 home runs.) Can you doubt that this alone — letting home runs stand on their own — provides a truer picture of a batter's contributions to team offense?

Beyond that, Bob has created a logical statistic similar to the batting average that measures production. It is the product of home runs, runs scored, and runs batted in (the latter two figures minus the already-counted home runs) divided by times at bat. Bob calls it production per at bat (PAB). I call it a stroke of genius. Why hasn't it been thought of before?

PAB is a springboard for comparing batters' production within eras, and rating them as Most Valuable Producers and Most Talented Producers. Starting with the Introduction, you'll learn about Bob's technique — it's not complicated — as you read along.

A note about the two-decade era: This allows a true evaluation of players whose careers overlapped the tidy eras baseball historians usually carve out in their studies of the game's past.

Every fielder who was reasonably active and efficient during the years that Kelly examined appears somewhere within the covers of this volume, rated, discussed and compared with his peers.

For pure statistical history, shelves of bookstores are replete with encyclopedias and similar works. Do not place Kelly's book into that classification. To be sure, statistical displays are omnipresent, but only because that is the necessary language of player analysis. Kelly's work brings life to the dry statistical histories of players. Charts themselves are unique and informative in form. Accompanying essays about each player, some wide-ranging and analytical, others straight and simple, make this a readable book as well as an indispensable research tool.

This book has one more feature seldom, if ever, seen in a volume of this type. It examines the fabric of which baseball, so historians tell us, is so uniquely a part: The World Beyond the Ballpark, as Bob Kelly puts it. If baseball has been, and continues to be, part of the framework of America — and in the twenty-first century probably the globe — what more logical step in a book about baseball than to sketch that framework? Such cataclysmic events as World War I (1917–18) and the construction of the Panama Canal (1904–14) affected all of the nation's pursuits, including baseball. Kelly's short historical background will be a subtle reminder to you that baseball is indeed a part of life — that life indeed is larger than baseball.

More than seventy years ago, philosopher–baseball fan Cohen suggested that international rivalries could be defused and solved if baseball pennant races were substituted for wars. Mr. Cohen left one question unanswered: What would we do in the off-season? Perhaps Bob Kelly has provided the solution. Read on.

Leonard Levin is the former metro editor of the Providence Journal, Providence, Rhode Island, *and the former editor of the* Patriot Ledger, Quincy, Massachusetts. *He is custodian of the Research Library, Society for American Baseball Research.*

Introduction

Many readers whiz through the Introduction on their impatient way to page one of the main body of work. They will be cheated if they do so with this volume. It contains much information, some of it in unique form, and it uses unique analytical methods that ought to be reviewed. Tips and explanations contained in this section will assist those who seek to turn these pages productively and enjoyably.

The Purpose of the Book

The baseball encyclopedia that provided historical data for this survey weighs nine pounds and boasts 2781 pages, an awesome work. It sits on the desks of fans and professionals who finger through it timidly, carefully, lovingly, searching for little-known facts that win arguments, round out a sportswriter's column, or complete an author's sentence.

Useful though it is, however, many wish that within its fatness there existed a section that summarized the contents, made it clearer who was important and who wasn't, and provided a key to the relative greatness of those whose careers are enumerated on its endless pages.

It is the purpose of this book to respond to that sense of frustration—to provide partial answers to those who want to know who were the best players, and who did they compete against. All of this is presented in some format that truly informs the reader.

Each chapter contains four summaries for each fielding position (first basemen, catchers, infielders and outfielders).

- Player records for the period separated as follows.
- The best production year of each player.
- The most talented producers (MTP).
- The most valuable producers (MVP).

And in the final remarks an All-Star team for the era will be presented for consideration that is mostly based on the analysis, but is conditioned by the author's knowledge that pure numbers sometimes obscure the truth.

Scope

The deadball era is the essential area of interest of this survey. Investigation of it was limited to the period 1901–1919, which captures the beginnings of the American League (1901) and the initial decades of competition between the two leagues that has continued until this day.

This book is offense oriented. Pitching, pitchers and fielding are mentioned only tangentially.

Time Period

For the purposes of this analysis, a period of two decades (actually 19 years, from the rise of a second major league through the end of the deadball era) was selected as the most appropriate analytical time span. Why this span? Common sense, mostly.

A decade is too short a time in which to measure careers of prominent players. Other favored analytical eras, like prewar or postwar, are handy ways to allocate time but, otherwise, have no particular significance.

On the other hand, a two-decade period relates to the career duration of most baseball players who arrive on the scene in their early twenties and depart close to their fortieth birthdays.

All Hall of Fame players were active for more than ten years. Most prominent athletes were on the field for a period of less than twenty but more than ten years.

In short, when twenty-year eras are established as analytical blocks of time, the full careers (or the best years) of players are eventually shown in full flower when succeeding eras are progressively scanned. For example, the 1910–29 era would be the next most logical analysis, and in it the careers of those who started their careers in 1910–19 would be shown in full. But it would be useless to conduct such a study because the game from the deadball era, 1910–19, was entirely different from the one played thereafter, a fact that distorts comparisons between deadball and live-ball records. That lost "split-ball era" must be left to subjective analysis.

Interlocking Periods

Interlocking periods are an issue **only when a book like this is extended to subsequent periods.** If that occurs, the first question will be: What years should the next book of this type cover?

The 1910–29 era is out of the question for reasons previously given. The same logic does not apply to 1920–39. True, it embraces careers of some deadball players whose records are distorted by having one leg in both periods, but the era itself is a coherent whole — the game was played end to end with the live ball. For that reason it qualifies as the next reasonable interlocking period to examine by analysts who remain sensitive to split-era issues raised, and who inform readers accordingly.

For those slow to accept the fact that the new ball created, in effect, a new game with new strategies, one need only review comparative home run statistics. For example, home run leaders during 1915–19 (excluding Babe Ruth's numbers) won that distinction with 24, 12, 12, 11 and 10 four-baggers, respectively. But during 1920–24, leaders (still excluding Ruth) won with 19, 24, 42, 41 and 27 homers — a collective increase in the latter period of 122 percent. The live-ball game was different, more powerful and more dramatic.

Ruth's numbers are excluded from the above comparison because his talent was so transcendent that the inclusion of them would totally exaggerate the comparison being made between eras. For example, Ruth, an American League player, had full seasons in 1920, 1921, 1923 and 1924. In those four years he hit 200 home runs. The runner-up in the same league hit 99 home runs, about half as many as the Titan of Swat. He was above the game — he was from another planet.

Pure analysis will begin with the 1930–1939 period because all players will be from the live-ball era. Thereafter, linear studies can continue without special comment, using interlocking decades. Interlocking periods recognize that players don't arrive on the scene to serve the convenience of historians. Like newborn babes, they appear when ready. As a consequence, fractions of careers commonly fall into more than one decade.

For example, assume Tom Baseball had 4,000 at bats in the 1950s and 5,000 in the 1960s. In the twenty-year period 1940–1959, Tom would show 4,000 at bats. In the next sequential twenty-year period, 1960–1979, 5,000 at bats for Tom would appear.

Under that approach, neither period would examine Tom's career fully. An interlocking period, 1950–69, solves the problem. Within it, Tom's 9,000 at bats will be found. Under such a system, all or most of a player's career eventually gets analyzed.

The decision to use interlocking periods as a device to capture full careers causes the activities of many athletes to appear in more than one period. When this occurs (it's common), only activities within the subject period are appraised. Thus it is common to find long-careered athletes ranked low in a period during which they are moderately active, and high in the one in which their prime years appears. In this book, Ray Schalk (HOF) was such a player. About half of his at bats fell into the subject period; the rest took place in the 1920s. To show his full career would require the creation of a 1910–29 analytical period.

The Sample

A total of 120 player records was examined and rated in this book, including 44 infielders, 48 outfielders and 15 first basemen, all of whom had 3,500-plus at bats during the period and who generated batting or slugging averages at least as high as the averages for the leagues during the same period. The 13 catchers included had a different standard to meet, five or more 300+ at bat seasons. The qualification standard for catchers was lowered because the one applied to other position players excluded too many of them.

To identify these players—the ones who made baseball great during the era—hundreds of records were reviewed. **Alert readers will realize that, everything else aside, this player sort is of enormous benefit to the fan and the researcher—it immediately presents to them only the records of those who were relatively important, and it discards the relatively unimportant records of hundreds of men who flowed in and out of the big leagues for short periods of time, or who lingered despite poor production records.**

The result is a sample of durable athletes who were the best producers. Phrased in a negative way, the sample ignores short-careered men, or those with poor batting skills.

The sample size is primarily an indication of how difficult it was (and still is) to survive as a major league player. Also, the pay scale for start-up players, or for those with marginal skills, cannot be overlooked as a causative factor—commonly below $1,000 (the equivalent of $21,000 in 2007). This was not an income to lure men away from more staid occupations—as is the case today—nor did it tend to keep slow-developing players without the patience to wait for the average ($2,500), or the superstar ($12,000) contract, which in 2007 was worth $52,000 and $251,000, respectively.

This book is production oriented. It seeks and measures great producers of the subject era realizing that, in so doing, non–productive defensive geniuses were ignored.

Production

"Production" is an important word in a book that seeks to identify and rate great producers. Definition is needed.

In this book, production is the total of home runs, runs scored excluding home runs, and runs batted in excluding home runs (normally, home runs are included as part of total runs scored and total runs batted in). In the player activity charts appearing in this book, home runs are counted once, and separately.

The result is a record which presents clearly and more meaningfully the elements of each athlete's production contribution.

No other source for such career statistics is known. (To adjust charts to conventional form, add home runs to runs scored and runs-batted-in columns.)

It can be said with assurance that the view of career records afforded by this format will surprise many. Players with great production reputations may not have been so great after all; men with no production reputations may have been more efficient than many believed at the time.

A final note on production: To many, the word describes home runs and runs-batted-in activity. For reasons that defy logic, runs scored are ignored (as are, usually, prolific scorers). This is not the case here.

The offensive purpose of a baseball team is to score runs. Players who contribute to that end as scorers, power hitters or RBI men are, to that extent, producers and are so treated in evaluations.

Measuring Player Performance

The best available measurement of player ability is the objective opinion of contemporary baseball men, and members of the press who cover the game regularly.

But statistical systems also help — presenting records in a comparative way is of assistance in forming judgments about players.

- What is a good measuring system? For the purposes of this book:
- It's understandable; it doesn't bore one to death.
- It provides answers baseball men can accept.
- Its conclusions parallel, in most cases, decisions made by those who vote on HOF appointments, or they can be logically defended when differences appear in a way that informed enthusiasts can accept as reasonable — even when they disagree.

This is not a book about systems or statistics. Numbers are used, of course, as they must be in baseball to express relationships, but it's the conclusions that are important, not the methods of calculation.

Those interested in arcane analytical techniques proving how Lefty Bigbat would hit more doubles in Boston than in Texas should look elsewhere for entertainment.

Most data in this analysis are available to all. With few exceptions, the originality of the work is due to how material is assembled and used, not to mathematical pyrotechnics.

H (hits) divided by AB (at bats) = BA (batting average). This simple equation is understood by all baseball fans. P (production) is the sum of runs scored, home runs and runs batted in; when P is divided by AB (at bats), PAB is the result (production average, or production per at bat). Just as a BA reports a player's fundamental batting record, so does a PAB report a player's fundamental production record.

The PAB of each player for each of his active years appears on all career activity charts.

For each twenty-year period, average performance for first basemen, catchers, infielders and outfielders was calculated. An objective of the study was to separate careers by degrees of excellence. An arbitrary factor could have been selected (for example, average plus or minus 10 percent is a popular construction) and career years could have been grouped according to such an interval. Instead, however, a statistical device (standard deviation) was used to develop five PAB ranges as follows:

- All players in a sample group (e.g., first basemen) are listed in a single chart and the average (Avg) PAB is calculated.
- The standard deviation (SD) of the PAB column is calculated (using Excel stdevp).

The result of the above is shown at the bottom of the schedule of the players who were active at the particular position being examined, for example, the first basemen, as shown on the following page:

	AB	H	R	HR	RBI	BA	SA	PAB
Avg	5072	1424	624	35	588	.281	.376	.246
SD	940							.027

The following PAB classification structure is built from these numbers, as follows:

Class I	.302
Class II	.274-.301
Class III	.246-.273
Class IV	.218-.245
Class V	.217-

The career years of players are then slotted into these classifications (see sample player chart below).

AB (at bats) is the "durability" factor used throughout the survey; PAB (production average) is the "class" factor. Within each period, all but the ABs in Class V were multiplied by PABs for each classification to calculate DP (domination points). The players with the highest DPs represent the best combination of Class + Durability on the field during that period — they are the Most Valuable Producers (MVP).

A word about the exclusion of ABs associated with Class V: Some players, as a result of contract, luck, emotion or poor management build "most of" records (most hits, most games, most anything) by hanging on for years performing at levels well below average — levels that, most likely, a promising rookie could duplicate or exceed. It is the attitude of this book that such career padding should not be recognized in the evaluation system — that this aspect of the durability factor when encountered should be ignored. The welcomed result of this procedure is that no long-careered and low-skilled player attains a relatively high rating simply because he hung around longer than he should have.

With this brief explanation of evaluation systems used, and in the belief that pictures instruct better than words, a sample chart of a relatively modern player follows:

HAROLD BAINES

Born 1959; Height 6.02; Weight 175; T-L; B-L

* = Net of home runs

	G	AB	H	R	HR	RBI	BA	SA	PAB
CLASS I PAB .290+									
None									
CLASS II PAB .268-.289									
1982	161	608	165	64	25	80	.271	.469	.278
1985	160	640	198	64	22	91	.309	.467	.277
Total	321	1248	363	128	47	171	.291	.468	.277
CLASS III PAB .245-.267									
1981	82	280	80	32	10	31	.286	.482	.261
1983	156	596	167	56	20	79	.280	.443	.260
1987	132	505	148	39	20	73	.293	.479	.261
1989	146	505	156	57	16	56	.309	.465	.255
Total	516	1886	551	184	66	239	.292	.464	.259

	G	AB	H	R	HR	RBI	BA	SA	PAB
CLASS IV									
PAB .223-.244									
1984	147	569	173	43	29	65	.304	.541	.241
1986	145	570	169	51	21	67	.296	.465	.244
Total	292	1139	342	94	50	132	.300	.503	.242
CLASS V									
PAB .222-									
1980	141	491	125	42	13	36	.255	.405	.185
1988	158	599	166	42	13	68	.277	.411	.205
Total	299	1090	291	84	26	104	.267	.408	.196
Period	1428	5363	1547	490	189	646	.288	.462	.247
Other	1402	4545	1319	425	195	598	.290	.375	.268
Career	2830	9908	2866	915	384	1244	.289	.465	.257
BEST 123+ GAMES									
1982	161	608	165	64	25	80	.271	.469	.278

CALCULATION OF DOMINATION POINTS, MTP/MVP

	AB	PAB	MVP	MTP
CLASS I	0	0	0	346
CLASS II	1248	.277	346	
CLASS III	1886	.259	489	
CLASS IV	1139	.242	276	
TOTAL	4373		1111	
CLASS V	1090		0	
PERIOD	5363		1111	

In light of the previous explanation, the career chart of Harold Baines is interpreted as follows:

- The average outfielder during the 1970–89 era (calculated elsewhere) had a PAB of .245. The five quality ranges calculated for the period appear on the Baines chart within which appropriate PAB years were assigned.
- Through 1989, Baines had 5,363 AB, all of which fell into a single period.
- His best season was 1982, during which he generated a Class II PAB of .278.
- As measured against his peers, Baines did not have Class I years, but in six out of ten seasons he was an above average producer.
- In calculating DP in the lower chart, about 20 percent (1090) of the Baines's ABs were ignored because his PAB during those seasons (Class V) fell below acceptable levels.
- Baines earned 1111 DP in the Most Valuable Producer (MVP) race, and 346 DP in the Most Talented Producer (MTP) contest — MTP points represent the total of Class I and Class II DP, which appears in the upper-right-hand box of the CALCULATION etc. chart.
- The MVP by position for the twenty-year era is the player who earns the most DP for BELOW AVERAGE or better at bats. The MTP is the man with the most STAR and SUPERSTAR DP.
- Those interested in a more detailed explanation of systems used should contact the author through the publisher.

The Reliability of the System

Former players and informed newsmen and baseball men select Hall of Fame (HOF) candidates based upon observation and the best information available. Readers will find that appraisal methods employed here yield results remarkably consistent with those of HOF electors. When this is not the case, reasons given should, at least, be found rational — perhaps compelling.

Where the system gives a high rank to players ignored by the HOF, readers may be encountering either a HOF oversight or a system weakness. Where it yields a low rank to players elected to the HOF, the reasons are most often the following:

- The player died prematurely and (probably) was an emotional choice made for human and laudable reasons.
- The player had a long career and, although not much of a producer, was a whiz in some baseball talent highly regarded by electors, for example, fielding, contact hitting and base stealing.
- Politics.

In short, systems used in this book are imperfect. Inevitably, they overlook someone and overrate someone else. Human interpretation by baseball experts represents the final touch needed. But as systems go, readers may agree that this one does a satisfactory job and it yields interesting and sometimes surprising results.

The Database

Player rankings contained herein may be controversial with some but the collection of player information by time period should not be. Researchers and others should find these data useful, especially when used in conjunction with a baseball encyclopedia.

Limitations of Survey

How would Ted Williams have performed had he played in New York or Detroit? How about Joe DiMaggio in Fenway Park? This survey doesn't indulge in such speculations. What players actually did is what is measured, not what they might have done in a different park, or from a different position in the batting order, or with so-and-so hitting ahead or behind him.

Such questions are left for others to ponder. Here, only what was — not what might have been — is examined and rated.

Glossary of Terms

Most readers are familiar with the typical headings of player and league charts of baseball data. In this book, terms used — or the meanings of them — are somewhat different. For that reason, the obvious and not-so-obvious definitions appear below.

AL American League
G Games
H Hits
HR Home Runs
PAB Production Per at Bat
MVP (in charts) Most Valuable Producer
SB Stolen Bases
FB First Base
INF Infield
SO Strikeouts
2B Doubles (or second base)
OBP On base percent
BWAA Baseball Writers Association of America

NL National League
AB At bats
R Runs (in charts, excluding home runs)
RBI Runs Batted In (in charts, excluding home runs)
MVP (in heading) Most Valuable Player*
MTP Most Talented Producer
FA Fielding Average
C Catcher
OF Outfield
SB Stolen Bases
3B Triples (or third base)
BB Base on Balls

*Chalmers Award, 1911–1921; League, 1922–1930; BWAA, 1931–

A Tribute

Not all players in this survey were stars. Under evaluation methods used to examine their careers, only a few came out on top—quite a few hugged the bottom.

But the fact remains they all qualified for the survey which, by itself, is a tribute to their abilities. Finally, players in the survey were better hitters than most who played the game at the same time.

This survey covers 19 years. Only 120 men qualified—an average six per year. No matter how lowly any were graded, when compared with talented peers, they stood tall. They were great athletes.

Readers may find that Joe Ballplayer has a BA of .305 in one section of the book and .306 in another. Variances of this type are minor, do not distort meaning, and are caused by the use of competing reference works, or to inconsistent rounding-off procedures of the author.

Larger differences and other distortions will no doubt be uncovered for which the author apologizes, hoping that readers will be forgiving—and will report mistakes for later correction.

The World Beyond the Ballpark, 1901–1919

Leon Czolgosz, a 28-year-old anarchist who shot and killed President William McKinley during the first year (1901) of McKinley's second term, unwittingly jump-started the career of the most dominant political figure of the first two decades of the twentieth century, vice president Teddy Roosevelt. Roosevelt was president for less than eight years. Then, in 1908, he stepped aside and supported William H. Taft.

Roosevelt reemerged in 1912 as a contender. Following a stormy Republican convention in the Chicago Coliseum, he ran as an Independent. His personal popularity scuttled Taft's bid for a second term, but it wasn't enough to stop Woodrow Wilson's opportunistic drive to capitalize on Republican division. Wilson became, in 1913, the first Democratic president of the century.

Russia was in turmoil during this era. Czar Nicholas II, through placebo tactics and occasional violence, had kept at bay demands of the people for a better life, but during World War I, the pot boiled over.

The Czar abdicated in March 1917; in April, Lenin was smuggled back to Russia by the Germans, who hoped (with justification) that he and his Bolshevik comrades-in-exile, Leon Trotsky and Joseph Stalin, would stir up the revolutionary spirit of their homeland.

In August of the same year the Czar and his family moved to Siberia under the "protection" of government troops. Lenin's Bolsheviks took over the government in November and moved quickly to satisfy the peace demands of their followers. In December 1917 they deserted the Allies and signed an armistice with Germany.

Fearing residual loyalty and sympathy for the Czar in some quarters, the Russians then executed Nicholas II and his son and heir, Alexis. This ended the Romanov dynasty that had ruled for three hundred years. Also slaughtered were his wife, four daughters and several servants. In such a way was the Soviet Union formed, an event of major importance during the first two decades, and a meaningful one that helped to shape twentieth-century history.

If the Russian revolution was an important subplot in history, World War I was its equal as a primary theme during the subject era. War talk was rife in early 1914. Winston Churchill saw danger, knew the enemy, spoke out and was hooted as a warmonger. In June, Archduke Ferdinand of Austria and his wife were gunned down. Europe shook, and the Germans, in August, launched World War I.

America was neutral, at times a difficult and unpopular stance, especially after the sinking of the British liner *Lusitania* in May 1915 by a German submarine. The United States severed relations with Germany in February 1917, and declared war (Senate, 90–6; House, 373–50) in April. Theodore Roosevelt publicly supported Wilson's policy. On that day, Germany lost the war. It was thereafter simply a matter of when the "Boche" would be collared. The Armistice was signed on November 11, 1918.

As presidential politics stimulated peaceful battles, and differences between nations caused violent ones, the world of ordinary people moved along customary paths. Ping-Pong, jigsaw puzzles and Raggedy Ann dolls appeared. Paper clips were patented. Men accepted the safety razor; women greeted lipstick. Smart people invented paper cups, Brillo pads and pop-up toasters. Merchandisers discovered the beauty of Mother's Day and, later, Father's Day.

Huge movie companies organized; a star system that promoted actors to growing audiences was established. Films produced by Mack Sennett were favored. D.W. Griffith's *Birth of a Nation* was a huge success. Big names included Fatty Arbuckle, Charlie Chaplin, Douglas Fairbanks and Mary Pickford.

In the heavyweight fight game, the period began with Jim Jeffries in charge and ended with Jack Dempsey holding the crown, after a one-sided battle with Jess Willard. Marvin Hart, Tommy Burns and Jack Johnson were champions in the middle years.

Enrico Caruso, internationally-known tenor, was fined $10 in November 1906 by a judge who found him guilty of "annoying" a woman in Central Park. At about the same time, Joseph F. Smith, president of the Mormon Church, announced the birth of his 43rd child (Mormons outlawed polygamy in 1896).

And the world turned another notch.

The World Within the Ballpark, 1901–1919

In 1900, only the eight-team National League (NL) was considered to be of major league quality. Then Ban Johnson, president of the Western League, challenged the status quo. He beefed up the quality of his teams, changed the name of his organization to the American League (AL), and invaded existing and former NL markets.

The NL wilted after two years of competition and, in the National Agreement of 1903, it recognized the AL as separate but equal. At that point, league franchises (in 1903 finishing order) were as follows:

NL	*AL*
Pittsburgh	Philadelphia
New York	Cleveland
Chicago	New York
Brooklyn	Detroit
Boston	St. Louis
Philadelphia	Chicago
St. Louis	Washington

The NL agreed to an eight-game playoff series at the end of the 1903 season between the pennant winners. Pittsburgh, led by magnificent Honus Wagner, and Boston, with indestructible Cy Young, locked horns.

To everyone's surprise (especially the NL), the AL won (5–3). As a result, the NL ducked a 1904 contest but in the next year returned to a post–season competition that has continued until this day. From 1903 to 1909, there were six World Series. The AL took one more championship in 1906 when the Chicago White Sox, led by Ed Walsh (2 wins; ERA 1.80) took the Chicago Cubs, 4–2.

The Giants, Cubs and Pirates were the best teams in the NL during the first decade; the Tigers of Detroit were the strongest AL team.

The AL, from 1910 to 1919, shifted into a position of clear dominance when measured by World Series results. In eight of ten post–season competitions, they took the prize — Red Sox (4); Athletics (3); White Sox (1). The Boston Braves and the Cincinnati Reds of the NL were the victors in 1914 and 1919 (the year of the White Sox scandal).

The Giants were also a top NL team during the second decade, but competition was reasonably balanced. Six teams won a pennant; seven finished second at least once. All feasted on the inept St. Louis club. The Red Sox dominated AL play. Only the White Sox and the Athletics joined them as pennant winners.

Rules were still being formed and standards set during the early years of the century. In 1901, the infield fly rule was clarified, and foul balls (less than two strikes) were called strikes. The height of the pitcher's mound was standardized in 1903 at not more than 15 inches higher than the base lines and home plate. The sacrifice fly rule was modified in 1908, and in 1909 it was ruled that an unsuccessful third-strike bunt was to be scored as a strikeout. An earned run charged to the pitcher was defined in 1912, and modified in 1917.

A new Federal League, it should be noted, entered the competition in 1914. Players shuffled around seeking opportunity that year and the next, but the league faded away as quickly as it had appeared. In 1916, the usual NL/AL competition resumed.

Selective Service went into effect on May 18, 1917; America mobilized its armed services. This had the expected impact on major league baseball. The development of young players slowed; some established athletes lost playing time. The 1918 and 1919 seasons were shortened. The White Sox scandal of 1919, in which eight White Sox players were accused of rigging World Series games, didn't break as a major story until 1920.

Diamonds were not uniform; ball gloves were small. The ball was dead. In the first decade of the century, two errors per game were usual; in the second, somewhat less. Four runs for a game was average. A good batter would hit .250–.260; a great one, .330–.340. On average, a home run was hit every six or seven games. Base stealing was an important offensive tool. A good earned run average was about 3.00; a great one, 1.80–1.90. A talented strikeout pitcher would register 170–180 whiffs. These statistics are remarkably similar to modern ones, despite the changes to the game that were caused by the live ball, improved gloves and better-conditioned players.

Christy Mathewson was the most durable pitcher of the era, Walter Johnson the toughest to score on. Rube Waddell was the strikeout king (per game); Addie Joss had the lowest base runner (per game) count. With men on base, Walter Johnson was the master.

From the standpoint of durability and class, the most valuable pitchers during the 1901–19 period were Walter Johnson, Christy Mathewson, Eddie Plank and Ed Walsh, all HOF pitchers.

Systems used in pitcher evaluation (beyond the scope of this book) selected Johnson as MVP and MTP (most valuable and most talented pitcher). The best season (ERA) of pitchers in the sample was Dutch Leonard's 1914 performance for the Boston Red Sox: 223 innings pitched, 174 strikeouts, ERA 1.01.

By fielding position, 120 men qualified for this survey during 1901–19.

SURVEY BASE

	TOTAL	FB	C	INF	OF
Sample	120	15	13	44	48
BA	.272	.281	.247	.275	.285
SA	.362	.376	.316	.372	.382

BA for major league baseball 1901–19 — .254; SA for major league baseball 1901–19 — .332

Statistics for survey players compared with those for all of baseball silently announce the superior talents of the selected athletes. They dominated the fielder positions. Twenty (17 percent) are in the Hall of Fame:

First Base (1) — Frank Chance
Catch (2) — Roger Bresnahan, Ray Schalk
Infield (8) — Honus Wagner, Nap Lajoie, Eddie Collins, Frank Baker, Joe Tinker, Johnny Evers, Bobby Wallace, Jimmy Collins
Outfield (9) — Ty Cobb, Sam Crawford, Tris Speaker, Fred Clarke, Harry Hooper, Elmer Flick, Zack Wheat, Max Carey, Willie Keeler

The final years of deadball baseball are covered in this book. Records established aren't comparable to subsequent periods because the live ball introduced in the 1920s changed all aspects of the game.

But it's interesting, nonetheless, to inspect deeds of athletes who did so much with so little, in a game that was characterized more by flamboyance and energy than contracts and dollar bills.

First Basemen — Analysis, 1901–1919

During the subject period, 15 men dominated first base play and generated an average PAB of .247, broken down as follows:

	PAB
Runs	.123
Home runs	.007
RBI	.116
Total	.246

Those first basemen who qualified for the survey appear below:

DOMINANT FIRST BASEMEN 1901–19 RECORD

* HOF
** = Net of home runs

PLAYER	LG	AB	H	R**	HR	RBI**	BA	SA	PAB
CLASS I									
PAB .302+									
Chance F*	N	3805	1131	685	18	529	.297	.396	.324
CLASS II									
PAB .275–.301									
Davis H	A	5373	1499	740	68	694	.279	.407	.280
CLASS III									
PAB .246–.274									
McGann D	N	3581	994	503	24	419	.278	.369	.264
Hoblitzel R	N	4706	1310	564	27	592	.278	.374	.251
Chase H	A	7417	2158	923	57	884	.291	.391	.251
McInnis S	A	4672	1442	520	14	632	.309	.380	.250
Miller D	N	5142	1344	602	31	634	.261	.360	.246
CLASS IV									
PAB .221–.245									
Konetchy E	N	6684	1856	788	58	789	.278	.396	.245
Merkle F	N	5437	1481	625	58	636	.272	.383	.243
Gandil C	A	4245	1176	438	11	546	.277	.362	.234
Luderus F	N	4819	1339	485	84	559	.278	.404	.234
Bransfield K	N	4994	1350	514	14	622	.270	.353	.230
Daubert J	N	5089	1535	692	35	424	.302	.390	.226
CLASS V									
PAB .220–									
Tenney F	N	4900	1362	744	14	313	.278	.336	.219
Stovall G	A	5219	1381	530	15	549	.265	.340	.210
Avg		5072	1424	624	35	588	.281	.376	.246
SD		940	.027						

(1) BA, PAB calculated horizontally; (2) AB, H, R, HR, RBI, SA, SD calculated vertically

Classifications

	Class (PAB)	Durability (AB)
CLASS I	.302+	6954+
CLASS II	.274–.301	6013–6953
CLASS III	.246–.273	5072–6012
CLASS IV	.218–.245	4131–5071
CLASS V	.217–	4130–

Player Analysis

Class I, PAB .302+

Frank Chance was the only first baseman to generate a Class I PAB. But, as analysis will show, numbers can sometimes be deceptive. In 1946 he was elected to the Hall of Fame (HOF).

Class II, PAB .274–.301

Harry Davis produced a PAB of .280 and, in 17 years, built a solid career. Analysis comparing him to Chance may surprise some.

Class III, PAB .246–.273

Five players qualified for this classification: McGann, Hoblitzel, Chase, McInnis and Miller. None are in the HOF. The Chase record stands out from the rest because he was so much more durable than the others. Durability plus an above-average PAB are a potent combination.

Class IV, PAB .218–.245

Six players were classified as Class IV: Konetchy, Merkle, Gandil, Luderus, Bransfield, and Daubert. Some had several quality seasons, but couldn't stabilize as quality players. There are no overlooked gems in this group.

Class V, PAB .217–

Tenney and Stovall fall into this classification. Tenney's poor numbers may reflect the poor quality of the team he spent 14 seasons with, the Boston Braves, more than they reflect his own ability — the Braves dependably finished at or close to the bottom of the league. Stovall, on the other hand, was consistently mediocre. Why he lasted 12 years is one of baseball's mysteries.

Frank Chance

Born 1877; Height 6.00; Weight 190; T-R; B-R; Led National League: 1903-SB; 1906-R, SB; HOF 1946

* = Net of home runs

	G	AB	H	R*	HR	RBI*	BA	SA	PAB
CLASS I									
PAB .302+									
1901	69	241	67	38	0	36	.278	.361	.307
1903	125	441	144	81	2	79	.327	.440	.367
1905	118	392	124	90	2	68	.316	.434	.408
1906	136	474	151	100	3	68	.319	.430	.361
1909	93	324	88	53	0	46	.272	.346	.306
1910	88	295	88	54	0	36	.298	.393	.305

	G	AB	H	R*	HR	RBI*	BA	SA	PAB
1911	31	88	21	22	1	16	.239	.409	.443
1912	2	5	1	2	0	0	.200	.200	.400
1913	11	24	5	3	0	6	.208	.208	.375
Total	673	2284	689	443	8	355	.302	.405	.353
CLASS II									
PAB .274-.301									
1902	75	236	67	39	1	30	.284	.369	.297
1904	124	451	140	83	6	43	.310	.430	.293
1907	111	382	112	57	1	48	.293	.361	.277
Total	310	1069	319	179	8	121	.298	.392	.288
CLASS III									
PAB .246-.273									
1908	129	452	123	63	2	53	.272	.363	.261
CLASS IV									
PAB .218-.245									
None									
CLASS V									
PAB .217-									
1914	1	0	0	0	0	0	0	0	0
Period	1113	3805	1131	685	18	529	.297	.396	.324
Other	173	488	140	93	2	47	.287	.370	.291
Career	1286	4293	1271	778	20	576	.296	.393	.320
BEST 123+ GAMES									
1903	125	441	144	81	2	79	.327	.440	.367

Calculation of Domination Points, MTP/MVP

	AB	PAB	MVP	MTP
CLASS I	2284	.353	806	1114
CLASS II	1069	.288	308	
CLASS III	452	.261	118	
CLASS IV	0	0	0	
TOTAL	3805		1232	
CLASS V	0		0	
PERIOD	3805		1232	

In 1898 Frank Chance, 21, wore the Chicago Cubs' uniform for the first time. He was used sparingly, mostly as a catcher, and showed signs of being an effective hitter.

In 1903 Chance, then 26, took over as the regular first baseman for the club and (except for three games) did no more catching for the balance of his career.

In 1905, when only 28 years old, Chance became field manager of the Cubs; his last year as a full-time player was 1908.

Chance managed the Chicago club until he moved to New York in 1913 to take over the Yankees who, in the previous season, finished in the AL cellar under the leadership of Harry Wolverton. He was succeeded in 1914 by Roger Pekinpaugh and, except for one more fling at managing in 1923 (Red Sox), he retired from major league baseball.

Frank Chance's first season as a regular (1903) was his best—PAB .367, well beyond anything produced by his competition. And for five more partial seasons, he posted impressive production numbers. For the final six years of his playing, however, he appeared in only 226 games with 736 at bats.

Chance was not as good as numbers say he was. He played in fewer than 100 games 11 times in his 17-year career; he appeared in 80 percent of scheduled games only four times—1903, 1904, 1906, 1908; he never posted 500+ at bats in a season.

In short, Chance's career was full of part-time seasons and it may be safely assumed that he, as manager, did not sit down when "easy" pitchers were throwing and play when "tough" ones were on the mound. In the 1901–19 era, he barely hurdled the survey screening level for durability (3500 at bats); in his entire career he registered 4,293 at bats, the lowest of all HOF first basemen.

What does this mean? There's every reason to suspect that Chance's production record would have suffered had he played a full schedule.

Frank Chance was, in fact, a part-time, short-careered first baseman with talent. When he played, he was impressive. The following graphic demonstrates this and also underlines the activity differential between him and other men in the survey group.

Per at Bat (PAB) 1901–19

	At Bat	R PAB	HR PAB	RBI PAB	Total PAB
Chase	3805	.180	.005	.139	.324
Chance	7417	.124	.008	.119	.251
Davis	5373	.138	.013	.129	.280
Sample avg.	5072	.123	.007	.116	.246

Chance played first base during 78 percent of his defensive appearances. His fielding record is a composite of his activity in three positions and is, therefore, meaningless. However, an inspection of individual years, when he played first base only, reveals that he boasted highly competitive fielding averages.

In 1907, he led the league with a FA of .992; in 1904, he tied with a FA of .990. Chance was a good glove man — for a short time — and a worthy member of the legendary Tinker to Evers to Chance double-play combination.

Harry Davis

Born 1873; Height 5.11; Weight 180; T-R; B-R; Led American League: 1902-2B; 1904-HR; 1905-2B, HR, R, RBI; 1906-HR, RBI; 1907-2B, HR

* = Net of home runs

	G	AB	H	R*	HR	RBI*	BA	SA	PAB
CLASS I PAB .302+									
1901	117	496	152	84	8	68	.306	.452	.323
1902	133	561	172	83	6	86	.307	.444	.312
1906	145	551	161	82	12	84	.292	.459	.323
1913	7	17	6	2	0	4	.353	.471	.353
1915	5	3	1	0	0	4	.353	.333	1.333
Total	407	1628	492	251	26	246	.302	.456	.321
CLASS II PAB .274–301									
1903	106	420	125	70	5	50	.298	.436	.298
1905	149	602	171	84	8	75	.284	.422	.277
1907	149	582	155	76	8	79	.266	.397	.280
1914	5	7	3	0	0	2	.429	.429	.286
Total	409	1611	454	230	21	206	.282	.417	.284
CLASS III PAB .246-.273									
1904	102	404	125	44	10	52	.309	.490	.262

	G	AB	H	R*	HR	RBI*	BA	SA	PAB
1909	149	530	142	69	4	71	.268	.374	.272
1911	57	183	36	26	1	21	.197	.273	.262
Total	308	1117	303	139	15	144	.271	.399	.267
CLASS IV									
PAB .218–.245									
1908	147	513	127	60	5	57	.248	.357	.238
CLASS V									
PAB .217–									
1910	139	492	122	60	1	40	.248	.309	.205
1912	2	5	0	0	0	0	0	.000	.000
1916	1	0	9	0	0	0	.000	.000	.000
1917	1	1	0	0	0	0	0	.000	.000
Total	143	498	131	60	1	40	.245	.305	.203
Period	1414	5367	1498	740	68	693	.279	.407	.280
Other	340	1281	341	184	6	184	.266	.412	.292
Career	1754	6648	1839	924	74	877	.277	.408	.282
Best 123+ Games									
1906	145	551	161	82	12	84	.292	.459	.323

CALCULATION OF DOMINATION POINTS, MTP/MVP

	AB	PAB	MVP	MTP
CLASS I	1628	.321	523	981
CLASS II	1611	.284	458	
CLASS III	1117	.267	298	
CLASS IV	513	.238	122	
TOTAL	4869		1401	
CLASS V	498		0	
PERIOD	5367		1401	

When Ban Johnson's AL went into business in 1901, Harry Davis was one of the first to jump. Leaving a so-so five-year NL career behind, Davis (28) joined Nap Lajoie and others on the Athletics of Connie Mack. It took Davis four seasons to nail the first base job down. In 1905, now 32, he carried a full load and continued to do so through the 1910 season. During those seasons he garnered most of his batting honors.

Stuffy McInnis took his job in 1911 and in 1912 he moved to Cleveland as manager and occasional player. This didn't work out (the Indians finished fifth, 30+ games behind first-place Boston). And in 1913, he returned to the Athletics and played little for five more years. Davis, 44, retired in 1917.

Davis had impressive battle ribbons indicating his prominent offensive skills as a power hitter. Additionally, from 1905 through 1909, he stole 20 or more bases per season. Speed was another of his many talents. His BA was slightly below the average of this elite group but he had the highest SA and the second highest PAB.

A good contact hitter with power and speed boasts the array of talents which, when they jell, can produce great production years. It was so with Davis. For two seasons in particular (1902, 1906), he was among the best in the business, and for two others (1904, 1907), he was a class act. Only one of his years (1910) was a bummer. The great weakness of Davis' record is the number of partial seasons he played which cost him at bats and kept him from production greatness.

He was a well-rounded producer.

Per at Bat (PAB) 1901–19

	At Bat	R PAB	HR PAB	RBI PAB	Total PAB
Davis	5373	.138	.013	.129	.289
Sample avg.	5072	.123	.007	.116	.246

Davis played first base during 93 percent of his career games and he was, arguably, the poorest fielder of the group. In range, only two others handled fewer chances per game and, aside from Miller — a part-time first baseman — his fielding average (.978) was the lowest.

Was Davis an HOF player?

His weak durability has already been noted and need not be repeated. As a defensive player, his record was not impressive. A player with that profile would have to be offensively brilliant to gain HOF status. Competent he was; brilliant, he wasn't.

Also, qualification for HOF status based on comparisons with Chance's record is a weak crutch indeed. Standing alone, neither man was an obvious HOF choice.

Dan McGann

Born 1871; Height 6.00; Weight 190; T-R; B-B

* = Net of home runs

	G	AB	H	R*	HR	RBI*	BA	SA	PAB
CLASS I PAB .302+									
1905	136	491	147	83	5	70	.299	.434	.322
CLASS II PAB .274–.301									
1901	103	426	123	67	6	50	.289	.411	.289
1904	141	517	148	75	6	65	.286	.387	.282
Total	244	943	271	142	12	115	.287	.398	.285
CLASS III PAB .246–.273									
1902	129	477	147	67	0	63	.308	.403	.273
1903	129	482	130	72	3	47	.270	.357	.253
Total	258	959	277	139	3	110	.289	.380	.263
CLASS IV PAB .218–.245									
1906	134	451	107	62	0	37	.237	.304	.220
1907	81	262	78	27	2	34	.298	.363	.240
1908	135	475	114	50	2	53	.240	.291	.221
Total	350	1188	299	139	4	124	.252	.312	.225
CLASS V PAB .217– None									
Period	988	3581	994	503	24	419	.278	.369	.264
Other	468	1717	517	308	18	275	.301	.412	.350
Career	1456	5298	1511	811	42	694	.285	.383	.292
BEST 123+ GAMES									
1905	136	491	147	83	5	70	.299	.434	.322

Calculation of Domination Points, MTP/MVP

	AB	PAB	MVP	MTP
CLASS I	491	.322	158	427
CLASS II	943	.285	269	
CLASS III	959	.263	252	
CLASS IV	1188	.225	267	
TOTAL	3581		946	
CLASS V	0		0	
PERIOD	3581		946	

McGann was 30 in 1901 with five major league seasons behind him. To do his career justice, one would have to analyze the 1891–1909 period, which is beyond the scope of this survey.

Within the subject period, McGann was active for eight years in the NL with the Cardinals, the Giants and the Braves—over five with the Giants. He was 37 when he retired in 1908.

McGann did everything well and nothing brilliantly. He played first base acceptably in 94 percent of his games (FA .986). But he was not active enough during the period to make a strong impression.

Per At Bat (PAB) 1901–19

	At Bat	R PAB	HR PAB	RBI PAB	Total PAB
McGann	3581	.140	.007	.117	.264
Sample avg.	5072	.123	.007	.116	.246

McGann, a good contact hitter, was a competitive scorer. Otherwise, his offensive record is undistinguished.

Dick Hoblitzell

Born 1888; Height 6.00; Weight 172; T-L; B-R; Led National League: 1910-AB; 1911–AB

* = Net of home runs

	G	AB	H	R*	HR	RBI*	BA	SA	PAB
CLASS I PAB .302+ None									
CLASS II PAB .274–.301									
1912	148	558	164	71	2	83	.294	.405	.280
1915	124	399	113	52	2	59	.283	.396	.283
Total	272	957	277	123	4	142	.289	.401	.281
CLASS III PAB .246–.273									
1911	158	622	180	70	11	86	.289	.415	.268
1910	155	611	170	81	4	66	278	.380	.247
1913	137	502	143	56	3	65	285	.376	.247
1914	146	477	125	62	0	62	.262	.342	.260
1916	130	417	108	57	0	50	.259	.305	.257
Total	726	2629	726	326	18	329	.276	.369	.256
CLASS IV PAB .218–.245									
1909	142	517	159	55	4	63	.308	.418	.236

	G	AB	H	R*	HR	RBI*	BA	SA	PAB
1917	120	420	108	48	1	46	.257	.343	.226
Total	262	937	267	103	5	109	.285	.384	.232
CLASS V PAB .217–									
1908	32	114	29	8	0	8	.254	316	140
1918	25	69	11	4	0	4	.159	.174	.116
Total	57	183	40	12	0	12	.219	.262	.131
Period	1317	4706	1310	564	27	592	.278	.374	.251
Career	1317	4706	1310	564	27	592	.278	.374	.251
BEST 123+ GAMES									
1915	124	399	113	52	2	59	.283	.396	.283

Calculation of Domination Points, MTP/MVP

	AB	PAB	MVP	MTP
CLASS I	0	0	0	269
CLASS II	957	.281	269	
CLASS III	2629	.256	673	
CLASS IV	937	.232	217	
TOTAL	4523		1159	
CLASS V	183		0	
PERIOD	4706		1159	

Dick Hoblitzel, a slender southpaw, joined the Reds in 1908 as a 20-year-old, and played 32 games at first base. John Ganzel was resident first baseman and manager at the time. In 1909 Ganzel was gone, Clark Griffith was manager and Hoblitzel became the regular first baseman. He played for the Reds for over seven years, then (surprisingly, for the waiver price) moved to the Boston Red Sox during the 1914 season.

Fritz Mollwitz (who couldn't carry Hoblitzel's glove) filled the Cincinnati job while Dick provided Boston with his steady brand of baseball until his retirement in 1918. Hoblitzell was 30 when he took his spikes off for the last time.

Hoblitzell spent 97 percent of his fielding time at first base. He had a career FA of .987 — better than most in the first base survey. He was solid defensively, with reasonably good speed.

Dick was a below average contact hitter. But he was a timely hitter who got the most from his ability. Only four percent of his at bats during the period were of poor quality.

Per at Bat (PAB) 1901–19

	At Bat	R PAB	HR PAB	RBI PAB	Total PAB
Hoblitzel	4706	.120	.006	.126	.251
Sample avg.	5072	.123	.007	.116	.246

He was an aggressive hitter, as his battle ribbons testify. But, as the above graphic makes clear, the weakness in his record is durability.

HAL CHASE

Born 1883; Height 6.00; Weight 175; T-L; B-R; Led Federal League: 1915-HR; Led National League: 1916-BA, H; 1917-AB

* = Net of home runs

	G	AB	H	R*	HR	RBI*	BA	SA	PAB
CLASS I									
PAB .302+									
None	0								
CLASS II									
PAB .274-.301									
1907	125	498	143	70	2	66	.287	.357	.277
1915	145	567	165	68	17	72	.291	.471	.277
Total	270	1065	308	138	19	138	.289	.418	.277
CLASS III									
PAB .246-.273									
1906	151	597	193	84	0	76	.323	.395	.268
1909	118	474	134	56	4	59	.283	.357	.251
1910	130	524	152	64	3	70	.290	.365	.261
1911	133	527	166	79	3	59	.315	.419	.268
1914	133	497	156	67	3	65	.314	.447	.272
1916	142	542	184	62	4	78	.339	.459	.266
1917	152	602	167	67	4	82	.277	.394	.254
1918	74	259	78	28	2	36	.301	.417	.255
Total	1033	4022	1230	507	23	525	.306	.406	.262
CLASS IV									
PAB .218-.245									
1905	126	465	116	57	3	46	.249	.329	.228
1919	110	408	116	53	5	40	.284	.397	.240
Total	236	873	232	110	8	86	.266	.361	.234
CLASS V									
PAB .217-									
1908	106	405	104	49	1	35	.257	.306	.210
1912	131	522	143	57	4	34	.274	.372	.220
1913	141	530	141	62	2	46	.266	.355	.208
Total	378	1457	388	168	7	135	.266	.347	.213
Period	1917	7417	2158	923	57	884	.291	.391	.251
Career	1917	7417	2158	923	57	884	.291	.391	.251
BEST 123+ GAMES									
1915	145	567	165	68	17	72	.291	.471	.277

CALCULATION OF DOMINATION POINTS, MTP/MVP

	AB	PAB	MVP	MTP
CLASS I	0	0	0	295
CLASS II	1065	.277	295	
CLASS III	4022	.262	1054	
CLASS IV	873	.234	204	
TOTAL	5960		1553	
CLASS V	1457		0	
PERIOD	7417		1553	

Hal Chase appeared in 1905 for the first time in a major league uniform. He replaced the aging Joe Ganzel at first base for the Yankees. In a bit more than eight seasons with that club, Chase produced batting marks consistently above average, and he stole over 20 bases in every season.

Chase moved to the Chicago White Sox in 1913; then he spent some time in the lower-quality Federal League (during which he generated his best season) before returning to the fold as a utility man with the Reds in 1916. He spent two more years in Cincinnati, mostly at first base; then he finished his 15-year career with the Giants in 1919.

Chase played 94 percent of his games at first base. In range, he compared favorably to all but Konetchy and Luderus, but his FA of .979 was lower than most — not much better than Davis's.

Chase's dominant characteristics were consistency and durability. In ten of his 15 seasons, his BA was higher than the average for this elite group (.281) and only once did it drop below the average for baseball (.254). In 11 of his 15 seasons, Chase stole over 20 bases. During the subject period, he registered 11 percent more at bats than his closest competitor — 95 percent more than HOF player Frank Chance.

Chase was no superstar, but for 12 seasons he played at impressive levels, two at Class II quality. Typically, he did a little better than the average of his peers in all elements of his PAB, but was not outstanding in any:

PER AT BAT (PAB) 1901–19

	At Bat	R PAB	HR PAB	RBI PAB	Total PAB
Chase	7417	.124	.008	.119	.251
Sample avg.	5072	.123	.007	.116	.246

Was Hal Chase a Hall of Fame player? On a career basis, he compares with Frank Chance (the only HOF first baseman from the period) as follows:

	AB	BA	SA	R PAB	HR PAB	RBI PAB	Total PAB
Chase	7417	.291	.391	.124	.008	.119	.251
Chance	4293	.296	.393	.181	.005	.134	.320

Chance had a higher PAB during his limited career. But would his level of superiority have continued had he played as long as Chase? Doubtful! Some view (and the evaluation system recognizes) the long-term steadiness of Chase as having more value than the short-term brilliance of Chance.

The proposed answer to the question is this: Chance didn't play enough to qualify; Chase didn't play well enough; there were no HOF first basemen during the subject period.

STUFFY McINNIS

Born 1890; Height 5.10; Weight 162; T-R; B-R

* = Net of home runs

	G	AB	H	R*	HR	RBI*	BA	SA	PAB
CLASS I									
PAB .302+									
1911	126	468	150	73	3	74	.321	.425	.321
1912	153	568	186	80	3	98	.327	.433	.319
1913	148	543	177	75	4	86	.326	.418	.304
Total	427	1579	513	228	10	258	.325	.425	.314
CLASS II									
PAB .274–.301									
1910	38	73	22	10	0	12	.301	.438	.301

	G	AB	H	R*	HR	RBI*	BA	SA	PAB
1914	149	576	181	73	1	94	.314	.368	.292
Total	187	649	203	83	1	106	.313	.376	.293
CLASS III									
PAB .246-.273									
None									
CLASS IV									
PAB .218-.245									
1918	117	423	115	40	0	56	.272	.322	.227
CLASS V									
PAB .217-									
1909	19	46	11	3	1	3	.239	.304	.152
1915	119	456	143	44	0	49	.314	.362	.204
1916	140	512	151	41	1	59	.295	.361	.197
1917	150	567	172	50	0	44	.303	.351	.166
1919	120	440	134	31	1	57	.305	.361	.202
Total	548	2021	611	169	3	212	.302	.357	.190
Period	1279	4672	1442	520	14	632	.309	.380	.250
Other	849	3150	964	332	6	408	.306	.382	.237
Career	2128	7822	2406	852	20	1040	.308	.381	.244
BEST 123+ GAMES									
1911	126	468	150	73	3	74	.320	.425	.321

Calculation of Domination Points, MTP/MVP

	AB	PAB	MVP	MTP
CLASS I	1579	.314	496	686
CLASS II	649	.293	190	
CLASS III	0	0	0	
CLASS IV	423	.227	96	
TOTAL	2651		782	
CLASS V	2021		0	
PERIOD	4672		782	

McInnis joined the Philadelphia Athletics in 1909 as a 19-year-old shortstop. First baseman Harry Davis was approaching the end of his career and in 1911 manager Connie Mack shifted the rookie to that position.

McInnis, though not as tall as many first sackers, played the position as well as anybody from 1912 to 1917 (career FA .991). Then he moved to the Red Sox for the final two years of the 1901–19 period.

In the 1920s, he spent three more seasons in the AL, then five in the NL. He was 37 when he ended his 19-year career with the Phillies.

The 1915 Athletics, absent the talents of Collins, Barry and Baker (sold/traded by Connie Mack), dropped from first place to last, and stayed in the cellar for the balance of the period. The PAB of McInnis went down simultaneously.

McInnis performed mostly in the 1910–29 era, a split period (deadball and live ball) that is beyond the scope of this survey. Within the subject period Stuffy had too few at bats and, of those he had, too many ranked as poor.

Per at Bat (PAB) 1901–19

	At Bat	R PAB	HR PAB	RBI PAB	Total PAB
McInnis	4672	.111	.003	.135	.250
Sample avg.	5072	.123	.007	.116	.246

McInnis was one of the most naturally talented first basemen of the time, offensively and defensively. He had the leading BA of the group (.309) and a better-than-average PAB and FA.

Overall, he had a 19-year career and more at bats than HOF first basemen like Bottomley, Brouthers, Chance, Connor, Greenberg, Kelly, Mize, and Terry. Over the years, HOF electors have at times been satisfied with far less than Stuffy had.

Dots Miller

Born 1886; Height 6.00; Weight 170; T-R; B-R

* = Net of home runs

	G	AB	H	R*	HR	RBI*	BA	SA	PAB
CLASS I PAB .302+									
1911	137	470	126	76	6	72	.268	.377	.328
CLASS II .274-301									
1909	151	560	156	68	3	84	.279	.396	.277
1912	148	567	156	70	4	83	.275	.397	.277
Total	299	1127	312	138	7	167	.277	.397	.277
CLASS III .246-.273									
1913	154	580	158	68	7	83	.272	.419	.272
1914	155	573	166	63	4	84	.290	.393	.264
1915	150	553	146	71	2	70	.264	.342	.259
Total	459	1706	470	202	13	237	.275	.385	.265
CLASS IV PAB .218-.245 None									
CLASS V PAB .217-									
1910	120	444	101	44	1	47	.227	.309	.207
1916	143	505	120	46	1	45	.238	.315	.182
1917	148	544	135	59	2	43	.248	.320	.191
1919	101	346	80	37	1	23	.231	.292	.176
Total	512	1839	436	186	5	158	.237	.311	.190
Period	1407	5142	1344	602	31	634	.261	.360	.246
Other	182	663	182	77	1	49	.275	.334	.192
Career	1589	5805	1526	679	32	683	.263	.357	.240
BEST 123+ GAMES									
1911	137	470	126	76	6	72	.268	.377	.328

Calculation of Domination Points, MTP/MVP

	AB	PAB	MVP	MTP
CLASS I	470	.328	154	466
CLASS II	1127	.277	312	
CLASS III	1706	.265	452	
CLASS IV	0		0	
TOTAL	3303		918	
CLASS V	1839		0	
PERIOD	5142		918	

Dots Miller joined Pittsburgh as an infielder in 1909. During his 12-year career, five each with the Pirates and Cardinals, and two final seasons with the Phillies, he never settled in a single defensive position. In 46 percent of his games, he played first base.

Because of the way he was handled, it may be safely assumed that he wasn't a great fielder. Miller retired in 1921 at 35 years of age.

Miller was reasonably durable and a timely hitter. His PAB was just below average.

Per at Bat (PAB) 1901–19

	At Bat	R PAB	HR PAB	RBI PAB	Total PAB
Miller	5142	.117	.006	.123	.246
Sample avg.	5072	.123	.007	.116	.246

Inconsistency was his major offensive problem. For the last half of his career, his production profile slumped badly — 36 percent of his at bats were poor.

Ed Konetchy

Born 1885; Height 6.03; Weight 195; T-R; B-R; Led National League: 1911–2B

* = Net of home runs

	G	AB	H	R*	HR	RBI*	BA	SA	PAB
CLASS I PAB .302+									
1910	144	520	157	84	3	75	.302	.425	.312
CLASS II PAB .274–.301									
1909	152	576	165	84	4	76	.286	.396	.285
1911	158	571	165	84	6	82	.289	.433	.301
1912	143	538	169	73	8	74	.314	.455	.288
1915	152	576	181	69	10	83	.314	.483	.281
Total	605	2261	680	310	28	315	.301	.442	.289
CLASS III PAB .246–.273									
1913	139	502	137	67	7	61	.273	.418	.269
1916	158	566	147	73	3	67	260	.373	.253
Total	297	1068	284	140	10	128	.266	.394	.260
CLASS IV PAB .218–.245									
1917	130	474	129	54	2	52	.272	.380	.228
CLASS V PAB .217–									
1907	90	330	83	31	3	27	.252	.361	.185
1908	154	545	135	41	5	45	.248	.354	.167
1914	154	563	140	52	4	47	.249	.343	.183
1918	119	437	103	31	2	54	.236	.307	.199
1919	132	486	145	45	1	46	.298	.391	.189
Total	649	2361	606	200	15	219	.257	.351	.184
Period	1825	6684	1856	788	58	789	.278	.396	.245
Other	258	962	292	109	16	129	.304	.444	.264
Career	2083	7646	2148	897	74	918	.281	.402	.247
BEST 123+ GAMES									
1910	144	520	157	84	3	75	.302	.425	.312

Calculation of Domination Points, MTP/MVP

	AB	PAB	MVP	MTP
CLASS I	520	.312	162	815
CLASS II	2261	.289	653	
CLASS III	1068	.260	278	
CLASS IV	474	.228	108	
TOTAL	4323		1201	
CLASS V	2361		0	
PERIOD	6684		1201	

Konetchy was an unusually large man for the times, hence his nickname, Big Ed.

In his first season (1907) with the St. Louis Cardinals, the young giant (22 years old) played a minor role with the club. Jake Beckley (HOF 1971, played 1888–1907), 40 years old at the time, was finishing his career with the Cardinals. When he retired in 1908, Konetchy took over at the first sack, a position he held with distinction through the 1913 season.

Before the 1914 season, Big Ed was traded to Pittsburgh in an eight-man deal which, among other things, brought Dots Miller to St. Louis.

Konetchy played a season with the Pirates, jumped to the Federal League in 1915, then in 1916 caught on with the Boston Braves; by then, Ed was 31 years old. He spent three seasons in Boston, then, in 1919, moved to Brooklyn; he played for the Dodgers and Phillies during the final three years of his 15-season career. He was 36 when he retired in 1921.

Konetchy was a top defensive player who, in 99 percent of his appearances, played first base (career FA .990).

As a contact hitter, Ed was a speck behind the rest of the survey group, but his SA (.396) was higher than that of his peers (.376). Also, despite his size, he stole more than 20 bases in six of his 15 years. Finally, only Hal Chase was more durable.

Konetchy spent 13 of his 15 career years in the subject period. In all but five he had competitive production numbers, including his best year (1910, PAB .312). In all elements of his PAB, he was competitive, but in home runs and runs batted in, he was above average.

Per at Bat (PAB) 1901–19

	At Bat	R PAB	HR PAB	RBI PAB	Total PAB
Konetchy	6684	.118	.009	.118	.245
Sample avg.	5072	.123	.007	.116	.246

The career of Konetchy provides a useful example of how, in the evaluation system being used, durability alone — that is to say, ABs below acceptable quality levels — have no value. Ed, one of the two most durable players in the sample, had 35 percent of his at bats (2361/6684) in the lowest classification, for which he got no credit — his DP (domination points) were less than they might otherwise have been had all at bats been valued.

Others might set different acceptable activity levels, but it's probable that most would agree that physical ability to play unaccompanied by adequate (major league) quality of play has little value in the game of skill known as baseball. When players reach the stage where they can no longer compete with their peers, they should make way for younger men who can produce as well or better.

Fred Merkle

Born 1888; Height 6.01; Weight 190; T-R; B-R; Led National League: 1914-SO

*= Net of home runs

	G	AB	H	R*	HR	RBI*	BA	SA	PAB
CLASS I **PAB .302+**									
1912	479	479	148	71	11	73	.309	.449	.324
CLASS II **PAB .274-.301**									
1908	38	41	11	5	1	6	.268	.439	.293
1910	144	506	148	71	4	66	.292	.441	.279
1911	149	541	153	68	12	72	.283	.438	.281
Total	331	1088	312	144	17	144	.287	.439	.280
CLASS III **PAB .246-.273**									
1913	153	563	147	75	3	66	.261	.373	.256
1914	146	512	132	64	7	56	.258	.375	.248
Total	299	1075	279	139	10	122	.260	.374	.252
CLASS IV **PAB .218-.245**									
1918	129	482	143	52	3	62	.297	.388	.243
1919	133	498	133	49	3	59	.267	.349	.223
Total	262	980	276	101	6	121	.282	.368	.233
CLASS V **PAB .217-**									
1907	15	47	12	0	0	5	.255	.277	.106
1909	78	236	45	15	0	20	.191	.237	.148
1915	140	505	151	48	4	58	.299	.384	.218
1916	135	470	111	44	7	39	.236	.336	.191
1917	148	557	147	63	3	54	.264	.368	.215
Total	516	1815	466	170	14	176	.257	.345	.198
Period	1537	5437	1481	625	58	636	.272	.383	.243
Other	100	345	99	34	3	36	.287	.400	.212
Career	1637	5782	1580	659	61	672	.273	.384	241
BEST 123+ GAMES									
1912	479	479	148	71	11	73	.309	.449	.324

Calculation of Domination Points, MTP/MVP

	AB	PAB	MVP	MTP
CLASS I	479	.324	155	460
CLASS II	1088	.280	305	
CLASS III	1075	.252	271	
CLASS IV	980	.233	228	
TOTAL	3622		959	
CLASS V	1815		0	
PERIOD	5437		959	

John McGraw was at the helm when the 19 year old Merkle joined the Giants in 1907; Dan McGann was the team's first baseman. The rookie played little.

McGann went to the Boston Braves in the winter of 1907 in an eight-man deal which, among other things, brought Fred Tenney to New York. McGraw immediately assigned the 37-year-old veteran to first base, leaving Merkle on the bench for most of a second season. This arrangement continued in 1909, but Merkle's playing time doubled; in 1910, McGraw gave him the full-time job.

Merkle was a Giant for over nine years. Then in 1916, he was traded to Brooklyn for Lew McCarty, a backup catcher. He began the 1917 season with the Dodgers but, in August, was sold to the Cubs. He finished that season and three others in Chicago.

Merkle's career was actually over when he left the Cubs in 1920, but he reappeared in 1925 with the New York Yankees as a part-time player and didn't quit for good until 1926 when he was 38 years old.

Merkle spent 95 percent of his games at first base. His fielding average (.985) was acceptable. Although a big man for the times, Merkle was fast. As a youngster, he seldom stole fewer than 20 bases in a season, and in 1911 he was fourth in the NL with 49 steals.

Per at Bat (PAB) 1901–19

	At Bat	R PAB	HR PAB	RBI PAB	Total PAB
Merkle	5437	.115	.011	.117	.243
Sample avg.	5072	.123	.007	.116	.246

Merkle was a below average contact hitter, but he was a timely hitter and showed above average durability. These were his strengths.

Chick Gandil

Born 1887; Height 6.02; Weight 190; T-R; B-R

* = Net of home runs

	G	AB	H	R*	HR	RBI*	BA	SA	PAB
CLASS I PAB .302+									
1912	117	443	135	57	2	79	.305	.431	.312
CLASS II PAB .274-.301									
None									
CLASS III PAB .246-.273									
1919	115	441	128	53	1	59	.290	.383	.256
CLASS IV PAB .218-.245									
1913	148	550	175	60	1	71	.318	.398	.240
1914	145	526	136	45	3	72	.259	.359	.228
1915	136	485	141	51	2	62	.291	.406	.237
1916	146	533	138	51	0	72	.259	.341	.231
1918	114	439	119	49	0	55	.271	.330	.237
Total	689	2533	709	256	6	332	.280	.368	.235
CLASS V PAB .217-									
1911	77	275	53	19	2	19	.193	.262	.145
1917	149	553	151	53	0	57	.273	.315	.199
Total	226	828	204	72	2	76	.246	.297	.181
Period	1147	4245	1176	438	11	546	.277	.362	.234
Career	1147	4245	1176	438	11	546	.277	.362	.234
BEST 123+ GAMES									
1913	148	550	175	60	1	71	.318	.398	.240

Calculation of Domination Points, MTP/MVP

	AB	PAB	MVP	MTP
CLASS I	443	.312	138	138
CLASS II	0		0	0
CLASS III	441	.256	113	
CLASS IV	2533	.235	595	
TOTAL	3417		846	
CLASS V	828		0	
PERIOD	4245		846	

Gandil played his nine-year career in the AL, all within the subject period. He, Daubert and Konetchy were the three best defensive first basemen in the survey group.

Gandil spent four years each with Washington and Chicago, and one with the Indians. He was 32 when he retired in 1919. He was a good journeyman who didn't last very long. His RBI profile was his strongest asset.

Per at Bat (PAB) 1901–19

	At Bat	R PAB	HR PAB	RBI PAB	Total PAB
Gandil	4245	.103	.003	.128	.234
Sample avg.	5072	.123	.007	.116	.246

Gandil, an opportunistic hitter, was otherwise an undistinguished offensive player.

Fred Luderus

Born 1885; Height 6.00; Weight 185; T-R; B-L

* = Net of home runs

	G	AB	H	R*	HR	RBI*	BA	SA	PAB
CLASS I PAB .302+									
1909	11	37	11	7	1	8	.297	.459	.432
CLASS II PAB .275-.301									
1911	146	551	166	53	16	83	.301	.472	.276
CLASS III PAB .246-.274									
1910	45	122	31	15	0	17	.254	.352	.262
1918	125	468	135	49	5	62	.288	.378	.248
Total	170	590	166	64	5	79	.281	.373	.251
CLASS IV PAB .221-.245									
1912	148	572	147	67	10	59	.257	.381	.238
1913	155	588	154	49	18	68	.262	.432	.230
1914	121	443	110	43	12	43	.248	.388	.221
1915	141	499	157	48	7	55	.315	.457	.220
1917	154	522	136	52	5	67	.261	.351	.238
Total	719	2624	704	259	52	292	.268	.402	.230
CLASS V PAB .220-									
1916	146	508	143	47	5	48	.281	.374	.197
1919	138	509	149	55	5	49	.293	.405	.214

	G	AB	H	R*	HR	RBI*	BA	SA	PAB
284	1017	292	102	10	97	.287	.390	.206	
Total Period	1330	4819	1339	485	84	559	.278	.404	.234
Other	16	32	5	1	0	4	.156	.252	.156
Career	1346	4851	1344	486	84	563	.277	.403	.234
BEST 123+ GAMES									
1911	146	551	166	53	16	83	.301	.472	.276

Calculation of Domination Points, MTP/MVP

	AB	PAB	MVP	MTP
CLASS I	37	.432	16	168
CLASS II	551	.276	152	
CLASS III	590	.251	148	
CLASS IV	2624	.230	604	
TOTAL	3802		920	
CLASS V	1017		0	
PERIOD	4819		920	

Fred Luderus, a fair fielding (FA .986), full-time first baseman, broke in with the Cubs in 1909 but soon went with the Phillies, where he spent 11 of his 12 seasons. He retired in 1920 at the age of 35.

Luderus was the slow-footed power hitter of the survey, and a fair RBI man. Scoring and durability were the weak spots in his record.

Per at Bat (PAB) 1901–19

	At Bat	R PAB	HR PAB	RBI PAB	Total PAB
Luderus	4819	.101	.017	.116	.234
Sample avg.	5072	.123	.007	.116	.246

Power, nothing else, defined Luderus as a hitter — he had four double-digit home runs seasons, rare for the times.

Kitty Bransfield

Born 1875; Height 5.11; Weight 207; T-R; B-R

* = Net of home runs

	G	AB	H	R*	HR	RBI*	BA	SA	PAB
CLASS I									
PAB .302+									
1901	139	566	167	92	0	91	.295	.398	.323
CLASS II									
PAB .274–.301									
1902	102	417	127	49	1	68	.305	.396	.283
CLASS III									
PAB .246–.273									
None									
CLASS IV									
PAB .218–.245									
1903	127	505	134	67	2	55	.265	.350	.246

	G	AB	H	R*	HR	RBI*	BA	SA	PAB
1905	151	580	150	52	3	73	.259	.345	.221
1908	144	527	160	50	3	68	.304	.395	.230
Total	422	1612	444	169	8	196	.275	.363	.231
CLASS V PAB .217-									
1904	139	520	116	47	0	60	.223	.290	.206
1906	140	524	144	46	1	58	.275	.353	.202
1907	94	348	81	25	0	38	.233	.287	.181
1909	140	527	154	46	1	59	.292	.372	.199
1910	123	427	102	36	3	49	.239	.319	.206
1911	26	53	15	4	0	3	.283	.377	.132
Total	662	2399	612	204	5	267	.255	.328	.198
Period	1325	4994	1350	514	14	622	.270	.353	.230
Other	5	9	2	2	0	1	.222	.353	.333
Career	1330	5003	1352	516	14	623	.270	.353	.230
BEST 123+ GAMES									
1901	139	566	167	92	0	91	.295	.398	.323

Calculation of Domination Points, MTP/MVP

	AB	PAB	MVP	MTP
CLASS I	566	.323	183	301
CLASS II	417	.283	118	
CLASS III	0	0	0	
CLASS IV	1612	.231	372	
TOTAL	2595		673	
CLASS V	2399		0	
PERIOD	4994		673	

Kitty Bransfield had a 12-year major league career, most of it in the subject period—four years with Pittsburgh, six and a fraction with the Phillies and just a touch with the Cubs. He was 36 when he quit in 1911.

In 1901 with the Pirates, Bransfield had one of the best production seasons of the era and it looked like he would become one of the stars of the NL. But he wasn't—he was rather ordinary at the plate and in the field.

Attentive readers will notice that many players had great seasons during the early years of this analytical period that were seldom equaled thereafter, which throws a legitimate cloud over the value of the early numbers that were calculated when the rules of the game were still being formed into those that applied in future decades.

Per at Bat (PAB) 1901–19

	At Bat	R PAB	HR PAB	RBI PAB	Total PAB
Bransfield	4994	.103	.003	.124	.230
Sample avg.	5072	.123	.007	.116	.246

Due to his burly physique, one assumes that few players made too much of Bransfield's nickname.

Jake Daubert

Born 1884; Height 5.11; Weight 160; T-L; B-L; MVP-NL, 1913; Led National League: 1913-BA; 1914-BA; 1918-3B

* = Net of home runs

	G	AB	H	R*	HR	RBI*	BA	SA	PAB
CLASS I PAB .302+ None									
CLASS II PAB .275–.301 None									
CLASS III PAB .246–.274									
1912	145	559	172	78	3	63	.308	.415	.258
1913	139	508	178	74	2	50	.350	.423	.248
1914	126	474	156	83	6	39	.329	.432	.270
Total	410	1541	506	235	11	152	.328	.423	.258
CLASS IV PAB .221–.245									
1911	149	573	176	84	5	40	.307	.391	.225
1916	127	478	151	72	3	30	.316	.397	.220
1918	108	396	122	48	2	45	.308	.429	.240
1919	140	537	148	77	2	42	.276	.350	.225
Total	524	1984	597	281	12	157	.301	.386	.227
CLASS V PAB .220–									
1910	144	552	146	59	8	42	.264	.389	.197
1915	150	544	164	60	2	45	.301	.381	.197
1917	125	468	122	57	2	28	.261	.299	.186
Total	419	1564	432	176	12	115	.276	.359	.194
Period	1353	5089	1535	692	35	424	.302	.390	.226
Other	661	2584	791	369	21	242	.306	.423	.245
Career	2014	7673	2326	1061	56	666	.303	.401	.232
BEST 123+ GAMES									
1914	126	474	156	83	6	39	.329	.432	.270

Calculation of Domination Points, MTP/MVP

	AB	PAB	MVP	MTP
CLASS I	0	0	0	0
CLASS II	0	0	0	
CLASS III	1541	.258	398	
CLASS IV	1984	.227	450	
TOTAL	3525		848	
CLASS V	1564		0	
PERIOD	5089		848	

Jake Daubert took over the first-base job during his first season (1910) with the Dodgers. He was 26 at the time. In nine years with them, he won the BA crown twice, the MVP award once, and he fielded his position as it's supposed to be done (FA .991).

Before the 1919 season, 35-year-old Daubert was traded to the Reds even up for Tommy Griffith, an outfielder of no great distinction. Daubert finished his career with the Reds, retiring in 1924 at the age of 40.

Daubert, one of the best contact hitters of the era, was also a superior fielder. The subject period encompasses only two-thirds of his career, which, like that of any player whose career overlapped into the live-ball era, does not get fully analyzed in this survey.

PER AT BAT (PAB) 1901–19

	At Bat	R PAB	HR PAB	RBI PAB	Total PAB
Daubert	5089	.136	.007	.083	.226
Sample avg.	5072	.123	.007	.116	.246

Daubert, with career ABs of 7673, had good speed and he hit better than most, but his full value as a player will always be clouded by the fact that he was a split-era player. The numbers, however, suggest this: If managers of the day were forced to choose between Chance, Davis, Chase or Daubert, the least known of the four — Daubert — would probably be the choice.

FRED TENNEY

Born 1871 Height 5.09; Weight 155; T-L; B-L

* = Net of home runs

	G	AB	H	R*	HR	RBI*	BA	SA	PAB
CLASS I PAB .302+ None									
CLASS II PAB .274-.301 None									
CLASS III PAB .246-.273									
1903	122	447	140	76	3	38	.313	.396	.262
1908	156	583	149	99	2	47	.256	.304	.254
Total	278	1030	289	175	5	85	.281	.344	.257
CLASS IV PAB .218-.245									
1902	134	489	154	86	2	28	.315	.376	.237
1911	102	369	97	51	1	35	.263	.328	.236
Total	236	858	251	137	3	63	.293	.355	.237
CLASS V PAB .217-									
1901	115	457	127	62	1	21	.278	.317	.184
1904	147	533	144	75	1	36	.270	.341	.210
1905	149	549	158	84	0	28	.288	.332	.204
1906	143	544	154	60	1	27	.283	.340	.162
1907	150	554	151	83	0	26	.273	.334	.197
1909	101	375	88	40	3	27	.235	.291	.187
Total	805	3012	822	404	6	165	.273	.328	.191
Period	1319	4900	1362	716	14	313	.278	.336	.213
Other	675	2701	869	537	8	353	.325	.401	.332
Career	1994	7602	2239	1253	22	666	.294	.359	.255
BEST 123+ GAMES									
1908	156	583	149	99	2	47	.256	.304	.254

Calculation of Domination Points, MTP/MVP

	AB	PAB	MVP	MTP
CLASS I	0	0	0	0
CLASS II	0	0	0	
CLASS III	1030	.257	265	
CLASS IV	858	.237	203	
TOTAL	1888		468	
CLASS V	3012		0	
PERIOD	4900		468	

Tenney was 30 when the subject period opened, with seven years of major league experience behind him with the Boston Braves. In 1901, he was still with that club and, for all but two of his 17 career years, stayed with them.

Like McInnis and Daubert, Tenney's durability looks weak only because the period being analyzed was not his period of peak activity (1891–1909, career ABs 7601). In the subject period, Fred was neither very active nor very productive.

As a production man, he was the second-best scorer in the group, but he had little power, and he had the lowest RBI yield.

Per at Bat (PAB) 1901–19

	At Bat	R PAB	HR PAB	RBI PAB	Total PAB
Tenney	4900	.146	.003	.064	.213
Sample avg.	5072	.123	.007	.116	.246

Tenney was small for a first basemen and not unusually skilled (FA .982). For three seasons (1905/1907), he was the playing manager.

George Stovall

Born 1878; Height 6.02; Weight 180; T-R; B-R

*= Net of home runs

	G	AB	H	R*	HR	RBI*	BA	SA	PAB
CLASS I PAB .302+ None									
CLASS II PAB .274-301									
1911	126	458	124	48	0	79	.271	.338	.277
CLASS III PAB .246-.273									
1904	52	182	54	17	1	30	.297	.379	.264
1914	124	450	128	44	7	68	.284	.398	.264
Total	176	632	182	61	8	98	.288	.393	.264
CLASS UV PAB .218-.245 None									
CLASS V PAB .217-									
1905	111	419	114	40	1	46	.272	.368	.208
1906	116	443	121	54	0	37	.273	.339	.205

	G	AB	H	R*	HR	RBI*	BA	SA	PAB
1907	124	466	110	37	1	35	.236	.305	.157
1908	138	534	156	69	2	43	.292	.380	.213
1909	145	565	139	58	2	47	.246	.322	.189
1910	142	521	136	47	0	52	.261	.313	.190
1912	115	398	101	35	0	45	.254	.322	.201
1913	89	303	87	33	1	23	.287	.363	.188
1915	130	480	111	48	0	44	.231	.288	.192
Total	1110	4129	1075	421	7	372	.260	.332	.194
Period	1412	5219	1381	530	15	549	.265	.340	.210
Career	1412	5219	1381	530	15	549	.265	.340	.210
BEST 123+ GAMES									
1911	126	458	124	48	0	79	.271	.338	.277

Calculation of Domination Points, MTP/MVP

	AB	PAB	MVP	MTP
CLASS I	0	0	0	127
CLASS II	458	.277	127	
CLASS III	632	.264	167	
CLASS IV	0		0	
TOTAL	1090		294	
CLASS V	4129		0	
PERIOD	5219		294	

George Stovall had a 12-year career, eight with Cleveland, two with the St. Louis Browns and two in Kansas City of the Federal League (1914–15). He was a journeyman ballplayer of no particular distinction who had a relatively short career in the subject period.

Per at Bat (PAB) 1901–19

	At Bat	R PAB	HR PAB	RBI PAB	Total PAB
Stovall	5219	.102	.003	.105	.210
Sample avg.	5072	.123	.007	.116	.246

The first baseman was made manager of the Indians in 1911, and he ultimately operated as the playing manager for five seasons, compiling a record as such of 313/376. When he retired in 1915, Stovall was 37 years old.

First Basemen — Analysis, Summary in Domination Point (DP) Sequence

* Net of home runs
** HOF

PLAYER	AB	R*	PAB HR	RBI*	TOTAL PAB	BA	SA	MTP	MVP
AVG. PLAYER	5072	.123	.007	.116	.246	.281	.376		
SUPERSTAR									
DP 1591+									
None									
STAR									
DP 1269–1590									
Chase H	7417	.124	.008	.119	.251	.291	.391	295	1553
Davis H	5367	.138	.013	.129	.280	.279	**.407**	981	1401
ABOVE AVG.									
DP 947–1268									
Chance F**	3805	**.180**	.005	**.139**	.324	.297	.396	1114	1232
Konetchy E	6684	.118	.009	.118	.245	.278	.396	815	1201
Hoblitzel R	4706	.120	.006	.126	.251	.278	.374	269	1159
Merkle F	5437	.115	.011	.117	.243	.272	.383	460	959
McGann D	3581	.140	.007	.117	.264	.278	.369	427	946
BELOW AVERAGE									
DP 625–946									
Luderus F	4819	.101	**.017**	.116	.234	.278	.404	168	920
Miller D	5142	.117	.006	.123	.246	.261	.360	466	918
Daubert J	5089	.136	.007	.083	.226	.302	.290	0	848
Gandil C	4245	.103	.003	.128	.234	.277	.362	138	846
McInnis S	4672	.111	.003	.135	.250	**.309**	.380	686	782
Bransfield K	4994	.103	.003	.124	.230	.270	.353	301	673
POOR									
DP 624									
Tenney F	4900	.146	.003	.064	.213	.278	.336	0	468
Stovall G	5219	.102	.003	.105	.210	.265	.340	127	294
Average									947
SD									321
10 BEST PAB SEASONS									
Chance**-1903	441	**.184**	.004	**.179**	.367	.327	.440		
Miller-1911	470	.162	.013	.153	.328	.268	.377		
Merkle-1912	479	.148	.023	.153	.324	.309	.449		
Bransfield K-1901>	**566**	.162	.000	.161	.323	.295	.398		
Davis-1906>	551	.149	.022	.152	.323	.292	**.459**		
McGann-1905	491	.169	.010	.143	.322	.299	.434		
McInnis-1911	468	156	.006	.158	.320	.321	.425		
Konetchy-1910	520	.162	.006	.144	.312	.302	.425		
Hoblitzell-1915	399	.130	.005	.148	.283	.283	.396		
Stovall-1911 >	458	.105	.000	.172	.277	.271	.338		
Chase-1915 >	567	.120	**.030**	.127	.277	.291	.471		
> Tie									

It is useful to note that in the listing of best PAB seasons only four men (Bransfield, Davis, Konetchy and Chase) had more than 500 AB. The performance of these fully-active players deserves special admiration. Questions about the records of selectively-active players will always remain.

Also, half of the best seasons fell in the first decade, and none went beyond 1915, another reminder that the early records should be viewed with caution.

The Best of the Best

Sample size	15
NL	10
AL	5
Most durable-top 5	Chase, Konetchy, Merkle, Davis, Miller
Top five BA	McInnis, Daubert, Chance, Chase, Davis
Top five SA	Davis, Luderus, Chance, Konetchy, Chase
Top five scorers (R)	Chance, McGann, Davis, Daubert, Chase
Top five power hitters (HR)	Luderus, Davis, Merkle, Konetchy, Chase
Top five clutch hitters (RBI)	Chance, McInnis, Davis, Gandil, Hoblitzel
Top five seasons	Chance, Miller, Merkle, Bransfield, Davis
Most talented producer (MTP)-top 5	Chance, Davis, Konetchy, McInnis, Miller
Most valuable producer (MVP)-top 5	Chase, Davis, Chance, Konetchy, Hoblitzel

The 1901–19 era featured short-careered players with lots of speed and little power. Only six players exceeded the average durability for the sample, 5072 AB — Chase, Konetchy, Merkle, Davis, Miller and Daubert. These were the backbone first basemen of the era, the men who day by day represented the quality of the times.

The MTP rating captures the players who produced at Class I and Class II levels for the longest time. The top five were Chance, Davis, Konetchy, McInnis and Miller.

But it's class (PAB) plus durability (AB) that determines the MVP ranking. The top five were Chase, Davis, Chance, Konetchy and Hoblitzel.

Careful readers will notice that it was Chase's Class III PAB weighted by his Class I durability that took him to the top of the heap. No matter how talented a player, to be of value to his team he must first be ready to play. In this respect, Chase was dominant with Konetchy close behind. Because of questions raised about the legitimacy of Chance's record, it is important to note that Chase was clearly the leading first baseman of the era.

It is the position of this analysis that position players with MVP ratings in the Superstar classification should be in the HOF, and those in the Star classification should get serious consideration, unless they were bypassed for some extraordinary reason. Those in lower MVP classifications who are in the HOF must have demonstrated obvious superiority in some aspect of the game, other than productivity, that made them stand out from the pack.

Based upon those criteria, Chase and Davis would have been understandable additions to the HOF; they were overlooked. On the other hand, Chance was elected, a decision that, from a comparable point of view, seems incorrect and unjust.

Analysis has demonstrated that Chance's MTP and MVP ratings are misleading — the product of a string of partial seasons that do not fairly and comparably reflect his full-time skills over an extended period. And the view is expressed here that his association with the famed Tinkers to Evers to Chance double-play combination was the questionable reason for his election.

The period did not produce a bumper crop of first basemen, and no superstar. Maybe Chase could have been chosen; maybe Davis. And it is just possible that McInnis and Daubert were the best of all split-era players, who can only be emotionally judged.

Catchers — Analysis, 1901–1919

With apologies to fans who follow baseball closely, it's useful to inform those who love the game as much, but study it less, that in developing a sample for catchers, screening levels used for other fielding positions were not fair or useful. The man behind the mask is special. The unique physical strains associated with his job reduce games played per season and shorten his career.

The judgment was made that using a specially designed durability factor (five or more seasons with at least 300 ABs) would provide a more meaningful sample — one more reflective of baseball managers' attitudes about player quality and value and, to be practical, one that would result in a sample of reasonable size.

During the 1901–19 period, 13 catchers met the test and generated an average PAB of .188. The elements of the PAB factor are summarized below:

	PAB
Runs	.091
Home runs	.003
RBI	.097
Total	.191

With the information dealing with first basemen fresh in mind, it's obvious that the catchers who qualified were a powerless, light-hitting and low-producing bunch. They are identified below:

Dominant Catchers, 1910–19 Record

* HOF
** Net of home runs

PLAYER	LG	AB	H	R**	HR	RBI**	BA	SA	PAB
CLASS I **PAB .263+**									
Bresnahan R*	N	4460	1245	656	26	501	.279	.378	.265
CLASS II **PAB .227–262**									
Kling J	N	4190	1127	447	20	486	.271	.357	.227
CLASS III **PAB .191–.226**									
Meyers C	N	2834	826	262	14	349	.291	.378	.221
Schalk R*	A	2830	707	292	5	279	.250	.306	.204
Schreckengost O	A	2588	693	235	7	274	.268	.338	.199
Wingo I	N	2562	658	235	15	259	.257	.359	.199
CLASS IV **PAB .155–.190**									
Sullivan B	A	3345	692	306	11	314	.207	.270	.189
McLean L	N	2647	694	177	6	292	.262	.323	.179
O'Neill S	A	2636	640	223	5	233	.243	.311	.175
Dooin R	N	4004	961	323	10	334	.240	.298	.167
Gibson G	N	3776	893	280	15	330	.236	.312	.166

PLAYER	LG	AB	H	R**	HR	RBI**	BA	SA	PAB
CLASS V									
POOR .154-									
Killefer B	N	2826	666	206	4	204	.236	.282	.146
Bergen B	N	3028	516	136	2	191	.170	.201	.109
Avg		3210	794	291	11	311	.247	.316	.191
SD		645					.035		

(1) BA, PAB calculated horizontally; (2) AB, H, R, HR, RBI, SA, SD calculated vertically

CLASSIFICATIONS

	Class (PAB)	Durability (AB)
CLASS I	.263+	4502+
CLASS II	.227–.262	3856–4501
CLASS III	.191–.226	3210–3855
CLASS IV	.155–.190	2564–3209
CLASS V	.154-	2563-

Player Analysis

Class I, PAB .263+

Roger Bresnahan, elected to the HOF in 1945, squeezed into this classification. Analysis reveals interesting information about this player, namely, that he was a part-time catcher who looks exceptional only when compared with full-time catchers.

Bresnahan was the first to use shin pads, for which his successors have been eternally grateful.

Before going forward, readers should pause and reflect upon the low threshold that catchers had to meet to acquire Class I status—much lower than the other positions.

Class II, PAB .227-.262

Johnny Kling is the only player so classified—and he barely made it. He was a durable player, better than most catchers, but not outstanding.

Class III, PAB .191–.226

Four catchers fell into this classification: Meyers, Schalk, Schreckengost and Wingo.

Schalk was elected to the HOF in 1945. That distinction was not justified by his production performance during the subject period and, on the surface, it doesn't appear he was any more fearsome at the plate during the live-ball era, in which he spent most of his career. The HOF blurb concentrates on his defensive skills.

The question raised is this: Should a great defensive catcher with poor offensive skills be in the HOF?

Class IV, PAB .155-.190

Sullivan, McLean, O'Neill, Dooin and Gibson were so classified. Dooin and Gibson had better-than-average durability and above-average power, skills that presumably kept their careers alive. The value of Sullivan, McLean and O'Neill may be revealed in analysis.

Class V, PAB .154-

Killefer and Bergen had the lowest production averages. They are in the sample only because the general quality of catchers during the era was so low.

Roger Bresnahan

Born 1879; Height 5.09; Weight 200; T-R; B-R; Led National League: 1908-BB

HOF 1945
* = Net of home runs

	G	AB	H	R*	HR	RBI*	BA	SA	PAB
CLASS I									
PAB .263+									
1903	113	406	142	83	4	51	.350	.493	.340
1904	109	402	114	76	5	28	.284	.410	.271
1905	104	331	100	58	0	46	.302	.375	.314
1906	124	405	114	69	0	43	.281	.356	.277
1907	110	328	83	53	4	34	.253	.360	.277
1908	140	449	127	69	1	53	.283	.359	.274
1910	88	234	65	35	0	27	.278	.368	.265
1911	81	227	63	19	3	38	.278	.463	.264
1914	86	248	69	42	0	24	.278	.351	.266
Total	955	3030	877	504	17	344	.289	.392	.285
CLASS II									
PAB .227–.262									
1901	86	295	79	39	1	31	.263	.369	.241
1902	116	413	116	42	5	51	.281	.414	.237
1913	68	161	37	19	1	20	.230	.304	.248
Total	270	869	232	100	7	102	.267	.378	.241
CLASS III									
PAB .191–.226									
1909	72	234	57	27	0	23	.244	.269	.214
1912	48	108	36	7	1	14	.333	.463	.204
Total	120	342	93	34	1	37	.272	.330	.211
CLASS IV,									
PAB .155-.190									
1915	77	221	45	18	1	18	.204	.262	.167
CLASS V,									
PAB .154-									
None									
Period	1422	4462	1247	656	26	501	.279	.382	.265
Other	8	18	6	1	0	3	.333	.368	.222
Career	1430	4480	1253	657	26	504	.280	.379	.265
BEST 123+ GAMES									
1906	124	405	114	69	0	43	.281	.356	.277

Calculation of Domination Points, MTP/MVP

	AB	PAB	MVP	MTP
CLASS I	3030	.285	864	1073
CLASS II	869	.241	209	
CLASS III	342	.211	72	
CLASS IV	221	.167	37	
TOTAL	4462		1182	
CLASS V	0		0	
PERIOD	4462		1182	

Bresnahan dropped into the major leagues in 1897 for a cup of coffee with Washington. He next appeared in 1900 as a catcher in two games for the Cubs. In 1901, then 22, he played for Baltimore as a utility man.

John McGraw, manager of Baltimore in those days, got into an argument with AL president Ban Johnson, at the end of which the disgruntled McGraw left the AL and hooked on with the Giants as manager. Bresnahan went with him.

For the next six seasons, Roger played a variety of positions for McGraw. In only one (1908) did he catch over 100 games.

Bresnahan was traded to the Cardinals in December 1908 for three players. He functioned in the 1909 season, and for the three following, as a playing manager. St. Louis let him go to the Cubs for cash in 1913; in Chicago, two years later, Bresnahan retired. He was 36 when he quit.

Like most things about Bresnahan's record, his defensive statistics are a hodgepodge of varying experiences in every position on the field. In only one year (1908) did he combine a full season of catching with a significant number of games. He came out of that unique (for him) experience with a FA of .985, better than the career FA of .981 of HOF catcher Ray Schalk, which seems to qualify him as a competent backstop. Further evidence of this is that he handled pitchers like Mathewson and McGinnity without complaint.

All catchers owe Bresnahan a debt of gratitude. In 1907, tired of the bumps and bruises, he introduced shin guards to the game. Players gave him a fierce ribbing, but he stuck it out and soon the equipment was formally approved by baseball.

Even for catchers, Bresnahan's durability record is lightweight. He appeared in 120 or more games only twice in his 17-year career, and he played in 100 or more games in only seven seasons.

In a situation of limited (managed?) exposure one must guard against undue enthusiasm over offensive statistics. That having been noted, Bresnahan functioned at a Class I level during his New York period which, for all practical purposes, constituted his career as an active player.

Roger had the second highest BA of the group and the highest SA. In terms of PAB elements, he was the top scorer, the top home run hitter and the third best RBI man in the sample.

He was also fast. He stole his share of bases (34 in 1903) and performed well as a leadoff hitter for McGraw's Giants, an unusual role for a catcher and one that explains his efficiency, when contrasted with other catchers, as a scorer (OBP .386).

In the following comparison of Bresnahan's statistics with those of the select catching sample, his total dominance of the scene becomes clearer.

Per at Bat (PAB) 1901–19

	AT BAT	R PAB	HR PAB	RBI PAB	TOTAL PAB
Bresnahan	4460	.147	.006	.112	.265
Sample avg.	3210	.091	.003	.097	.191

Bresnahan's offensive talent was indisputable. But his election to the HOF isn't. Only against catchers does his durability record appear strong. Against first basemen, for example, it's below average. Only against catchers does his PAB appear robust.

Actually, Bresnahan became the equivalent of a utility player when he was 23, and for all practical purposes he quit when he was 29—seven years. Thereafter, he was an occasional backup man.

Should a record like this be compared with those of regular catchers? Indeed, was Bresnahan a catcher at all, or was he just a multi-talented utility player?

Many might conclude that, with such questions in the air, Bresnahan was not a HOF player.

Johnny Kling

Born 1875; Height 5.10; Weight 160; T-R; B-R

* = Net of home runs

	G	AB	H	R*	HR	RBI*	BA	SA	PAB
CLASS I									
PAB .263+									
1903	132	491	146	64	3	65	.297	.428	.269
CLASS II									
PAB .227–.262									
1902	114	434	124	50	0	57	.286	.343	.247
1906	107	343	107	43	2	44	.312	.420	.259
1907	104	334	95	43	1	42	.284	.386	.257
1908	126	424	117	47	4	55	.276	.382	.250
Total	451	1535	443	183	7	198	.289	.380	.253
CLASS III									
PAB .191–.226									
1904	123	452	110	39	2	44	.243	.296	.188
1905	111	380	83	25	1	51	.218	.279	.203
1910	91	297	80	29	2	30	.269	.360	.205
1911	102	321	68	37	3	26	.212	.293	.206
1912	81	252	80	24	2	28	.317	.405	.214
1913	80	209	57	20	0	23	.273	.364	.206
Total	588	1911	478	174	10	202	.250	.324	.202
CLASS IV									
PAB .155-.190									
1901	74	253	70	26	0	21	.277	.324	.186
CLASS V									
PAB .154									
None									
Period	1245	4190	1137	447	20	486	.271	.357	.227
Other	15	51	15	8	0	7	.294	.357	.294
Career	1260	4241	1152	455	20	493	.272	.357	.228
BEST 123+ GAMES									
1903	132	491	146	64	3	65	.297	.428	.269

Calculation of Domination Points, MTP/MVP

	AB	PAB	MVP	MTP
CLASS I	491	.269	132	520
CLASS II	1535	.253	388	
CLASS III	1911	.202	386	
CLASS IV	253	.196	50	
TOTAL	4190		956	
CLASS V	0		0	
PERIOD	4190		956	

Johnny Kling was a late arrival. In 1900, as a 25-year-old, he played 15 games with the Cubs. He was behind the plate for almost half the schedule in the next season, and in 1902, he became the first-string backstop for the club. He continued in that capacity through the 1908 season.

Kling had squabbles with team management in 1909 and 1910, and in 1911 he went to the Boston Braves in an eight-man deal. In 1912, he was playing manager for Boston and finished in last place. Then he was sold to the Reds where he finished up in 1913 — 38 years old.

Kling was behind the plate for 100+ games in eight of his 13 years; he compiled a career FA of .970, which suggests that he was marginally competent as a glove man.

Competent contact hitters with some pop in their bats are always prized possessions in baseball. Kling qualified as such. He was a competent contact hitter (BA .271); he stroked the long ball more than most catchers and he was the second best clutch hitter in the sample.

Compared with his peers, Johnny Kling was well ahead as a producer.

PER AT BAT (PAB) 1901–19

	AT BAT	R PAB	HR PAB	RBI PAB	TOTAL PAB
Kling	4190	.107	.005	.115	.227
Sample avg.	3210	.091	.003	.097	.191

In terms of quality, Kling's durability was more real than Bresnahan's and (unlike Bresnahan) he was indisputably a catcher.

Was he of HOF caliber?

Doubtful. He had no battle ribbons to suggest that he was a league leader in anything of importance. Most would conclude that, although more effective than his peers, he was king of a weak crowd, and neither his durability nor his PAB was overly impressive in an absolute sense.

CHIEF MEYERS

Born 1880; Height 5.11; Weight 194; T-R; B-R

* = Net of home runs

	G	AB	H	R*	HR	RBI*	BA	SA	PAB
CLASS I									
PAB .263+									
1911	133	391	130	47	1	60	.332	.432	.276
1912	126	371	133	54	6	48	.358	.477	.291
Total	259	762	263	101	7	108	.345	.454	.283
CLASS II									
PAB .227–.262									
1910	127	365	104	24	1	61	.285	.342	.236
1914	134	381	109	32	1	54	.286	.354	.228
Total	261	746	213	56	2	115	.286	.348	.232
CLASS III									
PAB .191–.226									
1909	90	220	61	14	1	29	.277	.382	.200
1913	120	378	118	34	3	44	.312	.410	.214
Total	210	598	179	48	4	73	.299	.400	.209
CLASS IV									
PAB .155–.190									
1915	110	289	67	23	1	25	.232	.311	.170
1916	80	239	59	21	0	21	.247	.314	.176
Total	190	528	126	44	1	46	.239	.312	.172
CLASS V									
PAB .154–									
1917	72	200	45	13	0	7	.225	.300	.100
Period	992	2834	826	262	14	349	.291	.378	.221
Career	992	2834	826	262	14	349	.291	.378	.221
BEST 123+ GAMES									
1912	126	371	133	54	6	48	.358	.477	.291

CALCULATION OF DOMINATION POINTS, MTP/MVP

	AB	PAB	MVP	MTP
CLASS I	762	.283	216	389
CLASS II	746	.232	173	
CLASS III	598	.209	125	
CLASS IV	528	.172	91	
TOTAL	2634		605	
CLASS V	200		0	
PERIOD	2834		605	

Chief Meyers didn't play a game of major league baseball until he was 29 years old. In 1909, he was used behind the plate for 90 games by the Giants who, since the departure of Bresnahan, were looking for a catcher. The job was given to Meyers in 1910 and he held it through the 1915 season. In 1916, then 36 years old, Meyers moved on to the Dodgers, then the Braves for part-time duty. He was 37 when he retired in 1917.

The Chief posted a FA of .974 — not great but good. He handled pitchers like Christy Mathewson (HOF) and Rube Marquard (HOF), and he appeared effectively with such men in four World Series, a fact that perhaps says as much or more about his skills as a catcher than any defensive statistic does.

It isn't surprising to find that Meyers had the best offensive year of the group. He was its best contact hitter; he had long ball power, and he was a tough strikeout. His weakness as an offensive threat was speed—he was slow.

In 1912, his skills came together before age deteriorated his coordination. With a BA of .358 (2nd best in the NL) and an SA of .477, the Chief made New Yorkers forget about Roger Bresnahan. His PAB of .291 was the best turned in by any man in the elite group in the 19-year period. And it wasn't a freak. In a nine-year career, Meyers had only one poor season—four were star-studded.

Lack of foot speed subtracts from the scoring ability that customarily goes with superior hitting skills. It was so with Meyers, who was but a slice above average as a scorer:

PER AT BAT (PAB) 1901–19

	AT BAT	R PAB	HR PAB	RBI PAB	TOTAL PAB
Meyers	2834	.092	.005	.124	.221
Sample avg.	3210	.091	.003	.097	.191

It could well be the case that given an earlier start Meyers could have ended up in the HOF as the outstanding full-time catcher of the period.

RAY SCHALK

Born 1892; Height 5.09; Weight 165; T-R; B-R

HOF 1955
* = Net of home runs

	G	AB	H	R*	HR	RBI*	BA	SA	PAB
CLASS I PAB .263+									
None									
CLASS II PAB .227–.264									
1912	23	63	18	7	0	8	.286	.317	.238

	G	AB	H	R*	HR	RBI*	BA	SA	PAB
1915	135	413	110	45	1	53	.266	.327	.240
1917	140	424	96	45	3	48	.226	.295	.226
1919	131	394	111	57	0	34	.282	.320	.231
Total	429	1294	335	154	4	143	.259	.314	.233
CLASS III PAB .191–.226									
1916	129	410	95	36	0	41	.232	.305	.188
CLASS IV PAB .155–.190									
1913	128	401	98	37	1	37	.244	.314	.187
1914	135	392	106	30	0	36	.270	.314	.168
1918	108	333	73	35	0	22	.219	.255	.171
Total	371	1126	277	102	1	95	.246	.297	.176
CLASS V PAB .154– None									
Period	929	2830	707	292	5	279	.250	.306	.204
Other	831	2476	638	275	7	303	.258	.327	.236
Career	1760	5306	1345	567	12	582	.253	.316	.219
BEST 123+ GAMES									
1915	135	413	110	45	1	53	.266	.327	.240

Calculation of Domination Points, MTP/MVP

	AB	PAB	MVP	MTP
CLASS I	0	0	0	301
CLASS II	1294	.233	301	
CLASS III	410	.188	77	
CLASS IV	1126	.176	198	
TOTAL	2830		576	
CLASS V	0		0	
PERIOD	2830		576	

Ray Schalk joined the White Sox when he was 20 years old in 1912. A year later, he was the starting catcher and he held that job for all but one of his 18 career years, which is partly explained by his impressive career FA (.991).

During his final two seasons with Chicago, 1927–28, Schalk functioned as player-manager. He went to the Giants in 1929 and retired there — 37 years old.

This was not Schalk's era. It is only a record of his beginnings. Defensively, he showed superior ability. As a producer, he was better than the average of the sample group.

Judging by his early offensive record, one assumes Schalk is in the HOF because of his defensive abilities, and his career durability as a catcher. His PAB elements compare with the average of the sample group as follows:

Per at Bat (PAB) 1901–19

	AT BAT	R PAB	HR PAB	RBI PAB	TOTAL PAB
Schalk	2830	.103	.002	.099	.204
Sample avg.	3210	.091	.003	.097	.191

A small man for a catcher, Ray Schalk was unusually durable on a seasonal basis. During his eight seasons in the subject period, he caught over 100 games in all but one — in six seasons, he was active in more than 120 games.

The Schalk era was 1910–1929. As previously noted, that era was a mixture of deadball and live-ball baseball, and for that reason career numbers have little meaning. Schalk is one of the players who was caught up in this mixed-era problem.

His production numbers do not suggest a HOF player, so one must look elsewhere for hints of what it was that impressed voters. His durability record and his fielding averages provide the answer — he appeared in 1762 games with 5,306 at bats.

The logic for not selecting players like Schalk is this: Time has shown that there is such a thing as an above average producer who has above average defensive talent plus durability. That being the case, why raise up a defensive artist with few offensive skills? Reserve the HOF for those who do it all.

OSSE SCHRECKENGOST

Born 1875; Height 5.10; Weight 180; T-R B-R

* = Net of home runs

	G	AB	H	R*	HR	RBI*	BA	SA	PAB
CLASS I									
PAB .263+									
1901	86	280	85	37	0	38	.304	.386	.268
1902	97	358	117	48	2	50	.327	.402	.279
Total	183	638	202	85	2	88	.317	.395	.274
CLASS II									
PAB .227–.262									
None									
CLASS III									
PAB .191–.226									
1906	98	338	96	28	1	40	.284	.358	.204
1907	101	356	97	30	0	38	.272	.334	.191
Total	199	694	193	58	1	78	.278	.346	.197
CLASSS IV									
PAB .155–.190									
1903	92	306	78	23	3	27	.255	.353	.173
1905	121	416	113	30	0	45	.272	.346	.180
Total	213	722	191	53	3	72	.265	.349	.177
CLASS V									
PAB .154–									
1904	95	311	58	22	1	20	.186	.232	.138
1908	77	223	49	17	0	16	.220	.260	.148
Total	172	534	107	39	1	36	.200	.244	.142
Period	767	2588	693	235	7	274	.268	.338	.199
Other	126	465	135	60	2	55	.290	.384	.252
Career	893	3053	828	295	9	329	.271	.345	.207

BEST 123+ GAMES
None

CALCULATION OF DOMINATION POINTS, MTP/MVP

	AB	PAB	MVP	MTP
CLASS I	638	.274	175	175
CLASS II	0	0		
CLASS III	694	.197	137	

	AB	PAB	MVP	MTP
CLASS IV	722	.177	128	
TOTAL	2054		440	
CLASS V	534		0	
PERIOD	2588		440	

Schreckengost had three years of major league experience under his belt when he opened the 1901 season behind the plate for the Boston Red Sox. The next season, he was on his way to the Athletics, after a brief stop in Cleveland. During his final season he was traded to the White Sox where, in 1908, he ended his 11-year career. He was 33 years old.

Schreckengost was competitive behind the plate and with a bat in his hands. Something about him or his skills, something that doesn't show in his statistical history, restrained managers from playing him more during an era poor in receiver talent.

Per at Bat (PAB) 1901–19

	AT BAT	R PAB	HR PAB	RBI PAB	TOTAL PAB
Schreckengost	2588	.091	.003	.105	.199
Sample avg.	3210	.091	.000	.097	.188

Schreckengost appeared in more than 100 games only twice during the era. He was essentially a part-time catcher of no particular distinction.

Ivy Wingo

Born 1890; Height 5.10; Weight 160; T-R; B-L

* = Net of home runs

	G	AB	H	R*	HR	RBI*	BA	SA	PAB
CLASS I PAB .263+ None									
CLASS II PAB .227–.262									
1912	100	310	82	36	2	42	.265	.394	.258
1919	76	245	67	30	0	27	.273	.371	.233
Total	176	555	149	66	2	69	.268	.384	.247
CLASS III PAB .191–.226									
1914	80	237	71	20	4	22	.300	.426	.194
1916	119	347	85	28	2	38	.245	.349	.196
1918	100	323	82	36	0	31	.254	.337	.207
Total	299	907	238	84	6	91	.262	.365	.200
CLASS IV PAB .155–190									
1913	111	305	78	23	2	33	.256	.344	.190
1917	121	399	106	35	2	37	.266	.376	.185
Total	232	704	184	58	4	70	.261	.362	.188
CLASS V PAB .154-									
1911	25	57	12	4	0	3	.211	.246	.123
1915	119	339	75	23	3	26	.221	.316	.153
Total	144	396	87	27	3	29	.220	.306	.149

	G	AB	H	R*	HR	RBI*	BA	SA	PAB
Period	851	2562	658	235	15	259	.257	.359	.199
Other	475	1439	381	103	10	171	.265	.351	.197
Career	1326	4001	1039	338	25	430	.260	.356	.198

BEST 123+ GAMES
None

Calculation of Domination Points, MTP/MVP

	AB	PAB	MVP	MTP
CLASS I	0	0	0	137
CLASS II	555	.247	137	
CLASS III	907	.200	181	
CLASS IV	704	.188	132	
TOTAL	2166		450	
CLASS V	396		0	
PERIOD	2562		450	

Wingo broke in with the Cardinals in 1911 at 21 years of age. In 1915, he was traded to the Reds for Mike Gonzalez, a catcher-for-catcher deal. It was a good marriage for Wingo. He remained in Cincinnati for 13 years.

Wingo was not a top defensive catcher—his FA (.961) was below average. And he was not a durable performer. He retired in 1929—39 years old—which gives the appearance of durability, but actually he was a part-time player for the last eight years of his 17-year career.

Per at Bat (PAB) 1901–19

	AT BAT	R PAB	HR PAB	RBI PAB	TOTAL PAB
Wingo	2562	.092	.006	.101	.199
Sample avg.	3210	.091	.003	.097	.191

Within a group of weak producers, Wingo was competitive in the 1901–19 period.

Billy Sullivan

Born 1875; Height 5.09; Weight 155; T-R; B-R

* = Net of home runs

	G	AB	H	R*	HR	RBI*	BA	SA	PAB
CLASS I									
PAB .263+									
1901	98	367	90	50	4	52	.245	.351	.289
1912	39	91	19	9	0	15	.209	.253	.264
Total	137	458	109	59	4	67	.238	.332	.284
CLASS II									
PAB .227–.262									
1902	76	263	64	35	1	25	.243	.323	.232
CLASS III									
PAB .191–.226									
1904	108	371	85	28	1	43	.229	.307	.194
1907	112	339	59	30	0	36	.174	.221	.195
1911	89	256	55	26	0	31	.215	.273	.223
Total	309	966	199	84	1	110	.206	.268	.202

	G	AB	H	R*	HR	RBI*	BA	SA	PAB
CLASS IV									
PAB .155-.190									
1906	118	387	83	35	2	31	.214	.297	.176
1908	137	430	82	40	0	29	.191	.228	.160
Total	255	817	165	75	2	60	.202	.261	.168
CLASS V									
PAB .154-									
1903	32	111	21	9	1	6	.189	.252	.144
1905	99	323	65	23	2	24	.201	.269	.153
1909	97	265	43	11	0	16	.162	.174	.102
1910	45	142	26	10	0	6	.225	.225	.113
1914	1	0	0	0	0	0	.000	.000	.000
1916	1	0	0	0	0	0	.000	.000	.000
Total	275	841	155	53	3	52	.184	.229	.128
Period	1052	3345	692	306	11	314	.207	.270	.189
Other	94	312	85	36	10	43	.272	.387	.285
Career	1146	3657	777	342	21	357	.212	.280	.197
BEST 123+ GAMES									
1908	137	430	82	40	0	29	.191	.228	.160

Calculation of Domination Points, MTP/MVP

	AB	PAB	MVP	MTP
CLASS I	458	.284	130	191
CLASS II	263	.232	61	
CLASS III	966	.202	195	
CLASS IV	817	.168	137	
TOTAL	2504		523	
CLASS V	841		0	
PERIOD	3345		523	

Billy Sullivan, mostly a part-time catcher, began his 17-year career in 1899 with the Braves. After two seasons with that club, during which he played in 94 games, Sullivan moved to the White Sox, where he played for 13 years. In four of them he was active in his only 100+ game seasons. Billy signed with the Tigers in 1916 for a final season — 41 years old.

A journeyman catcher, Sullivan generated a PAB slightly above the average for the group.

Per at Bat (PAB) 1901–19

	AT BAT	R PAB	HR PAB	RBI PAB	TOTAL PAB
Sullivan	3345	.091	.003	.094	.189
Sample avg.	3210	.091	.003	.097	.191

Sullivan had a fling at managing the 1909 White Sox to a fourth-place finish. In 1910, he was succeeded in that job by Hugh Duffy. Oddly enough, he hung around as a backup catcher for a few more seasons.

LARRY McLEAN

Born 1881; Height 6.05; Weight 228; T-R; B-R

* = Net of home runs

	G	AB	H	R*	HR	RBI*	BA	SA	PAB
CLASS I									
PAB .263+									
1901	9	19	4	4	0	2	.211	.263	.316
CLASS II									
PAB .227–.262									
1903	1	4	0	0	0	1	.0	.0	.250
1907	113	374	108	35	0	54	.289	.361	.238
1910	127	423	126	25	2	69	.298	.378	.227
Total	241	801	234	60	2	124	.292	.368	.232
CLASS III									
PAB .191–.226									
None									
CLASS IV									
PAB .155–.190									
1908	99	309	67	23	1	27	.217	.282	.165
1909	55	324	83	24	2	34	.256	.324	.185
1911	107	328	94	24	0	34	.287	.320	.177
Total	301	961	244	71	3	95	.254	.309	.176
CLASS V									
PAB .154–									
1904	27	84	14	5	0	4	.167	.214	.107
1906	12	35	7	3	0	2	.200	.257	.143
1912	102	333	81	16	1	26	.243	.303	.129
1913	78	227	65	10	0	21	.286	.344	.137
1914	79	154	40	8	0	14	.260	.299	.143
1915	13	33	5	0	0	4	.152	.152	.121
Total	311	866	212	42	1	71	.245	.297	.132
Period	862	2647	694	177	6	292	.262	.323	.179
Career	862	2647	694	177	6	292	.262	.323	.179
BEST 123+ GAMES									
1910	127	423	126	25	2	69	.298	.378	.227

CALCULATION OF DOMINATION POINTS, MTP/MVP

	AB	PAB	MVP	MTP
CLASS I	19	.316	6	192
CLASS II	801	.232	186	
CLASS III	0		0	
CLASS IV	961	.176	169	
TOTAL	1781		361	
CLASS V	866		0	
PERIOD	2647		361	

Larry McLean started with the Boston Red Sox in 1901, dropped out in 1902, played with Chicago and St. Louis of the NL in 1903 and 1904, dropped out again in 1905 and then reappeared with the Cincinnati Reds in 1906—finally, a major league home. He served them for seven years. In 1913, McLean went to the Giants via St. Louis. At the age of 34, he retired in 1915.

McLean's FA (.973) was reasonably typical of his entire career behind the plate. He was a reliable receiver; his BA (.262) was one of the good ones among this weak-hitting group.

Per at Bat (PAB) 1901–19

	AT BAT	R PAB	HR PAB	RBI PAB	TOTAL PAB
McLean	2647	.067	.002	.110	.179
Sample avg.	3210	.091	.003	.097	.191

McLean appeared in at least 80 percent of scheduled games only once in his career. In an era of part-time catchers, he was just another mediocre face in the crowd.

Steve O'Neill

Born 1891; Height 5.10; Weight 165; T-R; B-R

* = Net of home runs

	G	AB	H	R*	HR	RBI*	BA	SA	PAB
CLASS I PAB .263+ None									
CLASS II PAB .227-.262									
1919	125	398	115	44	2	45	.289	.427	.229
CLASS III PAB .191-.226									
1913	78	234	69	19	0	29	.295	.376	.205
CLASS IV PAB .155-.190									
1914	86	269	68	28	0	20	.253	.312	.178
1915	121	386	91	30	2	32	.236	.298	.166
1916	130	378	89	30	0	29	.235	.296	.156
1918	114	359	87	33	1	34	.242	.312	.189
Total	451	1392	335	121	3	115	.241	.304	.172
CLASS V PAB .154-									
1911	9	27	4	1	0	1	.148	.185	.074
1912	68	215	49	17	0	14	.228	.247	.144
1917	129	370	68	21	0	29	.184	.222	.135
Total	206	612	121	39	0	44	.198	.229	.136
Period	860	2636	640	223	5	233	.243	.311	.175
Other	726	2159	619	212	8	.291	.287	.369	.237
Career	1586	4795	1259	435	13	524	.263	.337	.203
BEST 123+ GAMES									
1919	125	398	115	44	2	45	.289	.427	.229

Calculation of Domination Points, MTP/MVP

	AB	PAB	MVP	MTP
CLASS I	0		0	91
CLASS II	398	.229	91	
CLASS III	234	.205	48	
CLASS IV	1392	.172	239	
TOTAL	2024		378	
CLASS V	612		0	
PERIOD	2636		378	

Steve O'Neill was 20 when in 1911 he joined the Cleveland franchise of the AL. After 13 years with that club he was traded, in 1924, to the Red Sox. Boston let him go but he hung on for two more seasons with the Yankees and Browns. He was 37 when he dropped his mitt for the last time.

Durability was a problem for O'Neill during the 1901–19 period, but it was not so for his full career—he played for nine more seasons in the 1920s, and was a starting catcher in five of them. Of the catchers in this sample, only Ray Schalk caught more career games. O'Neill's career FA of .972 is not impressive.

He was also a weak hitter during the era (BA .243), and contributed little to team offense.

Per at Bat (PAB) 1901–19

	AT BAT	R PAB	HR PAB	RBI PAB	TOTAL PAB
O'Neill	2636	.085	.002	.088	.175
Sample avg.	3210	.091	.003	.097	.191

O'Neill remained in baseball when he stopped playing and in 1935 began a long managerial career with Cleveland, Detroit, Boston and Philadelphia.

Red Dooin

Born 1879; Height 5.10; Weight 165; T-R; B-R

* = Net of home runs

	G	AB	H	R*	HR	RBI*	BA	SA	PAB
CLASS I PAB .263+ None									
CLASS II PAB .227–.262									
1912	69	184	43	20	0	22	.234	.283	.228
CLASS III PAB .191–.226									
1904	108	355	86	35	6	30	.242	.346	.200
1905	113	380	95	45	0	36	.250	.311	.213
Total	221	735	181	80	6	66	.246	.328	.207
CLASS IV PAB .155–.190									
1902	94	333	77	20	0	35	.231	.270	.165
1903	62	188	41	18	0	14	.218	.255	.170
1906	113	351	86	25	0	32	.245	.305	.162
1908	133	435	108	28	0	41	.248	.306	.159
1909	141	468	105	40	2	36	.224	.271	.167
1910	103	331	80	30	0	30	.242	.305	.181
Total	646	2106	497	161	2	188	.236	.288	.167
CLASS V PAB .154–									
1907	101	313	66	18	0	14	.211	.262	.102
1911	74	247	81	17	1	15	.328	.409	.134
1913	55	129	33	6	0	13	.256	.302	.147
1914	53	118	21	9	1	7	.178	.220	.144
1915	56	155	37	11	0	9	.239	.277	.129
1916	15	17	2	1	0	0	.118	.118	.059

	G	AB	H	R*	HR	RBI*	BA	SA	PAB
Total	354	979	240	62	2	58	.245	.299	.125
Period	1290	4004	961	323	10	334	.240	.298	.167
Career	1290	4004	961	323	10	334	.240	.298	.167
BEST 123+ GAMES									
1909	141	468	105	40	2	36	.224	.271	.167

CALCULATION OF DOMINATION POINTS, MTP/MVP

	AB	PAB	MVP	MTP
CLASS I	0	0	0	42
CLASS II	184	.228	42	
CLASS III	735	.207	152	
CLASS IV	2106	.167	352	
TOTAL	3025		546	
CLASS V	979		0	
PERIOD	4004		546	

Red Dooin spent his entire 15-year career in the subject period and he had seven seasons in which he played in 100+ games.

It began for Red in 1902 with the Phillies. He became the premier catcher for that club in 1904, a position he held until 1911, when George Gibson took over. Dooin was also the manager of the club by that time.

Dooin left the Phillies in 1915, and spent his final two seasons with the Reds and Giants. He was 37 when he retired in 1916.

PER AT BAT (PAB) 1901–19

	AT BAT	R PAB	HR PAB	RBI PAB	TOTAL PAB
Dooin	4004	.081	.002	.084	.167
Sample avg.	3210	.091	.003	.097	.191

The durability of Red Dooin testifies to the sparsity of catching talent in the 1901–19 era. He was not exceptional defensively (FA .957), and his PAB was below average.

GEORGE GIBSON

Born 1880; Height 6.00; Weight 190; T-R; B-R

* = Net of home runs

	G	AB	H	R*	HR	RBI*	BA	SA	PAB
CLASS I PAB .263+ None									
CLASS II PAB .227–.262 None									
CLASS III PAB .191–.226									
1905	46	135	24	12	2	12	.178	.267	.193
1910	143	482	125	50	3	41	.259	.349	.195
Total	189	617	149	62	5	53	.241	.331	.194

	G	AB	H	R*	HR	RBI*	BA	SA	PAB
CLASS IV									
PAB .155–.190									
1907	113	382	84	25	3	32	.220	.301	.157
1908	143	486	111	35	2	43	.228	.296	.165
1909	150	510	135	40	2	50	.265	.361	.180
1911	100	311	65	32	0	19	.209	.260	.164
1912	95	300	72	21	2	33	.240	.327	.187
1914	102	274	78	19	0	30	.285	.354	.179
1915	120	351	88	27	1	29	.251	.336	.162
Total	823	2614	633	199	10	236	.242	.320	.170
CLASS V									
PAB .154–									
1906	81	259	46	8	0	20	.178	.208	.108
1913	48	118	33	6	0	12	.280	.347	.153
1916	33	84	17	4	0	4	.202	.274	.095
1917	35	82	14	1	0	5	.171	.207	.073
1918	4	2	1	0	0	0	.500	1.000	.000
Total	201	545	111	19	0	41	.204	.251	.110
Period	1213	3776	893	280	15	330	.236	.312	.166
Career	1213	3776	893	280	15	330	.236	.312	.166
BEST 123+ GAMES									
1910	143	482	125	50	3	41	.259	.349	.195

Calculation of Domination Points, MTP/MVP

	AB	PAB	MVP	MTP
CLASS I	0	0	0	0
CLASS II	0	0	0	
CLASS III	617	.194	120	
CLASS IV	2614	.170	444	
TOTAL	3231		564	
CLASS V	545		0	
PERIOD	3776		564	

George Gibson's 14-year career began in 1905 with the Pirates. He spent a dozen years with that club; in seven, he appeared in over 100 games.

Gibson played almost 99 percent of his games behind the plate — FA .977. During his final two seasons, he played for the Giants as a backup catcher; he was 38 when he retired in 1918.

George Gibson, defensively reliable, was one of the most active catchers during the era.

But his hitting was below average (BA .236), as was his PAB. How and why did Gibson hang on for so long? Defense and durability must be the answer.

Per at Bat (PAB) 1901–19

	AT BAT	R PAB	HR PAB	RBI PAB	TOTAL PAB
Gibson	3776	.074	.004	.087	.166
Sample avg.	3210	.091	.003	.097	.191

The era had a need for men with the strength, desire and defensive skill to undertake the physically punishing duties of the catcher. Gibson fit that profile.

BILL KILLEFER

Born 1887; Height 5.11; Weight 200; T-R; B-R

* = Net of home runs

	G	AB	H	R*	HR	RBI*	BA	SA	PAB
CLASS I PAB .263+									
1911	6	16	3	3	0	2	.188	.188	.313
CLASS II PAB .227–.262 None									
CLASS III PAB .191–.226 None									
CLASS IV PAB .155–.190									
1914	98	299	70	27	0	27	.234	.274	.181
1915	105	320	76	26	0	24	.238	.278	.156
1916	97	286	62	19	3	24	.217	.294	.161
1918	104	331	77	30	0	22	.233	.281	.157
Total	404	1236	285	102	3	97	.231	.282	.163
CLASS V PAB .154–									
1909	11	29	4	0	0	1	.138	.138	.034
1910	74	193	24	14	0	7	.124	.155	.109
1912	85	268	60	17	1	20	.224	.280	.142
1913	120	360	88	25	0	24	.244	.300	.136
1917	125	409	112	28	0	31	.274	.303	.144
1919	103	315	90	17	0	22	.286	.330	.124
Total	518	1574	378	101	1	105	.240	.283	.132
Period	928	2826	666	206	4	204	.236	.282	.146
Other	107	324	85	27	0	32	.262	.292	.182
Career	1035	3150	751	233	4	236	.238	.283	.150
BEST 123+ GAMES									
1917	125	409	112	28	0	31	.274	.303	.144

CALCULATION OF DOMINATION POINTS, MTP/MVP

	AB	PAB	MVP	MTP
CLASS I	16	.313	5	6
CLASS II	0	0	0	0
CLASS III	0	0	0	0
CLASS IV	1236	.163	201	
TOTAL	1252		206	
CLASS V	1574		0	
PERIOD	2826		206	

Bill Killefer spent 13 years in the majors with three clubs, the Browns, Phillies and Cubs. He broke in with the Browns in 1909 and retired in Chicago in 1921 after playing his final four seasons with the Cubs.

Per at Bat (PAB) 1901–19

	AT BAT	R PAB	HR PAB	RBI PAB	TOTAL PAB
Killefer	2826	.073	.001	.072	.146
Sample avg.	3210	.091	.003	.097	.191

Killefer appeared in 100+ games in five seasons. He was a good defensive catcher (FA .976), but a poor batsman.

Bill Bergen

Born 1878; Height 6.00; Weight 184; T-R; B-R

* = Net of home runs

	G	AB	H	R*	HR	RBI*	BA	SA	PAB
CLASS I PAB .263+ None									
CLASS II PAB .227-.262 None									
CLASS III PAB .191–.226									
1903	58	207	47	21	0	19	.227	.266	.193
CLASS IV PAB .155-.190									
1902	89	322	58	19	0	36	.180	.224	.171
CLASS V PAB .154-									
1901	87	308	55	14	1	16	.179	.234	.101
1904	96	329	60	17	0	12	.182	.207	.088
1905	79	247	47	12	0	22	.190	.219	.138
1906	103	353	56	9	0	19	.159	.184	.079
1907	51	138	22	2	0	14	.159	.181	.116
1908	99	302	53	8	0	15	.175	.215	.076
1909	112	346	48	15	1	14	.139	.156	.087
1910	89	249	40	11	0	14	.161	.177	.100
1911	84	227	30	8	0	10	.132	.154	.079
Total	800	2499	411	96	2	136	.164	.193	.094
Period	947	3028	516	136	2	191	.170	.201	.109
Career	947	3028	516	136	2	191	.170	.201	.109

BEST 123+ GAMES
None

Calculation of Domination Points, MTP/MVP

	AB	PAB	MVP	MTP
CLASS I	0	0	0	0
CLASS II	0	0	0	
CLASSS III	207	.193	40	
CLASS IV	322	.171	55	
TOTAL	529		95	
CLASS V	2499		0	
PERIOD	3028		95	

Bill Bergen broke in with the Reds in 1901, spent three seasons with that club, then went to the Dodgers for the last eight years of his 11-year career. He was essentially a backup catcher who appeared in more than 100 games only twice.

PER AT BAT (PAB) 1901–19

	AT BAT	R PAB	HR PAB	RBI PAB	TOTAL PAB
Bergen	3028	.045	.001	.063	.109
Sample avg.	3210	.091	.003	.097	.191

Bergen was unimpressive offensively.

Catchers — Summary in Domination Point (DP) Sequence

* Net of home runs
** HOF

PLAYER	AB	R*	PAB HR	RBI*	TOTAL PAB	BA	SA	MTP	MVP
AVG. PLAYER	3210	.091	.003	.097	.191	.247	.316		
SUPERSTAR									
DP 1078+									
Bresnahan R**	4462	.147	.006	.112	.265	.279	.382	1073	1182
STAR									
DP 801–1077									
Kling J	4190	.107	.005	.115	.227	.271	.357	520	956
ABOVE AVG.									
DP 524–800									
Meyers C	2834	.093	.005	.123	.221	.291	.378	389	605
Schalk R**	2830	.103	.002	.099	.204	.250	.306	301	576
Gibson G	3776	.074	.004	.088	.166	.236	.312	0	564
Dooin R	4004	.081	.002	.084	.167	.240	.298	42	546
BELOW AVERAGE-									
PAB 247–523									
Sullivan B	3345	.091	.004	.094	.189	.207	.270	191	523
Wingo I	2562	.092	.006	.101	.199	.257	.359	137	450
Schreckengost G	2588	.091	.003	.105	.199	.268	.338	175	440
O'Neill S	2636	.085	.002	.088	.175	.243	.311	91	378
McLean L	2647	.067	.002	.110	.179	.262	.323	192	361
POOR									
DP 246-									
Killefer B	2826	.073	.001	.072	.146	.236	.282	6	206
Bergen B	3028	.045	.001	.063	.109	.170	.201	0	95
Average	524								
SD	276								
10 BEST PAB SEASONS									
Meyers 1912	371	.146	.016	.129	.291	.358	.477		
Bresnahan ** 1906	405	.171	.000	.106	.277	.281	.356		
Kling 1903	491	.130	.006	.133	.269	.297	.428		
Schalk ** 1915	413	.109	.002	.129	.240	.266	.327		
O'Neill 1919	398	.111	.005	.113	.229	.289	.427		
McLean 1910	423	.059	.005	.163	.227	.298	.378		
Gibson 1910	482	.104	.006	.085	.195	.259	.349		
Dooin 1909	468	.086	.004	.077	.167	.224	.271		
Sullivan 1908	430	.093	.000	.067	.160	.191	.228		
Killefer 1917	409	.069	.000	.075	.144	.274	.303		

The one outstanding fact that emerges from this listing is the sparsity of talent at the catcher position during this 19-year period. The physical demands of the job were probably the major reason for this — reasonable men did not want to play the position.

Despite the equipment enjoyed by the modern player, the position is still difficult to fill because of its physical demands and the life of continual bruises that it promises. The same demands existed in the 1901–19 era, but equipment afforded even less protection.

Concerning the ten best seasons, the same point is being made in a different way. It was difficult in those years to recruit and hold good offensive players in the catcher position. For all practical purposes, only the best seasons of Meyers, Bresnahan and Kling have any significance — the others simply represent the best of many below average production years.

The Best of the Best

Sample size	13
NL	9
AL	4
Most durable-top 5	Bresnahan, Kling, Dooin, Gibson, Sullivan
Top five BA	Meyers, Bresnahan, Kling, Schreckengost, McLean
Top five SA	Bresnahan, Meyers, Wingo, Kling, Schreckengost
Top five scorers (R)	Bresnahan, Kling, Schalk, Meyers, Wingo
Top five power hitters (HR)	Bresnahan, Wingo, Kling, Meyers, Gibson
Top five clutch hitters (RBI)	Meyers, Kling, Bresnahan, McLean, Schreckengost
Top five seasons	Kling, Bresnahan, Meyers, Schalk, McLean
Most talented producer (MTP)-top 5	Bresnahan, Kling, Meyers, Schalk, McLean
Most valuable producer (MVP)-top 5	Bresnahan, Kling, Meyers, Gibson, Schalk

This continuing analysis demonstrates once again the differences that existed in the early game of baseball in the deadball era as compared with the slam-bang game of 2008. Speed and bat control were premium talents — home run hitting was rare.

Bresnahan seems to loom above all other catchers in the sample. But his talent stands out from the pack largely because of a classification curiosity, and because of his power (as manager) to assign himself to playing activity according to the quality of the opposition.

In assigning players to positions, the number of games during which the player is assigned to a given position determines his ultimate classification as a fielder. In Bresnahan's case, he was a catcher in 68 percent of his games and was assigned to that position and, indeed, is so classified in the Hall of Fame, to which he was elected in 1945. But as correct as that may be for purposes of classification, it is incorrect for comparison purposes. Full-time catchers expended far more energy at their defensive job than Bresnahan did in his various assignments as a player and as a player-manager. For that reason, in all cases where he was the statistical leader in the above charts, the second-place player was also indicated in bold type.

Bresnahan was a utility player. And he should be evaluated as such, not as a catcher. On that yardstick, with a PAB of .278, it is doubtful he would have, or should have, earned Hall of Fame status.

Johnny Kling, on the other hand, was a full-time catcher and the true leader, by a wide margin, of his group. He is not in the Hall of Fame — probably because Bresnahan is.

The other Hall of Fame catcher, Ray Schalk, was not a powerful presence in the subject period. His career straddled the 1910–29 era (deadball and live ball), one that is seldom analyzed because the number mix makes no sense — two different games. Only this can be said about Schalk's selection to the Hall of Fame: During his younger (and, theoretically, his best) years he was not as productive as Kling or Meyers.

Infielders — Analysis, 1901–1919

Infielders in this survey are considered to be the two middle infielders plus third basemen. During the subject period 44 infielders screened through: 12 shortstops, 17 second basemen and 15 third basemen. The average PAB of the group was .241, as follows:

	PAB
Runs	.129
Home runs	.005
RBI	.107
Total	.241

Some analysts object to grouping third basemen with the middle infielders. This is based upon the theory (hope?) that hot corner men are power hitters who should be appraised as such, and middle infielders are defensive geniuses who should be measured as much by their gloves as their bats.

This analysis expects all major league infielders to field well and to hit well, and history has demonstrated that offensive and defensive skills can be simultaneously found in all three positions. Indeed, to go even further, this analysis implies that defensive geniuses who are below average producers do not belong in the HOF, nor do those players who hit with considerable power but can't catch a cold.

Qualifiers and associated performance standards appear on the following charts:

Dominant Infielders, 1901–1919 Record

* HOF
** Net of home runs

PLAYER	LG	AB	H	R**	HR	RBI**	BA	SA	PAB
CLASS I									
PAB .301+									
Wagner H*	N	8518	2769	1335	78	1297	.325	.462	.318
Collins E*	A	6096	1979	1110	25	755	.325	.419	.310
Baker F*	A	5421	1676	731	80	826	.309	.442	.302
CLASS II									
PAB .271–.300									
Lajoie N*	A	7501	2523	1031	51	1090	.336	.451	.290
Zimmerman H	N	5304	1566	637	58	742	.295	.419	.271
CLASS III									
PAB .241–.270									
Doyle L	N	6038	1753	842	70	673	.290	.411	.263
Williams J	A	4448	1178	547	35	575	.265	.378	.260
Elberfeld K	A	4389	1192	613	10	496	.272	.340	.255
Davis G	N	3545	942	451	13	430	.266	.346	.252
Murphy D	A	5403	1557	655	44	658	.288	.404	.251
Steinfeldt H	N	4692	1266	567	25	585	.270	.362	.251
Collins J*	A	3770	1072	495	25	425	.284	.395	.251
Devlin A	N	4412	1185	593	10	494	.269	.338	.249

PLAYER	LG	AB	H	R**	HR	RBI**	BA	SA	PAB
LaPorte F	A	4212	1185	487	14	546	.281	.376	.249
Smith R	N	3907	1087	450	27	487	.278	.377	.247
Gardner L	A	4902	1395	594	19	593	.285	.378	.246
Fletcher A	A	4595	1267	560	21	539	.276	.357	.244
Dahlen B	N	4218	1043	497	22	506	.247	.322	.243
Delahanty J	A	4091	1159	502	18	471	.283	.373	.242
Pratt D	A	4398	1242	493	27	539	.282	.391	.241
CLASS IV PAB .211–240									
Lobert H	N	4563	1252	608	32	450	.274	.366	.239
Bush D	A	6058	1498	1077	8	359	.247	.298	.238
Tinker J*	N	6441	1695	742	31	751	.263	.354	.237
Evers J*	A	6131	1658	907	12	525	.270	.334	.236
Bradley B	A	4858	1307	641	26	459	.269	.367	.232
Groh H	N	3582	1054	516	17	297	.294	.391	.232
Isbell F	A	4060	1019	471	13	434	.251	.329	.226
Huggins M	N	5557	1474	938	9	309	.265	.314	.226
Ritchey C	N	4019	1083	450	8	435	.269	.338	.222
Wallace B*	A	6211	1612	670	11	693	.260	.337	.221
Cutshaw G	N	4141	1080	432	23	456	.261	.345	.220
Mowrey M	N	4290	1098	478	7	454	.256	.329	.219
Parent F	A	4976	1305	613	20	450	.262	.340	.218
Herzog B	N	4979	1311	646	20	406	.263	.341	.215
Lord H	A	3689	1024	491	14	280	.278	.356	.213
CLASS V PAB .210-									
Schaefer G	A	3783	972	488	9	299	.257	.320	.210
Foster E	A	4501	1188	578	6	350	.264	.327	.208
Ferris H	A	4800	1146	434	39	511	.239	.340	.205
Conroy W	A	5058	1256	583	22	430	.248	.329	.205
Byrne B	N	4830	1225	657	10	319	.254	.323	.204
Weaver B	A	4180	1100	502	19	327	.263	.345	.203
Hummel J	N	3906	991	392	29	365	.254	.352	.201
Bridwell A	N	4169	1064	455	2	346	.255	.295	.193
Olson I	N	3952	1007	468	7	276	.255	.311	.190
Avg		4832	1329	623	24	516	.275	.360	.241
SD		1038	.029						

CLASSIFICATIONS

	Class (PAB)	Durability (AB)
CLASS 1	.301+	6910+
CLASS II	.271–.300	5871–6909
CLASS III	.241–.270	4832–5870
CLASS IV.	.211–.240	3793–4831
CLASS V	.210-	3792-

Measuring offensive performance in the context of defensive assignment is important, as the following summary shows of comparative PABs:

	FIRST	CATCH	INFIELD
Class I	.302+	.263+	.301+
Class III	.246-.273	.191-.226	.241-.270
Class V	.217-	.154	.210

Obviously, these are different types of ballplayers whose records should not be directly compared. When they are, player value can be distorted beyond recognition.

During the subject period, for example, a Class V production record of an infielder or first baseman would have been regarded as Class III performance by a catcher.

Player Analysis

Class I, PAB .301+

Three sterling performers reached this classification: Honus Wagner, Eddie Collins and Frank Baker. All are in the HOF, Wagner the clear leader not only because his PAB was the highest, but also because his skills were tested by 40 percent more ABs than his closest rival, Eddie Collins.

Class II, PAB .271-.300

This classification contains two surprises: Nap Lajoie, a HOF player, because he is not in the highest classification, and Heinie Zimmerman, ignored by the HOF, because he is in such august company. Readers are cautioned when considering these apparent aberrations: These initial groupings measure class (PAB) only. The durability factor of the PAB will gradually appear to form a more complete picture of each player's relative value. It is interesting to note, however, that Zimmerman — historically forgotten — was 93 percent as productive as the acknowledged HOF great, Lajoie.

Class III, PAB .241-.270

Fifteen men — 34 percent of the sample — qualified for this classification, led by the forgotten Larry Doyle (second base) who was more productive than HOF third baseman Jimmy Collins. Why one and not the other? Analysis should provide hints as to why this was so.

Class IV, PAB .211-.240

Fifteen players appear in this group, including HOF players Joe Tinker (SS), Johnny Evers (2B) and Bobby Wallace (SS).

Tinker and Evers were two members of the much-ballyhooed double-play combination (Chance was the third) of the era, and that fact may ultimately explain why any one of them is in the HOF. Bobby Wallace was considered to be superior defensively.

Again the question of HOF standards arises. Are below average producers with good gloves HOF players? Does Evers vs. Eddie Collins make sense? Does Wagner vs. Wallace make sense? And if it does, why were men like Doyle and Bush ignored?

Class V, PAB .210-

Nine men fell into the lowest classification. None was very durable; Byrne was an above average scorer; Ferris and Hummel had above average power. Otherwise, these were journeymen ballplayers who managed to hang on long enough to be noticed.

The first HOF appointments were made in 1936 — Ty Cobb, Babe Ruth, Honus Wagner, Christy Mathewson and Walter Johnson. Other names on that first ballot, who also appear in this sample, were Nap Lajoie, Tris Speaker, Eddie Collins, Jimmy Collins, Roger Bresnahan and Willie Keeler, all of whom ultimately received the highest award.

Obviously, electors of that time were still feeling their way toward standards that would be generally applied to future candidates. Such a standard was set, de facto, for infielders when Tinker, Evers and Wallace were elected, to wit: A durable, talented defensive infielder who is a below average producer should get serious consideration.

Given that formula, one hopes that analysis will reveal why men like Doyle, Zimmerman (3B) and Bush (SS) were overlooked.

Honus Wagner

Born 1874; Height 5.11; Weight 200; T-R; B-R; Led National League: 1901–2B, RBI, SB; 1902-SA, 2B, R, RBI, SB; 1903-BA, 3B; 1904-BA, SA, 2B, SB; 1906-BA, 2B, R; 1907-BA, SA, 2B; 1908-BA, SA, H, 2B, 3B, RBI; 1909-BA, SA, 2B, RBI; 1910-H; 1911–BA

HOF 1936
* = Net of home runs

	G	AB	H	R*	HR	RBI*	BA	SA	PAB
CLASS I									
PAB .301+									
1901	141	556	196	94	6	120	.353	.491	.396
1902	137	538	177	102	3	88	.329	.467	.359
1903	129	512	182	92	5	96	.355	.518	.377
1904	132	490	171	93	4	71	.349	.520	.343
1905	147	548	199	108	6	95	.363	.505	.381
1906	142	516	175	101	2	69	.339	.459	.333
1907	142	515	180	92	6	76	.350	.513	.338
1908	151	568	201	90	10	99	.354	.542	.350
1909	137	495	168	87	5	95	.339	.489	.378
1911	130	473	158	78	9	80	.334	.507	.353
1912	145	558	181	84	7	95	.324	.496	.333
Total	1533	5769	1988	1021	63	984	.345	.501	.358
CLASS II									
PAB .271–.300									
1910	150	556	178	86	4	77	.320	.432	.300
CLASS III									
PAB .241–.270									
1913	114	413	124	48	3	53	.300	.385	.252
1915	151	566	155	62	6	72	.274	.422	.247
Total	265	979	279	110	9	125	.285	.406	.249
CLASS IV									
PAB .211–.240									
None									
CLASS V									
PAB .210-									
1914	150	552	139	59	1	49	.252	.317	.197
1916	23	432	124	44	1	38	.287	.370	.192
1917	74	230	61	15	0	24	.265	.304	.170
Total	347	1214	324	118	2	111	.267	.333	.190
Period	2295	8518	2769	1335	78	1297	.325	.462	.318
Other	494	1923	649	299	23	334	.337	.484	.346
Career	2789	10441	3418	1634	101	1631	.327	.466	.323
BEST 123+ GAMES									
1901	141	556	196	94	6	120	.353	.491	.396

Calculation of Domination Points, MTP/MVP

	AB	PAB	MVP	MTP
CLASS I	5769	.358	2065	2232
CLASS II	556	.300	167	
CLASS III	979	.249	244	
CLASS IV	0	0	0	
TOTAL	7304		2476	
CLASS V	1214		0	
PERIOD	8518		2476	

The Flying Dutchman was 23 when he broke in with Louisville as an outfielder in 1897. In 1900, Barney Dreyfus moved the NL club to Pittsburgh. Wagner, still playing the outfield, was hitting like gangbusters (BA .381).

In 1901, Honus Wagner played more games at shortstop than at any other position for the first time, but a permanent defensive home continued to elude him until Wid Conroy and Bones Ely, after failing to nail down the shortstop position, left the team. Management was slow to accept ungainly-appearing Wagner as the super, all-around athlete he truly was.

Honus was finally installed at shortstop in 1903, at which post he remained for the balance of his career as a full-time player. He was 43 when his 21-year odyssey ended in 1917.

Career records include him among the all-time best in at bats, hits, doubles, triples and stolen bases. Defensive statistics, inconclusive indicators of fielding ability, are less useful in the case of Wagner because of his unsettled defensive beginnings.

He didn't play as many as 100 games a season at shortstop until he was 29 years old. He showed good range, but the sure-handedness for which he later became famous evolved more slowly. Curiously, even after he had arrived as a major league shortstop, Wagner continued to appear at other positions with sufficient regularity to contaminate his defensive record.

Fortunately, in 1908 he played as a pure shortstop and generated a record of his defensive play that typified his talents. To give meaning to his numbers, they are juxtaposed with career statistics of two great HOF shortstops of the time, Joe Tinker and Bobby Wallace.

Player	TC/G*	FA
Wagner	5.8	.943
Tinker	5.8	.938
Wallace	5.5	.938

*Total chances per game

Wagner was a regular shortstop for 13 years, during which time there's no doubt that his range was at least the equal of the best shortstops, and he may have had the surest hands of all.

There's absolutely nothing obscure about Wagner's offensive record. During the subject period, he was active for 17 years. Until he was 40, his BA was always above .300. His battle ribbons (above) attest to his superiority in all aspects of the offensive game, except home run hitting—he never hit more than ten. But doubles and triples exploded from his bat with great regularity.

Wagner delivered these offensive feats year after year while filling the toughest defensive position on the field, accumulating in the process the best durability record of competing infielders. Elements of his PAB appear below in contrast with those for the entire sample.

Per at Bat (PAB) 1901-19-Infielders

	AT BAT	R PAB	HR PAB	RBI PAB	TOTAL PAB
Wagner	8518	.157	.009	.152	.318
Sample avg.	4832	.129	.005	.107	.241

Durability married to class equals a champion — a designation that aptly fits the Flying Dutchman, one of the immortal five (Wagner, Cobb, Ruth, Johnson, Mathewson) who were the first to enter baseball's Hall of Fame in 1936. His inclusion in the august group was most appropriate.

Eddie Collins

Born 1887; Height 5.09; Weight 175; T-R; B-L; MVP-AL 1914; Led the American League: 1910-SB; 1912/13/14-R; 1915-BB; 1919-SB; HOF 1939

* = Net of home runs

	G	AB	H	R*	HR	RBI*	BA	SA	PAB
CLASS I									
PAB .301+									
1911	132	493	180	89	3	70	.365	.481	.329
1912	153	543	189	137	0	64	.348	.435	.370
1913	148	534	184	122	3	70	.345	.453	.365
1914	152	526	181	120	2	83	.344	.452	.390
1915	155	521	173	114	4	73	.332	.436	.367
1919	140	518	165	83	4	76	.319	.405	.315
Total	880	3135	1072	665	16	436	.342	.443	.356
CLASS II									
PAB .271–.300									
1909	153	572	198	101	3	53	.346	.449	.274
1910	153	583	188	78	3	78	.322	.417	.273
1917	156	564	163	91	0	67	.289	.363	.280
Total	462	1719	549	270	6	198	.319	.410	.276
CLASS III									
PAB .241–.270									
1916	155	545	168	87	0	52	.308	.396	.255
CLASS IV									
PAB .211–.240									
1908	102	330	90	38	1	39	.273	.379	.236
1918	97	330	91	49	2	28	.276	.330	.239
Total	199	660	181	87	3	67	.274	.355	.238
CLASS V									
PAB .210-									
1906	6	17	4	1	0	0	.235	.235	.059
1907	14	20	5	0	0	2	.250	.350	.100
Total	20	37	9	1	0	2	.243	.297	.081
Period	1716	6096	1979	1110	25	755	.325	.419	.310
Other	1110	3853	1332	661	22	497	.346	.442	.306
Career	2826	9949	3311	1771	47	1252	.333	.428	.309
BEST 123+ GAMES									
1914	152	526	181	120	2	83	.344	.452	.390

CALCULATION OF DOMINATION POINTS, MTP/MVP

	AB	PAB	MVP	MTP
CLASS I	3135	.356	1116	1590
CLASS II	1719	.276	474	
CLASS III	545	.255	139	
CLASS IV	660	.238	157	
TOTAL	6059		1886	
CLASS V	37		0	
PERIOD	6096		1886	

Eddie Collins broke in with Connie Mack's Athletics in 1906 at 19 years of age. For two seasons the youngster played a few games, mostly at shortstop, with no great distinction. Danny Murphy, Mack's second baseman at the time, had held the keystone job for half a decade.

Collins took over in 1908. He was on the field for about two-thirds of the season, mostly at second base. Murphy became an outfielder on the day during the 1908 season that Mack became sold on Collins as his new second baseman.

As a member of the famous "$100,000 infield" (Stuffy McInnis; Eddie Collins; Frank Baker; Jack Barry) that had led the Philadelphia club to four World Series in five seasons (1910–1914), Collins was widely acclaimed for his all-around talent. But at the end of the 1914 season, he was sold to Chicago.

This was the beginning of the end for the marvelous Athletics as Mack, in his eternal search for cash, unloaded talent. Barry and Baker were also sold; McInnis, traded to Boston. Mack's dazzlers were gone, within four years, for cash plus a few players.

Collins performed for Chicago in classic style for the balance of the subject period. He became playing manager in 1924, a role he carried until 1927 when he was replaced by Ray Schalk. He caught on with his old boss, Connie Mack, in Philadelphia and continued as a part-time player with that club until his retirement in 1930. He was 43 when he finished his 25-year career as one of the top hit producers and base stealers in baseball history.

With a career BA of .333, it's easy to bypass the defensive record of a player. To do so with Collins would be an injustice. Like Wagner, he was as impressive with a glove as with a bat.

Collins' FA of .969 was the best of all keystone men in the sample. Baseball men rate him as one of the great all-time fielding second basemen.

A discriminating batting eye, contact hitting ability and speed are characteristics that one usually finds in a top scorer. Collins was in this mold. He took the base on balls. His BA during the period of .325 was the second best (tied with Wagner) in the survey group. He hit even better in the live-ball era, and lifted his career BA to .333.

Eddie could run. He stole over 40 bases in 10 seasons and appears in the record books as one of baseball's best all-time base stealers.

This combination of talents brought to Collins the best scoring record of those in the infield sample. This was his foremost offensive tool, although he was also an above average RBI man.

The elements of his PAB are compared with those of the group in the following graphic:

PER AT BAT (PAB) 1901–19 — INFIELDERS

	AT BAT	R PAB	HR PAB	RBI PAB	TOTAL PAB
Collins	6096	.182	.004	.124	.310
Sample avg.	4832	.129	.005	.107	.241

The importance of durability to a player's ultimate rating has been amply demonstrated. Obviously Collins was more durable than most, a fact which, when related to his PAB, will have a strong impact on his ultimate MVP rating. But that is not the end of the Collins story.

His career ABs were 9,949. The period that would show his career in full flower, 1910–29, will not be examined because it would mix deadball and live-ball performances—a toxic mix.

Collins played enough in the subject period to make his quality mark. One can only guess about the MVP rating his full career would have earned.

In this regard it's worth noting that his performance during the years following the subject period was outstanding. As a member of the Philadelphia Athletics, Collins played in four World Series.

He competed in the 1919 World Series between his White Sox and the Cincinnati Reds that featured the infamous Black Sox scandal. Collins was in no way involved in the scandal.

Collins hoped to manage the Athletics when his mentor, Connie Mack, retired. But Mack went on and on so, in 1933, Collins joined the Boston Red Sox as general manager. He was still on the job when he died in 1951.

FRANK BAKER

Born 1886; Height 5.11; Weight 173; T-R; B-L; Led American League: 1909–3B; 1911–HR; 1912/13–HR, RBI; 1914–HR

HOF 1955
* = Net of home runs

	G	AB	H	R*	HR	RBI*	BA	SA	PAB
CLASS I									
PAB .301+									
1911	148	592	198	85	11	104	.334	.505	.338
1912	149	577	200	106	10	123	.347	.541	.414
1913	149	565	190	104	12	114	.336	.492	.407
1914	150	570	182	75	9	88	.319	.442	.302
Total	596	2304	770	370	42	429	.334	.495	.365
CLASS II									
PAB .271–.300									
1909	148	541	165	69	4	81	.305	.447	.285
1910	146	561	159	81	2	72	.283	.392	.276
Total	294	1102	324	150	6	153	.294	.419	.280
CLASS III									
PAB .241–.279									
1916	100	360	97	36	10	42	.269	.428	.244
1918	126	504	154	59	6	62	.306	.409	.252
1919	141	567	166	60	10	73	.293	.388	.252
Total	367	1431	417	155	26	177	.291	.405	.250
CLASS IV									
PAB .211–.240									
1908	9	31	9	5	0	2	.290	.387	.226
1917	146	553	156	51	6	65	.282	.365	.221
Total	155	584	165	56	6	67	.283	.366	.221
CLASS V									
PAB .210–									
None									
Period	1412	5421	1676	731	80	826	.309	.442	.302
Other	163	564	162	60	16	91	.287	.442	.296
Career	1575	5985	1838	791	96	917	.307	.442	.301
BEST 123+ GAMES									
1912	149	577	200	106	10	123	.347	.541	.414

Calculation of Domination Points, MTP/MVP

	AB	PAB	MVP	MTP
CLASS I	2304	.365	841	1150
CLASS II	1102	.280	309	
CLASS III	1431	.250	358	
CLASS IV	584	.221	129	
TOTAL	5421		1637	
CLASS V	0		0	
PERIOD	5421		1637	

Frank Baker entered the major leagues in 1908 at 22 years of age with the Philadelphia Athletics. In a year, he became the anchor of the left side of the diamond in Connie Mack's fabled infield of McInnis, Collins, Jack Barry and Baker. He starred in that position until Mack went on one of his cash hunts and, one by one, disassembled his championship team.

Baker was sold in 1916 to the Yankees and he spent the final six years of his 13-year career with them. He was 36 when he retired.

Baker, mostly known for his offensive feats, was also a talented glove man. His range was adequate; his hands were sure. His career statistics are compared below with those of prominent third basemen of the time.

Player	G	TC/G	FA
Frank Baker	1575	3.6	.943
Jimmy Collins*	1728	3.8	.928
Bill Bradley	1461	3.7	.934

*His FA was heavily influenced by pre–1901 play, an era that was defensively loose.

In a day when infielders frequently moved from position to position, these men played over 95 percent of the time at third base. Baker didn't range quite as far as some, but his FA was superior. He was a steady and reliable defensive performer.

Baker had a history of hitting home runs against baseball's premier pitchers and because of this his nickname — Homerun Baker — was born. If the cognomen somewhat exaggerated his long-ball expertise, it is nevertheless true that he was one of the premier power hitters during a powerless time.

He was also a dependable contact hitter (career BA .307). Only Wagner, Collins and Lajoie had a higher BA within the infield group; only Wagner and Lajoie had a better SA. And his best production year (1912) would stand tall in any era.

The general superiority of Baker's production record is clarified by the following graphic:

Per at Bat (PAB) 1901–19 — Infielders

	AT BAT	R PAB	HR PAB	RBI PAB	TOTAL PAB
Baker	5421	.135	.015	.152	.302
Sample avg.	4832	.129	.005	.107	.241

Frank Baker in 1955 joined another member of Connie Mack's "$100,000 infield," Eddie Collins, in the Hall of Fame.

NAP LAJOIE

Born 1874; Height 6.01; Weight 195; T-R; B-R; Led the American League: 1901-BA, SA, H, 2B, HR, R, RBI; 1903-BA, SA; 1904-BA, SA, H, 2B, RBI; 1906-H, 2B; 1910-AB, H, 2B; HOF 1937

* = Net of home runs

	G	AB	H	R*	HR	RBI*	BA	SA	PAB
CLASS I									
PAB .301+									
1901	131	543	229	131	14	111	.422	.635	.471
1902	87	352	129	74	7	58	.366	.551	.395
1903	126	488	173	83	7	86	.355	.533	.361
1904	140	554	211	86	6	96	.381	.554	.339
1912	117	448	165	66	0	90	.368	.462	.348
Total	601	2385	907	440	34	441	.380	.550	.384
CLASS II									
PAB .271–.300									
1905	65	249	82	27	2	39	.329	.422	.273
1906	152	602	214	88	0	91	.355	.460	.297
1910	159	591	227	88	4	72	.384	.514	.277
1911	90	315	115	34	2	58	.365	.454	.298
1913	137	465	156	66	1	67	.335	.404	.288
Total	603	2222	794	303	9	327	.357	.458	.288
CLASS III									
PAB .241–.270									
1908	157	581	168	75	2	72	.289	.375	.256
CLASS IV									
PAB .211–.240									
1907	137	509	152	51	2	61	.299	.393	.224
1909	128	469	152	55	1	46	.324	.431	.217
Total	265	978	304	106	3	107	.311	.411	.221
CLASS V									
PAB .210-									
1914	121	419	108	37	0	50	.258	.305	.208
1915	129	490	137	39	1	60	.280	.355	.204
1916	113	426	105	31	2	33	.246	.312	.155
Total	363	1335	350	107	3	143	.262	.326	.190
Period	1989	7501	2523	1031	51	1090	.336	.451	.290
Other	490	2091	721	391	32	426	.345	.520	.405
Career	2479	9592	3244	1422	83	1516	.338	.466	.315
BEST 123+ GAMES									
1901	131	543	229	131	14	111	.422	.635	.471

CALCULATION OF DOMINATION POINTS, MTP/MVP

	AB	PAB	MVP	MTP
CLASS I	2385	.384	916	1556
CLASS II	2222	.288	640	
CLASS III	581	.256	149	
CLASS IV	978	.221	216	
TOTAL	6166		1921	
CLASS V	1335		0	
PERIOD	7501		1921	

Lajoie was 22 when he put the New England League behind him and joined the Philadelphia NL franchise in 1896. For the next five seasons (that pre-date this study) Nap played for the NL club. In three of those years he appeared in more than 100 games, his BA ranged from .324 to .378, and in 1898 he knocked in 121 runs (net of home runs).

Nat jumped to the newly-formed AL of Ban Johnson in 1901. And his record-setting BA of .422 was generated during that season. This reference to 1901 is not made to derogate his accomplishment, but it would be naïve to overlook the fact that this prodigious feat was accomplished against inferior competition.

When the subject period began, Nap was already a 27-year-old player facing complications. The Phillies sued for the return of the hard-hitting second baseman, the net effect of which was the sale in 1902 of Lajoie to Cleveland. There he was popular (the team was named the "Naps") and successful and, after a great season in 1904 (BA .381), the 31-year-old infielder was named playing manager. His personal effectiveness as an offensive force was thereafter less prominent. He remained a dangerous hitter until 1914, but never again with the awesome superiority of the 1901–04 period.

Deacon McGuire became manager during the 1909 season and, oddly enough, Lajoie remained as the second baseman, happily so it seems, because in 1910 his BA returned once more to the stratosphere (.384).

Lajoie continued with Cleveland as the regular second baseman through the 1914 season, when he was let go ("Naps" as a team name was dropped and "Indians" adopted). He caught on with the Athletics for two more years then, at 42 years of age, he retired in 1916.

The storied excellence of Lajoie in the field is solidly supported by records of the era. When his first two seasons are discounted (he mostly played first base), it would seem fair to say that he handled about 5.9 chances a game with a FA of .964, a stunning record for the times, as a comparison with two star HOF keystone men demonstrates:

Player	TC/G*	FA
Nap Lajoie	5.9	.964
Eddie Collins	5.2	.969
Johnny Evers	5.3	.953

*Total chances per game

The .422 BA of Lajoie still stands as an AL record. To some degree, however, it is tainted. The 1901 season was the first for the AL and the level of competition was presumably evolving. Such questions, however, in no way cast doubt on the extraordinary batting ability of the second baseman. In the five years prior to the record-setting 1901 season, he had demonstrated an ability to post high numbers, and over the balance of his 21-year career Lajoie hit over .350 seven times, and he slipped below .300 only five times (in three of those years, he was over 40). He is listed among historical leaders in career hits and doubles.

A comparison with his contemporaries clearly demonstrates Lajoie's talent:

Per at Bat (PAB) 1901–19 — Infielders

	AT BAT	R PAB	HR PAB	RBI PAB	TOTAL PAB
Lajoie	7501	.137	.007	.146	.290
Sample avg.	4832	.129	.005	.107	.241

Nap was the second most durable player in the infielder group, well above average as a home run hitter and the third best RBI man. This all-around capability plus the strength to perform at high efficiency over an extended period are the combined strengths that Lajoie brought to his team.

Finally, the Lajoie numbers are useful indicators of how difficult it was (and still is) to generate a career PAB of .300+. He is best remembered for his .422 BA in 1901, his furious BA race in 1910 with Ty Cobb (Cobb won, .385 vs. .384), and his graceful excellence in the field. He epitomized the all-around athlete of his time and his inclusion in the second class of HOF players (1937) was appropriate.

HEINIE ZIMMERMAN

Born 1887; Height 6.00; Weight 176; T-R; B-R; Led National League: 1912-BA, SA, H, 2B, HR, RBI; 1916/17-RBI

* = Net of home runs

	G	AB	H	R*	HR	RBI*	BA	SA	PAB
CLASS I									
PAB .301+									
1912	145	557	207	81	14	89	.372	.571	.330
1913	127	447	140	60	9	86	.313	.490	.347
Total	272	1004	347	141	23	175	.346	.535	.338
CLASS II									
PAB .271–.300									
1911	143	535	164	71	9	76	.307	.462	.292
1914	146	564	167	71	4	83	.296	.424	.280
1916	147	549	157	70	6	77	.286	.390	.279
Total	436	1648	488	212	19	236	.296	.425	.283
CLASS III									
PAB .241–.270									
1915	139	520	138	62	3	59	.265	.379	.238
1917	150	585	174	56	5	97	.297	.391	.270
1919	123	444	113	52	4	54	.255	.354	.248
Total	412	1549	425	170	12	210	.274	.376	.253
CLASS IV									
PAB .211–.240									
1908	46	113	33	17	0	9	.292	.345	.230
1909	65	183	50	23	0	21	.273	.344	.240
1918	121	463	126	42	1	55	.272	.363	.212
Total	232	759	209	82	1	85	.275	.356	.221
CLASS V									
PAB .210-									
1907	5	9	2	0	0	1	.222	.333	.111
1910	99	335	95	32	3	35	.284	.394	.209
Total	104	344	97	32	3	36	.282	.392	.206
Period	1456	5304	1566	637	58	742	.295	.419	.271
Career	1456	5304	1566	637	58	742	.295	.419	.271
BEST 123+ GAMES									
1913	127	447	140	60	9	86	.313	.490	.347

CALCULATION OF DOMINATION POINTS, MTP/MVP

	AB	PAB	MVP	MTP
CLASS I	1004	.338	339	805
CLASS II	1648	.283	466	
CLASS III	1549	.253	392	
CLASS IV	759	.221	168	

	AB	PAB	MVP	MTP
TOTAL	4960		1365	
CLASS V	344		0	
PERIOD	5304		1365	

Heinie Zimmerman, 20 years old, wore a Cubs uniform for the first time in 1907. Manager Frank Chance was well protected at the third base position — 30-year-old Harry Steinfeldt, recently acquired from the Reds, operated in that spot with his usual proficiency.

Chance, in 1911, decided to unload the aging Steinfeldt and give Zimmerman — then 24 — his chance. It was a good gamble offensively since the youngster was hitting in the high .200s as a swing player. But is was a huge gamble defensively — the young man, for example, made 33 errors in 99 games in 1910. But it worked. Zimmerman was a hitter from the beginning and this appeared to offset his liabilities as a fielder that, although less than before, continued throughout his career.

Zimmerman was traded to the Giants in 1916, where he continued to play almost exclusively at the hot corner.

Under Chance, it took Zimmerman four years to break into the lineup at a 100+ game rate per season — he was shuffled from position to position. The unwillingness of the manager to give more playing time to the hard-hitting youngster is an important clue to his evaluation of the defensive abilities of the young man. Heinie's FA improved toward the end of his career, but not enough to redeem a poor career defensive record (FA .933).

With a bat in his hands, Zimmerman had HOF credentials; less than a handful of players had his contact hitting ability, or generated an SA of equal quality; his production record was, comparatively, outstanding — his durability, adequate.

Per at Bat (PAB) 1901–19 — Infielders

	AT BAT	R PAB	HR PAB	RBI PAB	TOTAL PAB
Zimmerman	5304	.120	.011	.140	.271
Sample avg.	4832	.129	.005	.107	.241

HOF electors must have defensive ability in mind when they weigh the merits of HOF candidates. Offensive ability alone is not enough, particularly with infielders.

Heinie Zimmerman's offensive dynamite was not sufficient to offset his deficiencies with the glove. He played only 65 percent of his games at the hot corner. The HOF is no place for utility infielders — unless their batting performance is mind-boggling.

Larry Doyle

Born 1886; Height 5.10; Weight 165; T-R; B-L; MVP-NL 1912; Led National League: 1909-H; 1911-3B; 1915-BA, H, 2B

= Net of home runs

	G	AB	H	R*	HR	RBI*	BA	SA	PAB
CLASS I PAB .301+									
1911	143	526	163	89	13	64	.310	.527	.316
1912	143	558	184	88	10	80	.330	.471	.319
Total	286	1084	347	177	23	144	.320	.498	.317

	G	AB	H	R*	HR	RBI*	BA	SA	PAB
CLASS II									
PAB .271–.300									
1910	151	575	164	89	8	61	.285	.412	.275
1913	132	482	135	62	5	68	.280	.388	.280
1918	75	257	67	35	3	33	.261	.354	.276
1919	113	381	110	54	7	45	.289	.433	.278
Total	471	1695	476	240	23	207	.281	.401	.277
CLASS III									
PAB .241–.270									
1908	104	377	116	65	0	33	.308	.398	.260
1914	145	539	140	82	5	58	.260	.353	.269
1915	150	591	189	82	4	66	.320	.442	.257
Total	399	1507	445	229	9	157	.295	.399	.262
CLASS IV									
PAB .211–.240									
1909	146	570	172	80	6	43	.302	.419	.226
1916	122	479	133	58	3	51	.278	.403	.234
1917	135	476	121	42	6	55	.254	.353	.216
Total	403	1525	426	180	15	149	.279	.393	.226
CLASS V									
PAB .210-									
1907	69	227	59	16	0	16	.260	.273	.141
Period	1628	6038	1753	842	70	673	.290	.411	.263
Other	137	471	134	44	4	46	.285	.370	.200
Career	1765	6509	1887	886	74	719	..290	.408	.258
BEST 123+ GAMES									
1912	143	558	184	88	10	80	.330	.471	.319

Calculation of Domination Points, MTP/MVP

	AB	PAB	MVP	MTP
CLASS I	1084	.317	344	814
CLASS II	1695	.277	470	
CLASS III	1507	.262	395	
CLASS IV	1525	.226	345	
TOTAL	5811		1554	
CLASS V	227		0	
PERIOD	6038		1554	

Larry Doyle was 21 when in 1907 he joined the Giants of John McGraw as a second baseman. The job was wide open and the young man went for it. By 1909, he had cleared away the competition.

This condition continued until 1916 when a five-man deal brought Heinie Zimmerman to New York and sent Doyle to the Chicago Cubs. But not for long.

He was traded to Boston after the 1917 season. Before Doyle played a game for them, he was traded back to McGraw's Giants. He ended his 14-year career in New York at the age of 34, in 1920.

Doyle, a second baseman throughout his major league career, had good hands but limited range. A comparison with some of his competitors appears below:

Player	G	TC/G	FA
Larry Doyle	1765	4.9	.949
Johnny Evers	1783	5.3	.953
Dell Pratt	1835	5.8	.962

Offense was Doyle's strength. Only five men in the sample were more efficient producers. His general superiority to the average infielder is shown below:

Per at Bat (PAB) 1901–19 — Infielders

	AT BAT	R PAB	HR PAB	RBI PAB	TOTAL PAB
Doyle	6038	.139	.012	.112	.263
Sample avg.	4832	.129	.005	.107	.241

Like many players of the day Doyle could, and did, run. In six seasons, he stole 20+ bases. Speed plus batting eye is a combination that leads to scoring.

Only Baker had a better home run factor than Doyle in 1901–19, an amazing feat when one considers his size. The second baseman was also an effective RBI man.

On the basis of offensive ability, Doyle was a HOF prospect. But he was passed over by HOF electors, and many wonder why. His durability (AB) and class (PAB) were good, and his defensive skills appeared to be adequate. In this analysis, that adds up to a HOF appointment more convincingly than arguments advanced in support of men like Tinker, Evers and Wallace.

JIMMY WILLIAMS

Born 1876; Height 5.09; Weight 175; T-R B-R; Led American League: 1901/02–3B

* = Net of home runs

	G	AB	H	R*	HR	RBI*	BA	SA	PAB
CLASS I									
PAB .301+									
1901	130	501	159	106	7	89	.317	.495	.403
1902	125	498	156	75	8	75	.313	.500	.317
Total	255	999	315	181	15	164	.315	.497	.360
CLASS II									
PAB .271–.300									
1903	132	502	134	57	3	79	.267	.392	.277
1906	139	501	139	59	3	74	.277	.373	.271
Total	271	1003	273	116	6	153	.272	.383	.274
CLASS III									
PAB .241–.270									
None									
CLASS IV									
PAB .211–.240									
1904	146	559	147	60	2	72	.263	.354	.240
1905	129	470	107	48	6	54	.228	.343	.230
1907	139	504	136	51	2	61	.270	.359	.226
Total	414	1533	390	159	10	187	.254	.352	.232
CLASS V									
PAB .210-									
1908	148	539	127	59	4	49	.236	.321	.208
1909	110	374	73	32	0	22	.195	.235	.144
Total	258	913	200	91	4	71	.219	.286	.182
Period	1198	4448	1178	547	35	575	.265	.378	.260
Other	258	1033	329	184	14	170	.318	.474	.356
Career	1456	5481	1507	731	49	745	.275	.396	.278
BEST 123+ GAMES									
1901	130	501	159	106	7	89	.317	.495	.403

Calculation of Domination Points, MTP/MVP

	AB	PAB	MVP	MTP
CLASS I	999	.360	360	635
CLASS II	1003	.274	275	
CLASS III	0	0	0	
CLASS IV	1533	.232	356	
TOTAL	3535		991	
CLASS V	913		0	
PERIOD	4448		991	

Williams broke in with Pittsburgh in 1899 at 23 years of age as a third baseman. In 1901, like many players of the day, he jumped to the AL as a second baseman for Baltimore, his defensive position for the balance of his career. Two years later he went to the Yankees for five seasons, and then concluded an 11-year career with the Browns. He was 33 when he retired in 1909.

Defensively, Jimmy had a career FA of .945, well below the numbers turned in by the better keystone men (Eddie Collins, .969), but it probably understates his ability with the glove. Over his last five seasons, his FA was about .963, reflecting a marked improvement brought about, perhaps, by better playing conditions as the game gradually matured and professionalized.

Williams was above average in offensive talent that partially offset his weak durability.

Per at Bat (PAB) 1901–19 — Infielders

	AT BAT	R PAB	HR PAB	RBI PAB	TOTAL PAB
Williams	4448	.123	.008	.129	.260
Sample avg.	4832	.129	.005	.107	.241

He had the seventh highest PAB of any player in the infield group. His problem was durability. He was a commendable short-term producer.

Kid Elberfeld

Born 1875; Height 5.07; Weight 158; T-R; B-R

* = Net of home runs

	G	AB	H	R*	HR	RBI*	BA	SA	PAB
CLASS I									
PAB .301+									
1901	122	436	135	73	3	73	.310	.429	.342
CLASS II									
PAB .271–.300									
1902	130	488	127	69	1	63	.260	.326	.273
1903	125	481	145	78	0	64	.301	.383	.295
1908	19	56	11	11	0	5	.196	.250	.286
Total	274	1025	283	158	1	132	.276	.349	.284
CLASS III									
PAB .241–.271									
1905	111	390	102	48	0	53	.262	.318	.259
1906	99	346	106	57	2	29	.306	.384	.254
1907	120	447	121	61	0	51	.271	.336	.251
1911	127	404	110	58	0	47	.272	.339	.260
Total	457	1587	439	224	2	180	.277	.343	.256

	G	AB	H	R*	HR	RBI*	BA	SA	PAB
CLASS IV PAB .211–.240									
1904	122	445	117	53	2	44	.263	.328	.222
CLASS V PAB .210–									
1909	106	379	90	47	0	26	.237	.288	.193
1910	127	455	114	51	2	40	.251	.292	.204
1914	30	62	14	7	0	1	.226	.242	.129
Total	263	896	218	105	2	67	.243	.287	.194
Period	1238	4389	1192	613	10	496	.272	.340	.255
Other	55	176	45	24	0	29	.256	.314	.301
Career	1293	4565	1237	637	10	525	.271	.339	.257
BEST 123+ GAMES									
1903	125	481	145	78	0	64	.301	.383	.295

Calculation of Domination Points, MTP/MVP

	AB	PAB	MVP	MTP
CLASS I	436	.342	149	440
CLASS II	1025	.284	291	
CLASS III	1587	.256	406	
CLASS IV	445	.222	99	
TOTAL	3493		945	
CLASS V	896		0	
PERIOD	4389		945	

Elberfeld played a few games with the Phillies and Reds before the turn of the century. In 1901, 26 years old, he became the starting shortstop for the Tigers as that club and others tried to get the AL organized.

He moved to the Yankees in 1903 and stayed with them for about six years as a part-time shortstop and utility infielder. Washington and the Brooklyn Dodgers used him in the same fashion; for two seasons (1912–13) he was idle. He retired in 1914 at the age of 39.

Per at Bat (PAB) 1901–19—Infielders

	AT BAT	R PAB	HR PAB	RBI PAB	TOTAL PAB
Elberfeld	4389	.140	.002	.113	.255
Sample avg.	4832	.129	.005	.107	.241

Elberfeld was essentially a part-time player with enough skill and versatility to hang on for 14 seasons. He was more valuable offensively than in the field (FA .923).

George Davis

Born 1870; Height 5.09; Weight 180; T-R; B-R

* = Net of home runs

	G	AB	H	R*	HR	RBI*	BA	SA	PAB
CLASS I PAB .301+									
1902	132	485	145	73	3	90	.299	.402	.342

	G	AB	H	R*	HR	RBI*	BA	SA	PAB
CLASS II									
PAB .271–.300									
1906	133	484	134	63	0	80	.277	.355	.295
CLASS III									
PAB .241–.270									
1901	130	495	153	62	7	58	.309	.428	.257
1904	152	563	142	74	1	68	.252	.359	.254
Total	282	1058	295	136	8	126	.279	.391	.255
CLASS IV									
PAB .211–.240									
1905	157	550	153	73	1	54	.278	.340	.233
1907	132	466	111	58	1	51	.238	.292	.236
Total	289	1016	264	131	2	105	.260	.318	.234
CLASS V									
PAB .210–									
1903	4	15	4	2	0	1	.267	.267	.200
1908	128	419	91	41	0	26	.217	.255	.160
1909	28	68	9	5	0	2	.132	.147	.103
Total	160	502	104	48	0	29	.207	.241	.153
Period	996	3545	942	451	13	430	.266	.346	.252
Other	1381	5505	1725	1019	61	931	.313	.448	.365
Career	2377	9050	2667	1470	74	1361	.295	.408	.321
BEST 123+ GAMES									
1902	132	485	145	73	3	90	.299	.402	.342

Calculation of Domination Points, MTP/MVP

	AB	PAB	MVP	MTP
CLASS I	485	.342	166	309
CLASS II	484	.295	143	
CLASS III	1058	.255	270	
CLASS IV	1016	.234	238	
TOTAL	3043		817	
CLASS V	502		0	
PERIOD	3545		817	

George Davis' career was almost over when the subject period began. He was 31 with 11 years as a full-time player behind him. His 20-year career began in 1890 with Cleveland. Three seasons with that club, then eight more with New York, preceded the opening of the 1901 season.

Except for one brief return visit to New York, Davis spent the rest of his career with the White Sox. He retired in 1909 at the age of 39.

Davis played 58 percent of his games at shortstop. For all practical purposes, he should be thought of as a utility man. His value was in his offensive contributions, especially as a base stealer. Over half of Davis' total career preceded the beginning of this period.

Per at Bat (PAB) 1901–19—Infielders

	AT BAT	R PAB	HR PAB	RBI PAB	TOTAL PAB
Davis	3545	.127	.004	.121	.252
Sample avg.	4832	.129	.005	.107	.241

Davis routinely stole 30–65 bases a season as a young man, and even in his later years, 20–30 steals was not unusual for him. Over his 20-year career Davis proved himself to be a competent but unremarkable baseball man.

Danny Murphy

Born 1876; Height 5.09; Weight 175; T-R; B-R

* = Net of home runs

	G	AB	H	R*	HR	RBI*	BA	SA	PAB
CLASS I									
PAB .301+									
1902	76	291	91	47	1	47	.313	.416	.326
1911	141	508	167	98	6	60	.329	.461	.323
1912	36	130	42	25	2	18	.323	.446	.346
Total	253	929	300	170	9	125	.323	.445	.327
CLASS II									
PAB .271–.300									
1914	52	161	49	12	4	28	.304	.435	.273
CLASS III									
PAB .241–.270									
1904	150	557	160	71	7	70	.287	.440	.266
1905	150	533	148	65	6	65	.278	.390	.255
Total	300	1090	308	136	13	135	.283	.416	.261
CLASS IV									
PAB .211–.240									
1903	133	513	140	64	1	59	.273	.382	.242
1906	119	448	135	46	2	58	.301	.404	.237
1907	124	469	127	49	2	55	.271	.345	.226
1908	142	525	139	47	4	62	.265	.364	.215
1909	149	541	152	56	5	64	.281	.412	.231
1910	151	560	168	66	4	60	.300	.436	.232
Total	818	3056	861	328	18	358	.282	.392	.230
CLASS V									
PAB .210-									
1901	28	102	19	6	0	6	.186	.216	.118
1913	40	59	19	3	0	6	.322	.441	.153
1915	5	6	1	0	0	0	.167	.167	.000
Total	73	167	39	9	0	12	.234	.294	.126
Period	1496	5403	1557	655	44	658	.288	.404	.251
Other	22	74	20	12	0	6	.270	.256	.243
Career	1518	5477	1577	667	44	664	.288	.402	.251
BEST 123+ GAMES									
1911	141	508	167	98	6	60	.329	.461	.323

Calculation of Domination Points, MTP/MVP

	AB	PAB	MVP	MTP
CLASS I	929	.327	304	348
CLASS II	161	.273	44	
CLASS III	1090	.261	284	
CLASS IV	3056	.230	703	
TOTAL	5236		1335	
CLASS V	167		0	
PERIOD	5403		1335	

Danny Murphy entered the major leagues at the turn of the century, and by 1902 had already completed two seasons as a part-time second baseman with the Giants. Connie Mack looked the 26-year-old over for a season then, in 1903, gave him the full-time job at the keystone position.

Baseball life stabilized for Murphy through 1907. Then, abruptly, he became an outfielder. What caused the radical change? Eddie Collins, the blossoming superstar, was ready and Mack made room for him.

Murphy played six more seasons for the Athletics as an outfielder. He spent his final two years in the ill-fated Federal League; he was 39 when he retired in 1915.

Defense was not the forte of Danny Murphy during his eight seasons at second base. His FA was not impressive (.950s). While few second basemen in baseball history could have kept Eddie Collins on the bench, Murphy was a minor defensive obstacle for the nimble, sure-handed Collins to overcome.

Over his full 16-year career, Murphy played only 57 percent of his games at the keystone sack. Ability with a bat (BA .288) was the talent that kept the young man at second base, and later justified his continued presence in the lineup as an outfielder.

PER AT BAT (PAB) 1901–19—INFIELDERS

	AT BAT	R PAB	HR PAB	RBI PAB	TOTAL PAB
Murphy	5403	.121	.008	.122	.251
Sample avg.	4832	.129	.005	.107	.241

Murphy hit well but was slow to take a base on balls. This over-aggressive attitude hurt his on-base percentage and his scoring ability. On the other hand, he was above average as a home run/RBI man, enough so to offset his scoring problems and to lift him into the above-average class of producers. As a contact hitter, he was among the ten best in the infielder group—his durability was also above average.

Murphy generated one of the ten best PAB ratings. He was a player with adequate durability who developed no defensive credentials to go with a good offensive record. A fine journeyman athlete, he was not HOF material.

HARRY STEINFELDT

Born 1877; Height 5.10; Weight 180; T-R; B-R; Led National League: 1903-2B; 1906-H, RBI

* = Net of home runs

	G	AB	H	R*	HR	RBI*	BA	SA	PAB
CLASS I									
PAB .301+									
1903	118	439	137	65	6	77	.312	.481	.337
CLASS II									
PAB .271–.300									
1906	151	539	176	78	3	80	.327	.430	.299
1910	129	448	113	68	2	56	.252	.317	.281
Total	280	987	289	146	5	136	.293	.379	.291
CLASS III									
PAB .241–.270									
1904	99	349	85	34	1	51	.244	.318	.246
1909	151	528	133	71	2	57	.252	.337	.246
Total	250	877	218	105	3	108	.249	.329	.246

	G	AB	H	R*	HR	RBI*	BA	SA	PAB
CLASS IV									
PAB .211–.240									
1901	105	382	95	34	6	41	.249	.380	.212
1902	129	479	133	52	1	48	.278	.355	.211
1905	114	384	104	48	1	38	.271	.367	.227
1907	152	542	144	51	1	69	.266	.336	.223
1908	150	539	130	62	1	61	.241	.306	.230
Total	650	2326	606	247	10	257	.261	.345	.221
CLASS V									
PAB .210-									
1911	19	63	16	4	1	7	.254	.365	.190
Period	1317	4692	1266	567	25	585	.270	.362	.251
Other	331	1207	312	165	2	150	.258	.352	.263
Career	1648	5899	1578	732	27	735	.268	.360	.253
BEST 123+ GAMES									
1906	151	539	176	78	3	80	.327	.430	.299

Calculation of Domination Points, MTP/MVP

	AB	PAB	MVP	MTP
CLASS I	439	.337	148	435
CLASS II	987	.291	287	
CLASS III	877	.246	216	
CLASS IV	2326	.221	514	
TOTAL	4629		1165	
CLASS V	63		0	
PERIOD	4692		1165	

Harry Steinfeldt, 24, was a utility infielder with three major league seasons behind him when the subject period opened. The Reds continued to use him in this capacity through the 1905 season.

He was traded to the Cubs in 1906 for two players, a fortunate deal for him in that it provided him with the opportunity to establish himself as full-time third baseman—which he did. He gave the Cubs five workmanlike seasons and then spent a final year with the Braves. He was 33 when he quit in 1911.

Steinfeldt was a utility infielder in all but five of his 14 active years. He proved to be defensively sound when he finally got a chance to play third base regularly—a surprisingly productive player given his limited batting skills (BA .268).

Per at Bat (PAB) 1901–19—Infielders

	AT BAT	R PAB	HR PAB	RBI PAB	TOTAL PAB
Steinfeldt	4692	.121	.005	.125	.251
Sample avg.	4832	.129	.005	.107	.241

Timely hitting was the key to Steinfeldt's impressive PAB.

Most baseball fans have heard about Tinker to Evers to Chance. Few are aware that Harry Steinfeldt anchored the left side of the diamond for that talented trio.

JIMMY COLLINS

Born 1870; Height 5.09; Weight 178; T-R B-R; HOF-1945

* = Net of home runs

	G	AB	H	R*	HR	RBI*	BA	SA	PAB
CLASS I PAB .301+									
1901	138	564	187	103	6	88	.332	.495	.349.
CLASS II PAB .271–.300									
1902	108	429	138	65	6	55	.322	.459	.294
1903	130	540	160	82	5	67	.296	.448	.285
Total	238	969	298	147	11	122	.308	.453	.289
CLASS III PAB .241–.270									
1905	131	508	140	62	4	61	.276	.368	.250
CLASS IV PAB .211–.240									
1904	156	631	168	82	3	64	.266	.374	.236
1906	37	142	39	16	1	15	.275	.408	.225
Total	193	773	207	98	4	79	.268	.380	.234
CLASS V PAB .210–									
1907	143	523	146	51	0	45	.279	.337	.184
1908	115	433	94	34	0	30	.217	.263	.148
Total	258	956	240	85	0	75	.251	.303	.167
Period	958	3770	1072	495	25	425	.284	.395	.251
Other	770	3026	925	495	40	493	.306	.424	.340
Career	1728	6796	1997	990	65	918	.294	.408	.290
BEST 123+ GAMES									
1901	138	564	187	103	6	88	.332	.495	.349.

CALCULATION OF DOMINATION POINTS, MTP/MVP

	AB	PAB	MVP	MTP
CLASS I	564	.349	197	477
CLASS II	969	.289	280	
CLASS III	508	.250	127	
CLASS IV	773	.234	181	
TOTAL	2814		785	
CLASS V	956		0	
PERIOD	3770		785	

Collins was 31 by the time the 1901 season began with six years of major league baseball behind him.

He started with the Boston Braves in 1895; then, when the AL opened up in 1901, he jumped cross-town to the Red Sox. He went to the Athletics to finish a 14-year career. Collins was 38 when he retired.

Collins' career FA of .928 was not impressive. HOF literature proclaiming his wizardry at third base seems at odds with his statistical record. But this is clarified when one notes that he led the American League in 1902 and 1903 with .954 and .952, respectively. As a fielder, his written reputation is more impressive than his overall statistical history, which was unusually burdened by pre–1901 activity.

Jimmy Collins was an above-average contact hitter (career BA .294). In 1901, he had one of the ten best production years of the era by an infielder.

Per at Bat (PAB) 1901–19 — Infielders

	AT BAT	R PAB	HR PAB	RBI PAB	TOTAL PAB
Collins	3770	.131	.007	.113	.251
Sample avg.	4832	.129	.005	.107	.241

Collins was playing manager with the Red Sox during most of his time in Boston. His election to the HOF in 1945 cannot be fairly appraised based upon his activities during the subject period. But it must be said that his offensive record does not justify the appointment, and one can rightly suspect that his election was related to one single aspect of his managerial career (1901–06) — his Red Sox whipped the highly favored Pirates in the 1903 World Series.

Art Devlin

Born 1879; Height 6.00; Weight 175; T-R; B-R; Led National League: 1905-SB

* = Net of home runs

	G	AB	H	R*	HR	RBI*	BA	SA	PAB
CLASS I									
PAB .301+									
1904	130	474	133	80	1	65	.281	.354	.308
CLASS II									
PAB .271–.300									
1906	148	498	149	74	2	63	.299	.390	.279
1910	147	493	128	69	2	65	.260	.327	.276
Total	295	991	277	143	4	128	.280	.359	.277
CLASS III									
PAB .241–.270									
1905	153	525	129	72	2	59	.246	.310	.253
1911	83	260	71	42	0	25	.273	.350	.258
1912	124	436	126	59	0	54	.289	.367	.259
Total	360	1221	326	173	2	138	.267	.339	.256
CLASS IV									
PAB .211–.240									
1907	143	491	136	60	1	53	.277	.324	.232
1909	143	491	130	61	0	55	.265	.336	.236
Total	286	982	266	121	1	108	.271	.330	.234
CLASS V									
PAB .219-									
1908	157	534	135	57	2	43	.253	.313	.191
1913	73	210	48	19	0	12	.229	.310	.148
Total	230	744	183	76	2	55	.246	.312	.179
Period	1301	4412	1185	593	10	494	.269	.338	.249
Career	1301	4412	1185	593	10	494	.269	.338	.249
BEST 123+ GAMES									
1904	130	474	133	80	1	65	.281	.354	.308

Calculation of Domination Points, MTP/MVP

	AB	PAB	MVP	MTP
CLASS I	474	.308	146	421
CLASS II	991	.277	275	
CLASS III	1221	.256	313	
CLASS IV	982	.234	230	
TOTAL	3668		964	
CLASS V	744		0	
PERIOD	4412		964	

Art Devlin came to the Giants in 1904 and anchored the hot corner for McGraw's club for eight years. He was sold to Boston in 1912 and he spent his final two seasons with them. He was 25 when he started his major league career and 34 when it ended in 1913.

A good third baseman at the time had a FA of about .938. Devlin was capable of such performance. In 92 percent of his games played, managers assigned him to third base.

On offense, Devlin was a timely hitter with explosive base-stealing speed. He pilfered an average of 28 bases per year and led the league once with 59.

Per at Bat (PAB) 1901–19—Infielders

	AT BAT	R PAB	HR PAB	RBI PAB	TOTAL PAB
Devlin	4412	.134	.002	.113	.249
Sample avg.	4832	.129	.005	.107	.241

Art Devlin was an above-average producer during a relatively brief career.

Frank LaPorte

Born 1880; Height 5.08; Weight 175; T-R; B-R

* = Net of home runs

	G	AB	H	R*	HR	RBI*	BA	SA	PAB
CLASS I **PAB .301+**									
1905	11	40	16	3	1	11	.400	.500	.375
1914	133	505	157	82	4	103	.311	.436	.374
Total	144	545	173	85	5	114	.317	.441	.374
CLASS II **PAB .271–.300**									
1911	136	507	159	69	2	89	.314	.446	.298
CLASS III **PAB .241–.270**									
1906	123	454	120	58	2	52	.264	.368	.247
1910	124	432	114	41	2	65	.264	.338	.250
1912	119	402	125	44	1	54	.311	.393	.246
Total	366	1288	359	143	5	171	.279	.366	.248
CLASS IV **PAB .211–.240**									
1907	130	470	127	56	0	48	.270	.360	.221
1909	89	309	92	35	0	31	.298	.379	.214
Total	219	779	219	91	0	79	.281	.368	.218

	G	AB	H	R*	HR	RBI*	BA	SA	PAB
CLASS V									
PAB .210-									
1908	101	301	75	21	0	30	.249	.316	.169
1913	79	242	61	25	0	18	.252	.306	.178
1915	148	550	139	53	2	54	.253	.351	.198
Total	328	1093	275	99	2	102	.252	.331	.186
Period	1193	4212	1185	487	14	546	.281	.376	.249
Career	1193	4212	1185	487	14	546	.281	.376	.249
BEST 123+ GAMES									
1914	133	505	157	82	4	103	.311	.436	.374

Calculation of Domination Points, MTP/MVP

	AB	PAB	MVP	MTP
CLASS I	545	.374	204	355
CLASS II	507	.298	151	
CLASS III	1288	.248	319	
CLASS IV	779	.218	170	
TOTAL	3119		844	
CLASS V	1093		0	
PERIOD	4212		844	

Frank LaPorte signed with the Yankees in 1905 when he was 25 years of age. He spent five full seasons with them during his 11-year career but, before his retirement in 1915, he also played for AL clubs in Boston, St. Louis and Washington. He finished in the Federal League.

LaPorte was a utility man who played a variety of positions, mostly second base. His value was in his bat — a good contact hitter (BA .281).

Per at Bat (PAB) 1901–19 — Infielders

	AT BAT	R PAB	HR PAB	RBI PAB	TOTAL PAB
LaPorte	4212	.116	.003	.130	.249
Sample avg.	4832	.129	.005	.107	.241

LaPorte put everything together in 1914 and generated one of the best production years by an infielder during the era. This feat must not be taken too seriously — it took place in the ill-fated Federal League.

Red Smith

Born 1890; Height 5.11; Weight 165; T-R; B-R; Led Nation al League: 1913–2B

*= Net of home runs

	G	AB	H	R*	HR	RBI*	BA	SA	PAB
CLASS I									
PAB .301+									
None									
CLASS II									
PAB .271–.300									
1914	150	537	146	62	7	78	.272	.395	.274
1918	119	429	128	53	2	63	.298	.373	.275
Total	269	966	274	115	9	141	.284	.385	.274

	G	AB	H	R*	HR	RBI*	BA	SA	PAB
CLASS III									
PAB .241–.270									
1911	28	111	29	10	0	19	.261	.333	.261
1912	128	486	139	71	4	53	.286	.393	.263
1913	151	540	160	64	6	70	.296	.441	.259
Total	307	1137	328	145	10	142	.288	.410	.261
CLASS IV									
PAB .211–.240									
1915	157	549	145	64	2	63	.264	.352	.235
1917	147	505	149	58	2	60	.295	.392	.238
Total	304	1054	294	122	4	123	.279	.371	.236
CLASS V									
PAB .210–									
1916	150	509	132	45	3	57	.259	.348	.206
1919	87	241	59	23	1	24	.245	.282	.199
Total	237	750	191	68	4	81	.255	.327	.247
Period	1117	3907	1087	450	27	487	.278	.377	.247
Career	1117	3907	1087	450	27	487	.278	.377	.247
BEST 123+ GAMES									
1914	150	537	146	62	7	78	.272	.395	.274

Calculation of Domination Points, MTP/MVP

	AB	PAB	MVP	MTP
CLASS I	0	0	0	265
CLASS II	966	.274	265	
CLASS III	1137	.261	297	
CLASS IV	1054	.236	249	
TOTAL	3157		811	
CLASS V	750		0	
PERIOD	3907		811	

Red Smith had a short career, all of it in the subject period. It started in Brooklyn in 1911, moved to Boston in 1914 and ended in the same town five years later. Smith was only 29 when he retired in 1919.

Unlike many contemporaries, Red Smith started at third base and stayed there throughout his career except for four games as an outfielder during his final season. His FA (.933) was below that of the top hot corner men of the day. But Smith was a good contact hitter (BA .278) and an above-average producer.

Per at Bat (PAB) 1901–19—Infielders

	AT BAT	R PAB	HR PAB	RBI PAB	TOTAL PAB
Smith	3907	.115	.007	.125	.247
Sample avg.	4832	.129	.005	.107	.241

Timely hitting and above-average middle-distance power were the offensive characteristics that kept Smith in the lineup.

Larry Gardner

Born 1886; Height 5.08; Weight 165; T-R; B-L

* = Net of home runs

	G	AB	H	R*	HR	RBI*	BA	SA	PAB
CLASS I PAB .301+									
1909	19	37	11	8	0	5	.297	.432	.351
1912	143	517	163	85	3	83	.315	.449	.331
Total	162	554	174	93	3	88	.314	.448	.332
CLASS II PAB .271–.300									
1919	139	524	157	65	2	77	.300	.393	.275
CLASS III PAB .241–.270									
1911	138	492	140	76	4	40	.285	.376	.244
1913	131	473	133	64	0	63	.281	.359	.268
1915	127	430	111	50	1	54	.258	.326	.244
Total	396	1395	384	190	5	157	.275	.355	.252
CLASS IV PAB .211–.240									
1910	113	413	117	53	2	34	.283	.375	.215
1916	148	493	152	45	2	60	.308	.387	.217
1917	146	501	133	52	1	60	.265	.345	.226
1918	127	463	132	49	1	51	.285	.365	.218
Total	534	1870	534	199	6	205	.286	.368	.219
CLASS V PAB .210-									
1908	2	6	3	0	0	1	.500	.500	.167
1914	155	553	143	47	3	65	.259	.385	.208
Total	157	559	146	47	3	66	.261	.386	.208
Period	1388	4902	1395	594	19	593	.285	.378	.246
Other	534	1782	536	246	8	309	.301	.404	.316
Career	1922	6684	1931	840	27	902	.289	.385	.265
BEST 123+ GAMES									
1912	143	517	163	85	3	83	.315	.449	.331

Calculation of Domination Points, MTP/MVP

	AB	PAB	MVP	MTP
CLASS I	554	.332	184	328
CLASS II	524	.275	144	
CLASS III	1395	.252	352	
CLASS IV	1870	.219	410	
TOTAL	4343		1090	
CLASS V	559		0	
PERIOD	4902		1090	

When 22-year-old Larry Gardner joined the Red Sox in 1908, Harry Lord was the third baseman and Fred Lake the newly-appointed manager. In 1910, Patsy Donovan succeeded Lake and a shift at third base also took place — Lord was traded to Chicago and Gardner took over the hot corner.

After a decade with Boston, Gardner was traded, in 1918, to Philadelphia, which sent Gardner and two players to the Athletics for Stuffy McInnis. After a cup of coffee in Philly, Gardner was traded to Cleveland, where he spent his last six seasons. When he retired in 1924, he was 38 years old.

Jimmy Collins and Frank Baker played better than 97 percent of their games at third base and they provide a useful defensive standard at that position for the times. Gardner played 86 percent of his games at the hot corner and the balance at short or second. The career fielding statistics of all three players, therefore, are reasonably reliable indicators of defensive abilities.

Player	G	TC/G	FA
Larry Gardner	1922	3.4	.948
Jimmy Collins	1728	3.8	.929
Frank Baker	1575	3.6	.943

The indicated range of Jimmy Collins was real, especially in his early years. It's also true that his FA is a mixture of pre-1901 and post-1901 activity (he led the league twice after 1901 with an FA in the .950s). Baker, best remembered for his offense, was a steady third baseman with good range. Gardner had fair range, good hands, and a competitive record in the field.

Gardner was one of the top ten contact hitters in the group during the subject period (BA .285). His PAB, the elements of which are summarized below, was above average.

PER AT BAT (PAB) 1901–19—INFIELDERS

	AT BAT	R PAB	HR PAB	RBI PAB	TOTAL PAB
Gardner	4902	.121	.004	.121	.246
Sample avg.	4832	.129	.005	.107	.241

He was an unspectacular, versatile offensive performer. Not as speedy as many contemporaries, he was a steady contact hitter who hit well in the clutch.

Only 73 percent of Gardner's career ABs fell into the 1901–19 period. As a consequence, the value of his full career is not seen here, nor will it be calculated. The deadball/live-ball mixture would be useless.

It speaks well for the quality of Gardner's career that he ranked high with only a portion of his career exposed to analysis. Given the fact that men like Tinker, Evers and Wallace were selected for the HOF, one tends to wonder why he was overlooked. Do electors expect more of third basemen than middle infielders? If so, why? And is it historically justified?

ART FLETCHER

Born 1885; Height 5.11; Weight 170; T-R; B-R

* = Net of home runs

	G	AB	H	R*	HR	RBI*	BA	SA	PAB
CLASS I PAB .301+									
1911	112	326	104	72	1	36	.319	.429	.334
CLASS II PAB .271–.300									
1912	129	419	118	63	1	56	.282	.372	.286
CLASS III PAB .241–.270									
1913	136	538	160	72	4	67	.297	.390	.266
1914	135	514	147	60	2	77	.286	.379	.270
Total	271	1052	307	132	6	144	.292	.385	.268

	G	AB	H	R*	HR	RBI*	BA	SA	PAB
CLASS IV									
PAB .211–.240									
1915	149	562	143	56	3	71	.254	.326	.231
1916	133	500	143	50	3	63	.286	.382	.232
1917	151	557	145	66	4	52	.260	.343	.219
1919	127	488	135	51	3	51	.277	.357	.215
Total	560	2107	566	223	13	237	.269	.351	.224
CLASS V									
PAB .210-									
1909	29	98	21	7	0	6	.214	.235	.133
1910	51	125	28	12	0	13	.224	.256	.200
1918	124	468	123	51	0	47	.263	.314	.209
Total	204	691	172	70	0	66	.249	.292	.197
Period	1276	4595	1267	560	21	539	.276	.357	.244
Other	253	946	267	92	11	104	.282	.404	.219
Career	1529	5541	1534	652	32	643	.277	.365	.239
BEST 123+ GAMES									
1912	129	419	118	63	1	56	.282	.372	.286

Calculation of Domination Points, MTP/MVP

	AB	PAB	MVP	MTP
CLASS I	326	.334	109	229
CLASS II	419	.286	120	
CLASS III	1052	.268	282	
CLASS IV	2107	.224	472	
TOTAL	3904		983	
CLASS V	691		0	
PERIOD	4595		983	

Art Fletcher joined the New York Giants in 1909. He was 24 at the time. In two years, he was the regular shortstop and remained so through the 1919 season. He was traded to the Phillies in 1920 in a deal that brought Dave Bancroft (HOF) to the Giants.

Anybody who could satisfy John McGraw at shortstop for over a decade must have been pretty good at the job. Fletcher had a half-dozen seasons during which he handled more than 6.0 chances per game. His career FA (.938) was as good as most shortstops of the era could deliver. And he was a better-than-average producer.

Per at Bat (PAB) 1901–19—Infielders

	AT BAT	R PAB	HR PAB	RBI PAB	TOTAL PAB
Fletcher	4595	.122	.005	.117	.244
Sample avg.	4832	.129	.005	.107	.241

A fine defensive shortstop who is an above-average contact hitter and PAB man is a great asset to a manager. As usual, McGraw knew what he was doing when he kept Fletcher in the middle of his infield.

Fletcher's talent was shy of HOF standards, and his career was short compared to men like Tinker, Evers and Wallace, but during his day he was a highly respected ballplayer.

BILL DAHLEN

Born 1870; Height 5.09; Weight 180; T-R; B-R

* = Net of home runs

	G	AB	H	R*	HR	RBI*	BA	SA	PAB
CLASS I PAB .301+ None									
CLASS II PAB .271–.300									
1901	131	513	134	65	4	78	.261	.357	.287
1903	138	474	124	70	1	63	.262	.342	.283
1904	145	523	140	68	2	78	.268	.337	.283
1905	148	520	126	60	7	74	.242	.337	.271
Total	562	2030	524	263	14	293	.258	.343	.281
CLASS III PAB .241–.270									
1902	138	527	139	65	2	72	.264	.351	.264
CLASS IV PAB .211–.240									
1906	143	471	113	62	1	48	.240	.297	.236
CLASS V PAB .210-									
1907	143	464	96	40	0	34	.207	.254	.159
1908	144	524	125	47	3	45	.239	.307	.181
1909	69	197	46	20	2	14	.234	.305	.183
1910	3	2	0	0	0	0	.0	.0	.0
1911	1	3	0	0	0	0	.0	.0	.0
Total	360	1190	267	107	5	93	.224	.285	.172
Period	1203	4218	1043	497	22	506	.247	.322	.243
Other	1240	4821	1417	1009	62	643	.294	.434	.356
Career	2443	9039	2460	1506	84	1149	.272	.382	.303
BEST 123+ GAMES									
1901	131	513	134	65	4	78	.261	.357	.287

CALCULATION OF DOMINATION POINTS, MTP/MVP

	AB	PAB	MVP	MTP
CLASS I	0	0	0	570
CLASS II	2030	.281	570	
CLASS III	527	.264	139	
CLASS IV	471	.236	111	
TOTAL	3028		820	
CLASS V	1190		0	
PERIOD	4218		820	

An analysis of the 1901–19 period doesn't do justice to the career of Bill Dahlen. Almost half of his career was over and he was 31 when the 1901 season began with him at shortstop for Brooklyn. A decade earlier he had started with the Cubs and had matured into an efficient player by the time he was traded (1899) to Brooklyn. Dahlen went on to complete two more seasons with them, four with the Giants and two with the Braves. Then he returned to Brooklyn as playing manager for a two-year windup of a 21-year career. He was 41 when he stopped playing, but remained for two more seasons as manager.

Dahlen appeared in more games at shortstop than any other player in the survey, but in the subject period he didn't play long enough to make a deep impression. His career FA of .920 is heavily influenced by the high-error years of early baseball, and exaggerates what appear to be his notable weaknesses as a defensive player.

PER AT BAT (PAB) 1901–19 — INFIELDERS

	AT BAT	R PAB	HR PAB	RBI PAB	TOTAL PAB
Dahlen	4218	.118	.005	.120	.243
Sample avg.	4832	.129	.005	.107	.241

Despite his age, Dahlen was an above-average producer during the subject period.

JIM DELAHANTY

Born 1879; Height 5.11; Weight 170; T-R; B-R

* = Net of home runs

	G	AB	H	R*	HR	RBI*	BA	SA	PAB
CLASS I									
PAB .301+									
1911	144	542	184	80	3	91	.339	.463	.321
CLASS II									
PAB .271–.300									
1910	106	378	111	65	2	43	.294	.368	.291
1912	78	266	76	34	0	41	.286	.346	.282
Total	184	644	187	99	2	84	.290	.359	.287
CLASS III									
PAB .241–.270									
1906	115	379	106	62	1	38	.280	.364	.266
CLASS IV									
PAB .211–.240									
1902	7	26	6	3	0	3	.231	.269	.231
1904	142	499	142	53	3	57	.285	.389	.226
1905	125	461	119	45	5	50	.258	.349	.217
1907	142	499	139	50	2	58	.279	.361	.220
1908	83	287	91	32	1	29	.317	.394	.216
Total	499	1772	497	183	11	197	.280	.370	.221
CLASS V									
PAB .219-									
1901	17	63	12	4	0	4	.190	.222	.127
1909	136	452	105	46	1	40	.232	.316	.192
1914	74	214	62	28	0	15	.290	.397	.201
1915	17	25	6	0	0	2	.240	.280	.080
Total	244	754	185	78	1	61	.245	.330	.186
Period	1186	4091	1159	502	18	471	.283	.373	.242
Career	1186	4091	1159	502	18	471	.283	.373	.242
BEST 123+ GAMES									
1911	144	542	1845	80	3	91	.339	.463	.321

CALCULATION OF DOMINATION POINTS, MTP/MVP

	AB	PAB	MVP	MTP
CLASS I	542	.321	174	359
CLASS II	644	.287	185	

	AB	PAB	MVP	MTP
CLASS III	379	.266	101	
CLASS IV	1772	.221	392	
TOTAL	3337		852	
CLASS V	754		0	
PERIOD	4091		852	

Jim's brother, Ed, an outfielder with a 16-year career, retired in 1903 with a BA of .346 and was elected in 1945 to the HOF. Brother Tom took a shot at infield play for three seasons and retired in 1897. And brother Joe tried it for three years in the outfield — he quit in 1909. Another brother, Frank, an outfielder, had a six-year career that ended in 1915.

Jim was the only one of the baseball Delahantys to challenge brother Ed as a bona fide major league ballplayer. His career as a utility infielder (mostly second base) began in 1901 and ended in 1915. In the NL, he played for Chicago, New York, Boston and Cincinnati. St. Louis, Washington and Detroit were his AL stops. In his final two seasons, Jim labored for Brooklyn in the Federal League. He spent over three seasons with the Tigers; otherwise his stays with each club were for one or two years. He was literally one of baseball's gypsies.

Delahanty had defensive problems but he was flexible, and good enough to operate in most positions without causing undue damage. Offensively, he was a good hitter (BA .283) and a useful production man.

Per at Bat (PAB) 1901–19 — Infielders

	AT BAT	R PAB	HR PAB	RBI PAB	TOTAL PAB
Delahanty	4091	.123	.004	.115	.242
Sample avg.	4832	.129	.005	.107	.241

Hitting has always been the key ingredient of a major league baseball player. There were only four infielders in the subject period who were .300-plus hitters — superstars Wagner, Collins, Baker and Lajoie. And Delahanty, at .283, was not far behind. That's why managers found him useful. In spots, he was a productive hitter.

Del Pratt

Born 1888; Height 5.11; Weight 175; T-R; B-R; Led American League: 1916-RBI

* = Net of home runs

	G	AB	H	R*	HR	RBI*	BA	SA	PAB
CLASS I PAB .301+ None									
CLASS II PAB .271–.300									
1916	158	596	159	59	5	98	.267	.391	.272
CLASS III PAB .241–.270									
1912	151	570	172	71	5	64	.302	.426	.246
1913	155	592	175	58	2	85	.296	.402	.245
1914	158	584	165	80	5	60	.283	.411	.248
1918	126	477	131	63	2	53	.275	.356	.247
Total	590	2223	643	272	14	262	.289	.401	.247

	G	AB	H	R*	HR	RBI*	BA	SA	PAB
CLASS IV									
PAB .211–.240									
1915	159	602	175	58	3	75	.291	.394	.226
1919	140	527	154	65	4	52	.292	.393	.230
Total	299	1129	329	123	7	127	.291	.394	.228
CLASS V									
PAB .210–									
1917	123	450	111	39	1	51	.247	.338	.202
Period	1170	4398	1242	493	27	539	.282	.391	.241
Other	665	2428	754	320	16	384	.311	.425	.297
Career	1835	6826	1996	813	43	923	.292	.403	.261
BEST 123+ GAMES									
1916	158	596	159	59	5	98	.267	.391	.272

CALCULATION OF DOMINATION POINTS, MTP/MVP

	AB	PAB	MVP	MTP
CLASS I	0	0	0	162
CLASS II	596	.272	162	
CLASS III	2223	.247	549	
CLASS IV	1129	.228	257	
TOTAL	3948		968	
CLASS V	450		0	
PERIOD	4398		968	

Del Pratt in 1912 walked right into the keystone job with the Browns—he was 24. In his first season he hit .302. For a half-dozen years he labored in the baseball hell that was the Browns, and then heaven beckoned. In 1918 he went with Eddie Plank (HOF) to the Yankees in a seven-man deal and ended the subject period in New York.

Before Pratt retired in 1924, he spent five additional seasons in the majors, one more in New York and two each in Boston and Detroit. He was 36 when he quit.

Del Pratt was a fine fielding second baseman. A quick comparison of his career numbers with those of Johnny Evers makes this point.

Player	G	TC/G	FA
Pratt	1835	5.8	.962
Evers	1783	5.3	.953

He was also a superior hitter and a fast man on the bases, regularly stealing 20–40 bases per year. He generated an above average PAB. A continuation of the comparison with Evers in the offensive arena follows:

PER AT BAT (PAB) 1901–19—INFIELDERS

	AT BAT	R PAB	HR PAB	RBI PAB	TOTAL PAB
Pratt	4398	.112	.006	.123	.241
Evers	6131	.148	.002	.086	.236
Sample avg.	4832	.129	.005	.107	.241

Defensively, Pratt was equal to or better than Evers. His career extended into the 1920s. At the end, he had 6,826 at bats, more than Evers; he outproduced Evers. And there is no doubt that he would have scored more often had he played for almost anybody else but the Browns.

The suspicion exists that some players with careers with one foot in the deadball era and one in that of the live-ball were overlooked by HOF electors who, for example, found Evers to be worthy. Pratt may have been such an unfortunate player. Given the choice between Evers and Pratt, many would choose Pratt.

HANS LOBERT
Born 1881; Height 5.09; Weight 170; T-R; B-R

* = Net of home runs

	G	AB	H	R*	HR	RBI*	BA	SA	PAB
CLASS I PAB .301+ None									
CLASS II PAB .271–.300									
1911	147	541	154	85	9	63	.285	.405	.290
CLASS III PAB .241–.270									
1910	93	314	97	40	3	37	309	.395	.255
1912	65	257	84	35	2	31	.327	.436	.265
1913	150	573	172	91	7	48	.300	.424	.255
1914	135	505	139	82	1	51	.275	.349	.265
Total	443	1649	492	248	13	167	.298	.397	.260
CLASS IV PAB .211–.240									
1906	79	268	83	39	0	19	.310	.366	.216
1908	155	570	167	67	4	59	.293	.407	.228
1909	122	425	90	46	4	48	.212	.294	.231
1915	106	386	97	46	0	38	.251	.319	.218
1916	48	76	17	6	0	11	.224	.316	.224
Total	510	1725	454	204	8	175	.263	.349	.224
CLASS V PAB .210–									
1903	5	13	1	1	0	0	.077	.154	.077
1905	14	46	9	7	0	1	.196	.239	.174
1907	148	537	132	60	1	40	.246	.313	.188
1917	50	52	10	3	1	4	.192	.269	.154
Total	217	648	152	71	2	45	.235	.301	.182
Period	1317	4563	1252	608	32	450	.274	.366	.239
Career	1317	4563	1252	608	32	450	.274	.366	.239
BEST 123+ GAMES									
1911	147	541	154	85	9	63	.285	.405	.290

CALCULATION OF DOMINATION POINTS, MTP/MVP

	AB	PAB	MVP	MTP
CLASS I	0	0	0	157
CLASS II	541	.290	157	
CLASS III	1649	.260	429	
CLASS IV	1725	.224	386	
TOTAL	3915		972	
CLASS V	648		0	
PERIOD	4563		972	

Hans Lobert came to the majors for a cup of coffee in 1903 with Pittsburgh. He next appeared in 1905 in a few games with the Cubs. In 1906, he became a secure big leaguer — the Reds took him on as a utility infielder and gradually made a third baseman out of him.

A 1911 trade involving eight players sent him to the Phillies, where he remained for three seasons. A final trade in 1915 sent him to the Giants, where he spent his final three years. Lobert was 36 when he retired in 1917.

He spent 76 percent of his career games at third base. He appeared in more than 100 games in only seven of his 14 years. He was an acceptable defensive player.

Lobert was a good hitter (BA .274) who ran well (20–40 stolen bases per year) with better than average production credentials.

Per at Bat (PAB) 1901–19 — Infielders

	AT BAT	R PAB	HR PAB	RBI PAB	TOTAL PAB
Lobert	4563	.133	.007	.099	.239
Sample avg.	4832	.129	.005	.107	.241

Lobert had good legs and a reliable bat, a combination that often accompanies a healthy scoring record. In four seasons, he stole over 40 bases.

Donnie Bush

Born 1887; Height 5.06; Weight 140; T-R; B-B; Led American League: 1909/10/11/12/14-BB; 1917-R

* = Net of home runs

	G	AB	H	R*	HR	RBI*	BA	SA	PAB
CLASS I PAB .301+ None									
CLASS II PAB .271–.300									
1909	157	532	145	114	0	33	.273	.314	.277
1911	150	561	130	125	1	35	.232	.287	.287
1912	144	511	118	105	2	36	.231	.301	.280
Total	451	1604	393	344	3	104	.245	300	.281
CLASS III PAB .241–.270									
1908	20	68	20	13	0	4	.294	.338	.250
1910	142	496	130	87	3	31	.262	.323	.244
1915	155	561	128	98	1	43	.228	.283	.253
Total	317	1125	278	198	4	78	.247	.304	.249
CLASS IV PAB .211–.240									
1913	153	593	149	97	1	39	.251	.322	.231
1914	157	596	150	97	0	32	.252	.295	.216
1917	147	581	163	112	0	24	.281	.322	.234
1919	129	509	124	82	0	26	.244	.289	.212
Total	586	2279	586	388	1	121	.257	.308	.224
CLASS V PAB .210-									
1916	145	550	124	73	0	34	.225	.267	.195
1918	128	500	117	74	0	22	.234	.266	.192

Infielders—Analysis, 1901–1919

	G	AB	H	R*	HR	RBI*	BA	SA	PAB
Total	273	1050	241	147	0	56	.230	.267	.193
Period	1627	6058	1498	1077	8	359	.247	.298	.238
Other	319	1148	305	194	1	68	.266	.311	.229
Career	1946	7206	1803	1271	9	427	.250	.300	.237
BEST 123+ GAMES									
1911	150	561	130	125	1	35	.232	.287	.287

Calculation of Domination Points, MTP/MVP

	AB	PAB	MVP	MTP
CLASS I	0	0	0	451
CLASS II	1604	.281	451	
CLASS III	1125	.249	280	
CLASS IV	2279	.224	510	
TOTAL	5008		1241	
CLASS V	1050		0	
PERIOD	6058		1241	

The Detroit Tigers welcomed the 20-year-old Bush in 1908. Hughie Jennings, manager, moved peripatetic Germany Schaefer to second in 1909 and installed the youngster at short, the most critical defensive position on the field. Bush held the job for more than 13 years. He ended up as a utility infielder in Washington. He was 36 when he retired in 1923.

Defense was Bush's reason for being. Except for his final years as a utility man, he spent all of his time at shortstop. His impressive tenure at that sensitive position qualifies him for comparison with HOF shortstop Joe Tinker.

	BUSH			TINKER		
Year	G	TC/G	FA	G	TC/G	FA
1909	157	6.0	.925	143	5.9	.940
1910	142	6.0	.940	133	5.5	.942
1911	150	6.7	.925	144	6.1	.937
1912	144	6.5	.929	142	6.2	.943
Career	1946	5.7	.937	1805	5.8	.938

Tinker was 29 at the beginning of this period; Bush, 22. It would appear that Bush covered his position as well as Tinker, but was not as steady. He played more games at the shortstop position than Tinker, and he is in no way embarrassed by this comparison with the HOF shortstop.

Bush was a below average contact hitter but the number two scorer of all infielders in the sample. How come? He was the walking man—in over 13 percent of his plate appearances he took a base on balls. In five years he led the AL in walks; his career OBP was a respectable .356. And he was aggressive—in 11 seasons he stole 375 bases. Finally, Ty Cobb and Sam Crawford were in the Detroit lineup, a duo designed to give the scoring record of any teammate an uplift.

Per at Bat (PAB) 1901–19—Infielders

	AT BAT	R PAB	HR PAB	RBI PAB	TOTAL PAB
Bush	6058	.178	.001	.059	.238
Sample avg.	4832	.129	.005	.107	.241

Some men join the right team at the right time and get what are sometimes the very considerable benefits of the association. Bush may have been one of these. His PAB is at least in part a reflection of the top-grade company he kept. But he was more than that — he was a skilled and durable shortstop who outproduced three men who were elected to the HOF, Tinker, Evers and Wallace. If they were chosen, why wasn't he? If he wasn't chosen, why were they?

JOE TINKER

Born 1880; Height 5.09; Weight 175; T-R; B-R

* = Net of home runs

	G	AB	H	R*	HR	RBI*	BA	SA	PAB
CLASS I									
PAB .301+									
None									
CLASS II									
PAB .271–.300									
1903	124	460	134	65	2	68	.291	.380	.293
1912	142	550	155	80	0	75	.282	.351	.282
Total	266	1010	289	145	2	143	.286	.364	.287
CLASS III									
PAB .241–.270									
1905	149	547	135	68	2	64	.247	.320	.245
1906	148	523	122	74	1	63	.233	.289	.264
1910	133	473	136	45	3	66	.288	.397	.241
1913	110	382	121	46	1	56	.317	.445	.270
Total	540	1925	514	233	7	249	.267	.355	.254
CLASS IV									
PAB .211–.240									
1902	133	501	137	52	2	52	.273	.343	.212
1908	157	548	146	61	6	62	.266	.392	.235
1909	143	516	132	52	4	53	.256	.372	.211
1911	144	536	149	57	4	65	.278	.390	.235
1914	126	438	112	48	2	44	.256	.349	.215
1915	31	67	18	7	0	9	.269	.328	.239
Total	734	2606	694	277	18	285	.266	.360	.223
CLASS V									
PAB .210-									
1904	141	488	108	52	3	38	.221	.318	.191
1907	117	402	89	35	1	35	.221	.271	.177
1916	7	10	1	0	0	1	.100	.100	.100
Total	265	900	198	87	4	74	.220	.294	.183
Period	1805	6441	1695	742	31	751	.263	.354	.237
Career	1805	6441	1695	742	31	751	.263	.354	.237
BEST 123+ GAMES									
1903	124	460	134	65	2	68	.291	.380	.293

CALCULATION OF DOMINATION POINTS, MTP/MVP

	AB	PAB	MVP	MTP
CLASS I	0	0	0	290
CLASS II	1010	.287	290	
CLASS III	1925	.254	489	
CLASS IV	2606	.223	581	
TOTAL	5541		1360	

	AB	PAB	MVP	MTP
CLASS V	900		0	
PERIOD	6441		1360	

Joe Tinker walked right into the shortstop job of the Cubs when he was 22 years of age, so much did he impress manager Frank Selee in 1902. This wasn't quite as impressive as it sounds because the man he replaced, Barry McCormick, was a leaky shortstop with a FA of .913 in his career, and worse at that particular time.

Tinker didn't do much better defensively for two years but, in 1905, settled in at a superior skill level for more than a decade. He led all shortstops in the National League in 1906, '08, '09, and '10.

As Tinker was developing experience, Johnny Evers was mastering second base and Frank Chance was maturing at first. And the famous combination of Tinker to Evers to Chance was a fully efficient reality when Chance became playing manager in 1905.

In 1912, 32 years old, Tinker went to Cincinnati as playing manager. He personally played well in the 1913 season but the club finished seventh and Tinker's relationship with ownership soured. He jumped the league.

For two seasons Joe operated as playing manager of the Chicago Whales of the Federal League. This managerial tour was successful (second place, 1914; pennant, 1915), but the league wasn't. When it folded, Tinker spent one more season with the Cubs as manager, and then retired in 1916 at 36 years of age.

Joe Tinker was one of the great defensive shortstops of the time. He seldom appeared at a different position — over 96 percent of his games were played at shortstop. A comparison with other defensive stalwarts of the period follows:

Player	G	TC/G	FA
Joe Tinker	1805	5.8	.938
Donie Bush	1946	5.7	.937
Art Fletcher	1528	5.7	.938

The edge would seem to go to Tinker.

Perhaps the best shortstop of the era (and a HOF selection) was Rabbit Maranville (FA .952) — he was the best in the NL in five different seasons, and he played for 23 years. He is not otherwise included in this analysis of infielders because it is production oriented, and Rabbit did not survive the BA and SA screens established for the era (see Introduction). The glove, not the bat, won him his seat at the HOF table. Some dispute this, including this analyst, on the grounds that the HOF is not the place for one-dimensional ballplayers. A special award honoring special skills would be more appropriate.

Tinker was not an offensive force of consequence. He produced an average PAB of .237.

PER AT BAT (PAB) 1901–19 — INFIELDERS

	AT BAT	R PAB	HR PAB	RBI PAB	TOTAL PAB
Tinker	6441	.115	.005	.117	.237
Sample avg.	4832	.129	.005	.107	.241

Timely hitting was Tinker's outstanding offensive credential. But it was the durability of a star and high defensive skills that boosted Tinker into the HOF.

The Tinker formula (durability + class) demonstrates that mercurial talent has less baseball value than more ordinary, but omnipresent, ability — the hare vs. the tortoise. Tinker wasn't an obvious HOF choice in 1946 but he was an understandable one. Unfortunately, however, when good but marginal players are so honored, a case is immediately built for others players of comparable ability.

JOHNNY EVERS

Born 1883; Height 5.09; Weight 125; T-R; B-L; MVP-NL 1914

* = Net of home runs

	G	AB	H	R*	HR	RBI*	BA	SA	PAB
CLASS I PAB .301+									
None									
CLASS II PAB .271–.300									
1908	126	416	125	83	0	37	.300	.375	.288
1912	143	478	163	72	1	62	.341	.441	.282
1913	135	444	126	78	3	46	.284	.372	.286
Total	404	1338	414	233	4	145	.309	.398	.286
CLASS III PAB .241–.270									
1903	124	464	136	70	0	52	.293	.381	.263
1910	125	433	114	87	0	28	.263	.321	.266
1914	139	491	137	80	1	39	.279	.338	.244
Total	388	1388	387	237	1	119	.279	.347	.257
CLASS IV PAB .211–.240									
1905	99	340	94	43	1	36	.276	.329	.235
1906	154	533	136	64	1	50	.255	.315	.216
1907	151	508	127	64	2	49	.250	.313	.226
1909	127	463	122	87	1	23	.263	.337	.240
1911	46	155	35	29	0	7	.226	.290	.232
1915	83	278	73	37	1	21	.263	.295	.212
Total	660	2277	587	324	6	186	.258	.317	.227
CLASS V PAB .210–									
1902	26	89	20	7	0	2	.225	.225	.101
1904	152	532	141	49	0	47	.265	.318	.180
1916	71	241	52	33	0	15	.216	.241	.199
1917	80	266	57	24	1	11	.214	.252	.135
Total	329	1128	270	113	1	75	.237	.278	.168
Period	1781	6131	1658	907	12	525	.270	.334	.236
Other	2	3	0	0	0	1	.0	.0	.333
Career	1783	6134	1658	907	12	526	.270	.334	.236
BEST 123+ GAMES									
1908	126	416	125	83	0	37	.300	.375	.288

CALCULATION OF DOMINATION POINTS, MTP/MVP

	AB	PAB	MVP	MTP
CLASS I	0	0	0	383
CLASS II	1338	.286	383	
CLASS III	1388	.257	357	
CLASS IV	2277	.227	517	

	AB	PAB	MVP	MTP
TOTAL	5003		1257	
CLASS V	1128		0	
PERIOD	6131		1257	

Johnny Evers, a 19-year-old skinny kid, joined the Cubs in 1902 as a utility infielder. The club was managed by Frank Selee and the infield was made up of Frank Chance, first base; Bobby Lowe, second base; Germany Schaefer, third base; and Joe Tinker, shortstop. It was Tinker's first year at shortstop and Chance's fifth at first base.

In the next season, 1903, Evers joined them and formed what was to become the most famous double-play combination in baseball history — Tinker to Evers to Chance.

Evers spent a dozen seasons with Chicago, then completed his final six years with the Braves, Phillies and White Sox. He played over 97 percent of his games at second base.

As a HOF second baseman, it's appropriate to compare his skills with those of an acknowledged master of the trade, fellow Hall of Famer Eddie Collins:

	EVERS			COLLINS		
Year	G	TC/G	FA	G	TC/G	FA
1909	127	5.1	.942	153	5.3	.967
1910	125	5.3	.950	153	5.7	.972
1911	46	4.2	.963	132	5.5	.967
1912	143	5.5	.959	153	5.6	.955
1913	135	5.6	.960	148	5.3	.965
Career	1783	5.3	.953	2826	5.2	.969

The edge would clearly go to Collins. He was more durable and, in his prime, more nimble and sure-handed than Evers.

Offensively, Evers' BA of .270 was below the sample average, as was his PAB.

PER AT BAT (PAB) 1901–19—INFIELDERS

	AT BAT	R PAB	HR PAB	RBI PAB	TOTAL PAB
Evers	6131	.148	.002	.086	.236
Sample avg.	4832	.129	.005	.107	.241

Scoring was the Evers forte. His OBP was an impressive .356, he was reasonably competent with the bat which, when combined with foot speed (he was a formidable base-stealing threat for eight seasons, in the 25–50 range), gave him an above average record as a scorer. But, in the end, doing what he did longer than most was his most outstanding offensive characteristic.

Evers was elected to the HOF in 1946, along with Tinker and Chance. Good fielding and impressive durability were the characteristics that could have impressed HOF electors. But the choice of all three players at the same time leads one to suspect that the double-play entity was more highly regarded than the individuals within it — that, standing alone, each man might not have been chosen. This feeling is buttressed when the record of Frank Chance is analyzed — he appeared in more than 100 games in only six seasons.

Of the three, Tinker was the best choice — but he was no way near as talented as Honus Wagner. Evers was not a bad selection but it's not unreasonable to suggest that he benefited by the company he kept — as an all-around player, he was significantly less competent than Eddie Collins.

Bill Bradley

Born 1878; Height 6.00; Weight 185; T-R; B-R

* = Net of home runs

	G	AB	H	R*	HR	RBI*	BA	SA	PAB
CLASS I									
PAB .301+									
1902	137	550	187	93	11	66	.340	.515	.309
1903	137	543	171	97	6	62	.315	.495	.304
1914	7	6	3	1	0	3	.500	.667	.667
Total	281	1099	361	191	17	131	.328	.506	.308
CLASS II									
PAB .271–.300									
1901	133	516	151	94	1	54	.293	.403	.289
1904	154	607	182	89	5	78	.300	.402	.283
Total	287	1123	333	183	6	132	.297	.402	.286
CLASS III									
PAB .241–.270									
None									
CLASS IV									
PAB .211–.240									
1905	145	537	144	63	0	51	.268	.354	.212
CLASS V									
PAB .210–									
1906	82	302	83	30	2	23	.275	.358	.182
1907	139	498	111	48	0	34	.223	.267	.165
1908	148	548	133	69	1	45	.243	.318	.210
1909	95	334	62	30	0	22	.186	.222	.156
1910	61	214	42	12	0	12	.196	.210	.112
1915	66	203	38	15	0	9	.187	.241	.118
Total	591	2099	469	204	3	145	.223	.278	.168
Period	1304	4858	1307	641	26	459	.269	.367	.232
Other	157	573	165	82	7	60	.288	.395	.260
Career	1461	5431	1472	723	33	519	.271	.370	.235
BEST 123+ GAMES									
1902	137	550	187	93	11	66	.340	.515	.309

Calculation of Domination Points, MTP/MVP

	AB	PAB	MVP	MTP
CLASS I	1099	.308	338	659
CLASS II	1123	.286	321	
CLASS III	0	0	0	
CLASS IV	537	.212	114	
TOTAL	2759		773	
CLASS V	2099		0	
PERIOD	4858		773	

In 1901, having spent two years with the Cubs as (mostly) a third baseman, Bradley jumped to the new AL and took over the hot corner for the Cleveland franchise. He spent his significant major league time with that club. After his 1910 retirement in Cleveland (32 years old) he returned in 1914 and 1915 to play (and manage) a few games in the Federal League — he was ineffective.

Bradley fielded his position well (FA .933), and led the league four times. His durability was about average — in his prime, he stole over 20 bases per year.

Overall, Bradley was a below average producer.

Per at Bat (PAB) 1901-19—Infielders

	AT BAT	R PAB	HR PAB	RBI PAB	TOTAL PAB
Bradley	4858	.132	.005	.095	.232
Sample avg.	4832	.129	.005	.107	.241

A fair contact hitter (BA .269), Bradley was also an above average scorer.

Heinie Groh

Born 1889; Height 5.08; Weight 158; T-R; B-R; Led National League: 1916-BB; 1917-H, 2B; 1918-2B, R

* = Net of home runs

	G	AB	H	R*	HR	RBI*	BA	SA	PAB
CLASS I PAB .301+									
1919	122	448	139	74	5	58	.310	.431	.306
CLASS II PAB .271-.300 None									
CLASS III PAB .241-.270									
1913	121	399	112	48	3	45	.281	.376	.241
1918	126	493	158	87	1	36	.320	.396	.252
Total	247	892	270	135	4	81	.303	.387	.247
CLASS IV PAB .211-.241									
1912	27	48	13	8	0	3	.271	.354	.229
1917	156	599	182	90	1	52	.304	.411	.239
Total	183	647	195	98	1	55	.301	.307	.238
CLASS V PAB .210-									
1914	139	455	131	57	2	30	.288	.358	.196
1915	160	587	170	69	3	47	.290	.390	.203
1916	149	553	149	83	2	26	.269	.374	.201
Total	448	1595	450	209	7	103	.282	.375	.200
Period	1000	3582	1054	516	17	297	.294	.391	.232
Other	676	2492	721	378	9	243	.289	.374	.253
Career	1676	6074	1774	894	26	540	.292	.384	.240
BEST 123+ GAMES									
1918	126	493	158	87	1	36	.320	.396	.252

Calculation of Domination Points, MTP/MVP

	AB	PAB	MVP	MTP
CLASS I	448	.306	137	137
CLASS II	0	0	0	
CLASS III	892	.247	220	
CLASS IV	647	.238	154	
TOTAL	1987		511	
CLASS V	1595		0	
PERIOD	3582		511	

Heinie Groh had a 16-year career beginning with the 1912 Giants and ending with the 1927 Pirates. Half of those years fell into the subject period.

Groh was traded to Cincinnati in 1913 and was still with them in 1919. He was always predominantly a third baseman but, especially during his first five seasons, frequently played other infield positions. During the 1901–19 period, he had only two seasons exclusively at third. He demonstrated a highly skilled glove (career FA .967; led the league five times).

Groh was a below-average producer.

PER AT BAT (PAB) 1901–19—INFIELDERS

	AT BAT	R PAB	HR PAB	RBI PAB	TOTAL PAB
Groh	3582	.144	.005	.083	.232
Sample avg.	4832	.129	.005	.107	.241

Only five men in the infield group had a higher BA than Groh (BA .294). His OBP (.373) indicates he was quite willing to take a base on balls. Such things, plus aggression on the bases (20–40 steals a year), helped to place him among the top scorers in the group.

Groh played for seven seasons beyond the sample period. He is one of several players in this study whose full career would be shown in a 1910–29 analysis. Unfortunately, such a study (as has been mentioned before) would be meaningless because it would be a mixture of deadball and live-ball records—apples and pears.

FRANK ISBELL

Born 1875; Height 5.11; Weight 190; T-R; B-L; Led American League: 1901-SB

* = Net of home runs

	G	AB	H	R*	HR	RBI*	BA	SA	PAB
CLASS I PAB .301+									
None									
CLASS II PAB .271–.300									
1901	137	556	143	90	3	67	.257	.329	.288
1905	94	341	101	53	2	43	.296	.440	.287
Total	231	897	244	143	5	110	.272	.371	.288
CLASS III PAB .241–.270									
1908	84	320	79	30	1	48	.247	.322	.247
CLASS IV PAB .211–.240									
1902	137	515	130	58	4	55	.252	.318	.227
1906	143	549	153	71	0	57	.279	.352	.233
Total	280	1064	283	129	4	112	.266	.336	.230
CLASS V PAB .210-									
1903	138	546	132	50	2	57	.242	.332	.200
1904	96	314	66	26	1	33	.210	.271	.191
1907	125	486	118	60	0	41	.243	.311	.208
1909	120	433	97	33	0	33	.224	.291	.152
Total	479	1779	413	169	3	164	.232	.306	.189
Period	1074	4060	1019	471	13	434	.251	.329	.226
Other	45	159	37	17	0	8	.233	.249	.157
Career	1119	4219	1056	488	13	442	.250	.326	.224
BEST 123+ GAMES									
1901	137	556	143	90	3	67	.257	.329	.288

Calculation of Domination Points, MTP/MVP

	AB	PAB	MVP	MTP
CLASS I	0	0	0	258
CLASS II	897	.288	258	
CLASS III	320	.247	79	
CLASS IV	1064	.230	245	
TOTAL	2281		582	
CLASS V	1779		0	
PERIOD	4060		582	

Frank Isbell had a cup of coffee in the major leagues in 1898 but didn't appear again until the AL opened up for business in 1901—he landed with the Cubs and stayed with them for the balance of his 10-year career. He was 34 when he retired in 1909.

Isbell never played one position for a full season. He played second, third, short and first base. He also caught, played outfield and pitched a few games (sold tickets?). In any event, his defensive record is murky. Trusting managers he played for, it's fair to estimate that Isbell was a good general purpose athlete (career FA .986) who was not good enough with the bat to keep in the lineup as a regular.

Offensively, Isbell was a below average producer:

Per at Bat (PAB) 1901–19—Infielders

	AT BAT	R PAB	HR PAB	RBI PAB	TOTAL PAB
Isbell	4060	.116	.003	.107	.226
Sample avg.	4832	.129	.005	.107	.241

Frank Isbell had base stealing ability (led the league in 1901).

Miller Huggins

Born 1879; Height 5.07; Weight 140; T-R; B-B; Led National League: 1905/07/10/14-BB; HOF 1964 (as a manager 1913–29)

* = Net of home runs

	G	AB	H	R*	HR	RBI*	BA	SA	PAB
CLASS I PAB .301 None									
CLASS II PAB .271–.300									
1905	149	564	154	116	1	37	.273	.326	.273
CLASS III PAB .241–.270									
1904	140	491	129	94	2	28	.263	.328	.253
1910	151	547	145	100	1	35	.265	.320	.249
1911	138	509	133	105	1	23	.261	.312	.253
1912	120	431	131	82	0	29	.304	.357	.258
1913	120	381	109	73	0	27	.286	.318	.262
Total	669	2359	647	454	4	142	.274	.326	.254
CLASS IV PAB .211–240									
1914	148	509	134	84	1	23	.263	.318	.212

	G	AB	H	R*	HR	RBI*	BA	SA	PAB
1915	107	353	85	55	2	22	.241	.283	.224
1916	18	9	3	2	0	0	.333	.333	.222
Total	273	871	222	141	3	45	.255	.304	.217
CLASS V									
PAB .210-									
1906	146	545	159	81	0	26	.292	.338	.196
1907	156	561	139	63	1	30	.248	.289	.168
1908	135	498	119	65	0	23	.239	.287	.177
1909	57	159	34	18	0	6	.214	.245	.151
Total	494	1763	451	227	1	85	.256	.300	.178
Period	1585	5557	1474	938	9	309	.265	.314	.226
Career	1585	5557	1474	938	9	309	.265	.314	.226
BEST 123+ GAMES									
1905	149	564	154	116	1	37	.273	.326	.273

Calculation of Domination Points, MTP/MVP

	AB	PAB	MVP	MTP
CLASS I	0	0	0	154
CLASS II	564	.273	154	
CLASS III	2359	.254	599	
CLASS IV	871	.217	189	
TOTAL	3794		942	
CLASS V	1763		0	
PERIOD	5557		942	

Miller Huggins joined the Cincinnati Reds in 1904 when he was 25 years of age. He stepped right into the keystone job. Six years later, he was traded to the Cardinals. Huggins spent his last seven years as an active player with them. He was 37 when he hung up his spikes in 1916.

Defensively, Huggins could be considered as a model of the average second baseman of the period: FA .956—a steady, unspectacular operator.

Per at Bat (PAB) 1901–19—Infielders

	AT BAT	R PAB	HR PAB	RBI PAB	TOTAL PAB
Huggins	5557	.168	.002	.056	.226
Sample avg.	4832	.129	.005	.107	.241

With a BA of .265, Huggins was a below average contact hitter. Despite this, he was the number three scorer. How come? He was on base more than 38 percent of the time—in four seasons he led the NL in walks. And Huggins was a runner. In 13 years, he stole 324 bases—an average of 24 per year. A good OBP plus speed is a run-producing duo.

As a player, Huggins earned his paycheck; but as a manager, he earned the HOF (1964). In his storied career in that position (1913–29), during which he handled the rambunctious Babe Ruth, he managed the Yankees for a dozen years to six pennants and three championships.

Miller Huggins died during the 1929 season.

CLAUDE RITCHEY

Born 1873; Height 5.07; Weight 167; T-R; B-B

* = Net of home runs

	G	AB	H	R*	HR	RBI*	BA	SA	PAB
CLASS I PAB .301+ None									
CLASS II PAB .271–.300 None									
CLASS III PAB .241–.270									
1901	140	540	160	65	1	73	.296	.354	.257
1902	115	405	112	52	2	53	.277	.328	.264
1903	138	506	145	66	0	59	.287	.381	.247
Total	393	1451	417	183	3	185	.287	.356	.256
CLASS IV PAB .211–.240									
1904	156	544	143	79	0	51	.263	.347	.239
1906	152	484	130	45	1	61	.269	.339	.221
Total	308	1028	273	124	1	112	.266	.343	.231
CLASS V PAB .210-									
1905	153	533	136	54	0	52	.255	.332	.199
1907	144	499	127	43	2	49	.255	.317	.188
1908	121	421	115	42	2	34	.273	.325	.185
1909	30	87	15	4	0	3	.172	.184	.080
Total	448	1540	393	143	4	138	.255	.317	.185
Period	1149	4019	1083	450	8	435	.269	.338	.222
Other	522	1900	535	240	10	220	.282	.350	.247
Career	1671	5919	1618	690	18	655	.273	.342	.230
BEST 123+ GAMES									
1901	140	540	160	65	1	73	.296	.354	.257

CALCULATION OF DOMINATION POINTS, MTP/MVP

	AB	PAB	MVP	MTP
CLASS I	0	0	0	0
CLASS II	0	0	0	
CLASS III	1451	.256	371	
CLASS IV	1028	.231	237	
TOTAL	2479		608	
CLASS V	1540		0	
PERIOD	4019		608	

Claude Ritchey joined Cincinnati in 1897. He appeared again with Louisville during the next season as a utility infielder. When Louisville folded in 1899, he moved to Pittsburgh with most of his teammates, including Honus Wagner.

With Wagner around, Ritchey's shortstop aspirations were forgotten. Thereafter he concentrated on second base and became the Dutchman's keystone partner through the 1906 season, after which he was traded to the Braves in a four-player deal. After three more seasons in Boston, Ritchey retired in 1909 — 34 years old.

Defensively, Ritchey was an appropriate partner for the marvelous Wagner. In a time when

5.3 chances per game were about average, he handled 5.5–6.0; when a FA of .956 was par, Ritchey delivered that and better for most of his career. He was a glove man.

Offensively, he was not dangerous—nor was he an automatic out (BA .269; OBP .348).

Per at Bat (PAB) 1901–19-Infielders

	AT BAT	R PAB	HR PAB	RBI PAB	TOTAL PAB
Ritchey	4019	.112	.002	.108	.222
Sample avg.	4832	.129	.005	.107	.241

Ritchey, 28 when the subject era began, had five major league seasons behind him, during which he was more effective on both sides of the ball, but not so much so to indicate that his profile as a player has been distorted in this analysis. From a career standpoint, he was a good journeyman ballplayer, with admirable defensive skills.

Bobby Wallace

Born 1873; Height 5.08; Weight 170; T-R; B-R; HOF 1953

* = Net of home runs

	G	AB	H	R*	HR	RBI*	BA	SA	PAB
CLASS I PAB .301+									
1915	9	13	3	1	0	4	.231	.385	.385
CLASS II PAB .271–.300									
1901	135	556	179	67	2	89	.322	.448	.284
1906	139	476	123	62	2	65	.258	.345	.271
Total	274	1032	302	129	4	154	.293	.400	.278
CLASS III PAB .241–.270									
1902	133	495	142	70	1	62	.287	.394	.269
1908	137	487	123	58	1	59	.253	.324	.242
Total	270	982	265	128	2	121	.270	.356	.256
CLASS IV PAB .211–.240									
1903	136	519	127	62	1	53	.245	.356	.224
1904	139	550	150	55	2	67	.273	.351	.225
1905	156	587	159	66	1	58	.271	.349	.213
1907	147	538	138	56	0	70	.257	.320	.234
1912	99	323	78	39	0	31	.241	.316	.217
1913	53	147	31	11	0	21	.211	.245	.218
Total	730	2664	683	289	4	300	.256	.335	.223
CLASS V PAB .210-									
1909	116	403	96	35	1	34	.238	.285	.174
1910	138	508	131	47	0	37	.258	.323	.165
1911	125	410	95	35	0	31	.232	.271	.161
1914	26	73	16	3	0	5	.219	.274	.110
1916	14	18	5	0	0	1	.278	.278	.056
1917	8	10	1	0	0	2	.100	.100	.200
1918	32	98	15	3	0	4	.153	.163	.171
Total	459	1520	359	123	1	114	.236	.284	.157
Period	1742	6211	1612	670	11	693	.260	.337	.221

	G	AB	H	R*	HR	RBI*	BA	SA	PAB
Other	641	2431	691	354	24	393	.284	.415	.317
Career	2383	8642	2303	1024	35	1086	.266	.359	.248
BEST 123+ GAMES									
1901	135	556	179	67	2	89	.322	.448	.284

CALCULATION OF DOMINATION POINTS, MTP/MVP

	AB	PAB	MVP	MTP
CLASS I	13	.385	5	292
CLASS II	1032	.278	287	
CLASS III	982	.256	251	
CLASS IV	2664	.223	594	
TOTAL	4691		1137	
CLASS V	1520		0	
PERIOD	6211		1137	

Wallace, 28 when the 1901–1919 period began, had seven years of major league experience behind him, two as a pitcher and five as a utility infielder.

In 1901, as he played under manager Patsy Donovan of the St. Louis Cardinals, it became plain that Wallace's calling was to be shortstop — his coverage of the position during that season was impressive (6.9 chances per game).

Wallace jumped in 1902 to the St. Louis Browns of the new AL. Through the 1908 season, he competed head to head with the best shortstops in baseball.

In 1909, then 36, Wallace began to slow down, and in 1911, still partially active, he replaced Jack O'Connor as manager of the Browns. George Stovall took over as manager in 1912, and the aging Wallace resumed his playing career as a utility infielder. He stayed with the Browns through 1916; then he moved back to the Cardinals for two years. He was 45 when in 1918 he retired.

Four men in the infielder group, including Wallace, played more than 1800 games at shortstop in their careers (Dahlen, Wagner, Bush and Wallace)—Dahlen was the most active of all (2132 games).

Always assuming that baseball men are the keenest judges of baseball talent, one must conclude that a man who lasted as long as Dahlen must be a good model to use for shortstops.

	WALLACE			DAHLEN		
Year	G	TC/G	FA	G	TC/G	FA
1901	135	6.9	.929	131	6.2	.930
1902	133	6.2	.949	138	5.7	.916
1903	136	6.0	.924	138	5.9	.948
1904	139	6.0	.947	145	6.0	.930
1905	156	6.1	.935	148	5.8	.928
Career	2383	5.5	.938	2443	5.6	.920

This is a glimpse of the comparative records of two talented and aggressive shortstops of the era. The edge, it appears, goes to Wallace.

PER AT BAT (PAB) 1901–19—INFIELDERS

	AT BAT	R PAB	HR PAB	RBI PAB	TOTAL PAB
Wallace	6211	.108	.002	.111	.221
Sample avg.	4832	.129	.005	.107	.241

Wallace, a below average contact hitter (BA .260) within this group of infielders, was not much of an offensive threat. His on-base average (.332) was good but not great; he was not unusually fast on the bases. In sum, he performed for a long time with mediocre offensive talent.

He spent most of his career with a doormat franchise, the St. Louis Browns. The club during his tenure finished better than fifth in only two seasons (1902, 1908). It's a tribute to Wallace that he maintained his skills in such a stifling environment.

HOF electors of the day must have been more impressed with defensive talent than they are today, and with the sheer endurance of some men. Certainly these were aspects of Wallace's career that in 1953 lifted him into the HOF — his was an avoidable appointment because 24 percent of his ABs were in Class V, an embarrassing number for a HOF player.

George Cutshaw

Born 1887; Height 5.09; Weight 160; T-R; B-R

* = Net of home runs

	G	AB	H	R*	HR	RBI*	BA	SA	PAB
CLASS I PAB .301+ None									
CLASS II PAB .271–.300 None									
CLASS III PAB .241–.270									
1913	147	592	158	65	7	73	.267	.385	.245
1914	153	583	150	67	2	76	.257	.346	.249
1918	126	463	132	51	5	63	.285	.395	.257
Total	426	1638	440	183	14	212	.269	.374	.250
CLASS IV PAB .211–.240									
1915	154	566	139	68	0	62	.246	.309	.230
CLASS V PAB .210–									
1912	102	357	100	41	0	28	.280	.342	.193
1916	154	581	151	56	2	61	.260	.320	.205
1917	135	487	126	38	4	45	.259	.347	.179
1919	139	512	124	46	3	48	.242	.320	.189
Total	530	1937	501	181	9	182	.259	.331	.192
Period	1110	4141	1080	432	23	456	.261	.345	.220
Other	406	1480	407	172	2	172	.275	.341	.234
Career	1516	5621	1487	604	25	628	.265	.344	.224
BEST 123+ GAMES									
1918	126	463	132	51	5	63	.285	.395	.257

Calculation of Domination Points, MTP/MVP

	AB	PAB	MVP	MTP
CLASS I	0	0	0	0
CLASS II	0	0	0	
CLASS III	1638	.250	409	
CLASS IV	566	.230	130	
TOTAL	2204		539	
CLASS V	1937		0	
PERIOD	4141		539	

George Cutshaw, a second baseman, was 25 when he joined the Dodgers in 1912. He gave that club a half-dozen years as a regular, then, in 1918, he and Casey Stengel were traded to Pittsburgh in a deal that brought Burleigh Grimes (HOF) to Brooklyn. Cutshaw played second base for the Pirates through the end of the subject period and into the next. He ended up with Detroit and, at 36, retired in 1923.

A career FA of .965 places Cutshaw among the most dependable keystone men of the era.

PER AT BAT (PAB) 1901–19 — INFIELDERS

	AT BAT	R PAB	HR PAB	RBI PAB	TOTAL PAB
Cutshaw	4141	.104	.006	.110	.220
Sample avg.	4832	.129	.005	.107	.241

Cutshaw's BA (.261) was below the average for the select group of infielders, but he had more pop in his bat than many and wings on his feet (20–40 range for steals), which, together with his good hands, kept his career alive.

MIKE MOWREY

Born 1884; Height 5.10; Weight 180; T-R; B-R

= Net of home runs

	G	AB	H	R*	HR	RBI*	BA	SA	PAB
CLASS I PAB .301+									
1905	7	30	8	4	0	6	.267	.300	.333
CLASS II PAB .271–.300									
1910	143	489	138	67	2	68	.282	.368	.280
CLASS III PAB .241–.270									
1911	137	471	126	59	0	61	.268	.359	.255
1912	114	408	104	57	2	48	.255	.341	.262
Total	251	879	230	116	2	109	.262	.351	.258
CLASS IV PAB .211–.240									
1916	144	495	121	57	0	60	.244	.313	.236
CLASS V PAB .210–									
1906	21	53	17	3	0	6	.321	.377	.170
1907	138	448	113	42	1	43	.252	.321	.192
1908	77	227	50	17	0	23	.220	.269	.176
1909	50	144	29	13	0	9	.201	.243	.153
1913	131	449	116	61	0	33	.258	.316	.209
1914	79	284	72	23	1	24	.254	.324	.169
1915	151	521	146	55	1	48	.280	.359	.200
1917	83	271	58	20	0	25	.214	.284	.166
Total	730	2397	601	234	3	211	.251	.316	.187
Period	1275	4290	1098	478	7	454	.256	.329	.219
Career	1275	4290	1098	478	7	454	.256	.329	.219
BEST 123+ GAMES									
1910	143	489	138	67	2	68	.282	.368	.280

Calculation of Domination Points, MTP/MVP

	AB	PAB	MVP	MTP
CLASS I	30	.333	10	147
CLASS II	489	.280	137	
CLASS III	879	.258	227	
CLASS IV	495	.236	117	
TOTAL	1893		491	
CLASS V	2397		0	
PERIOD	4290		491	

Mike Mowrey, 21, joined in 1905 the Cincinnati club. He operated for them as a utility man for four years; then he was traded in 1909 to the Cardinals, for whom he was the regular third baseman for four years.

An eight-man trade in 1914 sent Mowrey to Pittsburgh. A year later he jumped to the Dodgers of the Federal League. He ended his 13-year career in 1917 with them — 33 years old.

Mowrey played 93 percent of his games at third base. He had good hands — FA .944 (led the league twice).

Per at Bat (PAB) 1901–19 — Infielders

	AT BAT	R PAB	HR PAB	RBI PAB	TOTAL PAB
Mowrey	4290	.111	.002	.106	.219
Sample avg.	4832	.129	.005	.107	.241

Mowrey's fielding talents kept him on the field. He was a marginal offensive infielder who appeared in more than 100 games only seven times.

Freddy Parent

Born 1875; Height 5.07; Weight 154; T-R; B-R; Led American League: 1902-AB

* = Net of home runs

	G	AB	H	R*	HR	RBI*	BA	SA	PAB
CLASS I PAB .301+									
1911	3	9	4	2	0	3	.444	.556	.556
CLASS II PAB .271–.300									
1901	138	517	158	83	4	55	.306	.408	.275
1903	139	560	170	79	4	76	.304	.441	.284
Total	277	1077	328	162	8	131	.305	.425	.279
CLASS III PAB .241–.270									
1902	138	567	156	88	3	59	.275	.374	.265
1904	155	591	172	79	6	71	.291	.389	.264
Total	293	1158	328	167	9	130	.283	.382	.264
CLASS IV PAB .211–.240									
None									
CLASS V PAB .210-									
1905	153	602	141	55	0	33	.234	.277	.146

	G	AB	H	R*	HR	RBI*	BA	SA	PAB
1906	149	600	141	66	1	48	.235	.297	.192
1907	114	409	113	50	1	25	.276	.355	.186
1908	119	391	81	28	0	35	.207	.251	.161
1909	136	472	123	61	0	30	.261	.303	.193
1910	81	258	46	22	1	15	.178	.221	.147
Total	752	2732	645	282	3	186	.236	.289	.172
Period	1325	4976	1305	613	20	450	.262	.340	.218
Other	2	8	1	0	0	1	.125	.125	.125
Career	1327	4984	1306	613	20	451	.262	.340	.217
BEST 123+ GAMES									
1903	139	560	170	79	4	76	.304	.441	.284

Calculation of Domination Points, MTP/MVP

	AB	PAB	MVP	MTP
CLASS I	9	.556	5	305
CLASS II	1077	.279	300	
CLASS III	1158	.264	306	
CLASS IV	0	0		
TOTAL	2244		611	
CLASS V	2732		0	
PERIOD	4976		611	

Freddy Parent is another player who failed to crack the NL (1899) but found quick employment when (1901) the AL went into operation. He appeared as the regular shortstop for the Boston Red Sox and stayed with that club through the 1907 season. A trade sent him to the White Sox in 1908, and in 1911 he retired in that city at the age of 36.

Defensively, Parent was an acceptable shortstop (career FA .930).

Per at Bat (PAB) 1901–19—Infielders

	AT BAT	R PAB	HR PAB	RBI PAB	TOTAL PAB
Parent	4976	.123	.004	.091	.218
Sample avg.	4832	.129	.005	.107	.241

Parent was a fair hitter with modest power—a good journeyman player.

Buck Herzog

Born 1885; Height 5.11; Weight 160; T-R; B-R

* = Net of home runs

	G	AB	H	R*	HR	RBI*	BA	SA	PAB
CLASS I PAB .301									
1908	64	160	48	38	0	11	.300	.363	.306
CLASS II PAB .271–.300									
1911	148	541	157	84	6	61	.290	.418	.279
CLASS III PAB .241–.270									
1912	140	482	127	70	2	45	.263	.355	.243

	G	AB	H	R*	HR	RBI*	BA	SA	PAB
1913	96	290	83	43	3	28	.286	.390	.255
Total	236	772	210	113	5	73	.272	.368	.247
CLASS IV									
PAB .211–.240									
1910	106	380	95	48	3	29	.250	.342	.211
1916	156	561	148	69	1	48	.264	.333	.210
1917	114	417	98	67	2	29	.235	.312	.235
Total	376	1358	341	184	6	106	.251	.329	.218
CLASS V									
PAB .210-									
1909	42	130	24	16	0	8	.185	.200	.185
1914	138	498	140	53	1	39	.281	.347	.187
1915	155	579	153	60	1	41	.264	.328	.176
1918	118	473	108	57	0	26	.228	.279	.175
1919	125	468	130	41	1	41	.278	.348	.177
Total	578	2148	555	227	3	155	.258	.318	.179
Period	1402	4979	1311	646	20	406	.263	.341	.215
Other	91	305	59	39	0	19	.193	.237	.190
Career	1493	5284	1370	685	20	425	.259	.335	.214
BEST 123+ GAMES									
1911	148	541	157	84	6	61	.290	.418	.279

Calculation of Domination Points, MTP/MVP

	AB	PAB	MVP	MTP
CLASS I	160	.306	49	200
CLASS II	541	.279	151	
CLASS III	772	.247	191	
CLASS IV	1358	.218	296	
TOTAL	2831		687	
CLASS V	2148		0	
PERIOD	4979		687	

Buck Herzog started his wandering career in 1908 with the Giants and ended it in 1920 with the Cubs. Apart from a brief visit to Boston in 1911, Herzog stayed with New York through the 1913 season. In 1914, as playing manager of the Reds, he assigned himself to shortstop. This didn't work out and in 1916 Herzog renewed his New York-to-Boston shuttle routine. In 1919, he went to Chicago and retired in that city in 1920 — 35 years old.

A career as a utility man doesn't build useful defensive statistics. Herzog's career FA (.943) suggests he had good hands, but his assignments in the field imply even more powerfully that he wasn't a first class defensive player — he spent most of his time at second base.

Per at Bat (PAB) 1901–19 — Infielders

	AT BAT	R PAB	HR PAB	RBI PAB	TOTAL PAB
Herzog	4979	.130	.004	.081	.215
Sample avg.	4832	.129	.005	.107	.241

Herzog ran well (over 30 stolen bases in four seasons). That was his most useful offensive weapon.

HARRY LORD

Born 1882; Height 5.11; Weight 165; T-R; B-L

* = Net of home runs

	G	AB	H	R*	HR	RBI*	BA	SA	PAB
CLASS I PAB .301+ None									
CLASS II PAB .271–.300									
1911	141	561	180	100	3	58	.321	.433	.287
CLASS III PAB .241–.270 None									
CLASS IV PAB .211–.240									
1909	136	534	166	85	0	31	.311	.360	.217
1912	151	570	152	76	5	49	.267	.368	.228
Total	287	1104	318	161	5	80	.288	.364	.223
CLASS V PAB .210–									
1907	10	38	6	4	0	3	.158	.184	.184
1908	145	558	145	59	2	35	.260	.319	.172
1910	121	453	121	50	1	41	.267	.333	.203
1913	150	547	144	61	1	41	.263	.346	.188
1914	21	69	13	7	1	2	.188	.275	.145
1915	97	359	97	49	1	20	.270	.345	.195
Total	544	2024	526	230	6	142	.260	.330	.187
Period	972	3689	1024	491	14	280	.278	.356	.213
Career	972	3689	1024	491	14	280	.278	.356	.213
BEST 123+ GAMES									
1911	141	561	180	100	3	58	.321	.433	.287

CALCULATION OF DOMINATION POINTS, MTP/MVP

	AB	PAB	MVP	MTP
CLASS I	0	0	0	161
CLASS II	561	.287	161	
CLASS III	0	0	0	
CLASS IV	1104	.223	246	
TOTAL	1665		407	
CLASS V	2024		0	
PERIOD	3689		407	

Harry Lord spent eight years (1907–14) in the AL and one in the Federal League. He was with the Red Sox for more than three seasons and after a trade in 1910, the balance of his AL time was spent with the White Sox. In 1915, his last season, he was playing manager for Buffalo of the Federal League. He was 33 when he quit.

Lord was a third baseman and played 93 percent of his games at that position (FA .924). Compared to talented hot corner men like Frank Baker and Bill Bradley, he was not in the lineup because of defensive ability.

Per at Bat (PAB) 1901–19—Infielders

	AT BAT	R PAB	HR PAB	RBI PAB	TOTAL PAB
Lord	3689	.133	.004	.076	.213
Sample avg.	4832	.129	.005	.107	.241

A good contact hitter has always been a prized characteristic in big league baseball. Lord was blessed with that ability (BA .278), although not to the extent that his early years suggested. And his reluctance to take a base on balls kept him off the bases and minimized his base stealing abilities (20–40 range).

Germany Schaefer

Born 1877; Height 5.09; Weight 175; T-R; B-R

* = Net of home runs

	G	AB	H	R*	HR	RBI*	BA	SA	PAB
CLASS I									
PAB .301+									
1918	1	5	0	2	0	0	.000	.0	.400
CLASS II									
PAB .271–.300									
1914	25	29	7	6	0	2	.241	.276	.276
CLASS III									
PAB .241–.270									
1908	153	584	151	93	3	49	.259	.342	.248
1911	125	440	147	74	0	45	.334	.398	.270
1912	60	166	41	21	0	19	.247	.325	.241
1913	52	100	32	17	0	7	.320	.350	.240
Total	390	1290	371	205	3	120	.288	.360	.254
CLASS IV									
PAB .211–.240									
1915	59	154	33	26	0	8	.214	.286	.221
CLASS V									
PAB .210-									
1901	2	5	3	0	0	0	.600	.800	.000
1902	81	291	57	32	0	14	.196	.223	.158
1905	153	554	135	62	2	45	.244	.318	.197
1906	124	446	106	46	2	40	.238	.296	.197
1907	109	372	96	44	1	31	.258	.315	.204
1909	124	408	101	38	1	25	.248	.301	.157
1910	74	229	63	27	0	14	.275	.345	.179
1916	1	0	0	0	0	0	.0	.0	.0
Total	668	2305	561	249	6	169	.243	.302	.184
Period	1143	3783	972	488	9	299	.257	.320	.210
Career	1143	3783	972	488	9	299	.257	.320	.210
BEST 123+ GAMES									
1911	125	440	147	74	0	45	.334	.398	.270

Calculation of Domination Points, MTP/MVP

	AB	PAB	MVP	MTP
CLASS I	5	.400	2	10
CLASS II	29	.276	8	

	AB	PAB	MVP	MTP
CLASS III	1290	.254	328	
CLASS IV	154	.221	34	
TOTAL	1478		372	
CLASS V	2305		0	
PERIOD	3783		372	

Schaefer's 15-year career started with two seasons for the Cubs. He disappeared for two years, and then came back with the Tigers for over four years before being traded in 1909 to Washington. He jumped to the Federal League in 1915, then was back in the AL with the Yankees in 1916. He dropped out in 1917, then returned for a moment with Cleveland in 1918. He was 41 when he retired.

Mostly a second baseman, Schaefer played a variety of positions well enough (FA .954) to keep him on the squad. At the plate he was adequate.

Per at Bat (PAB) 1901–19—Infielders

	AT BAT	R PAB	HR PAB	RBI PAB	TOTAL PAB
Schaefer	3783	.129	.002	.079	.210
Sample avg.	4832	.129	.005	.107	.241

Offensively, Schaefer ran well and he was a fair contact hitter.

Eddie Foster

Born 1887; Height 5.07; Weight 145; T-R; B-R; Led American League: 1912/14/15/18-AB

* = Net of home runs

	G	AB	H	R*	HR	RBI*	BA	SA	PAB
CLASS I PAB .301+ None									
CLASS II PAB .271–.300 None									
CLASS III PAB .241–.270									
1912	154	618	176	96	2	68	.285	.379	.269
CLASS IV PAB .211–.240									
1913	106	409	101	55	1	40	.247	.306	.235
1914	156	616	174	80	2	48	.282	.351	.211
Total	262	1025	275	135	3	88	.268	.333	.220
CLASS V PAB .210-									
1910	30	83	11	5	0	1	.133	.157	.072
1915	154	618	170	75	0	52	.275	.348	.206
1916	158	606	153	74	1	43	.252	.317	.195
1917	143	554	130	66	0	43	.235	.292	.197
1918	129	519	147	70	0	29	.283	.320	.191
1919	120	478	126	57	0	26	.264	.310	.174
Total	734	2858	737	347	1	194	.258	.314	.190

Period	1150	4501	1188	578	6	350	.264	.327	.208
Other	348	1151	302	148	0	90	.262	.322	.207
Career	1498	5652	1490	726	6	440	.264	.326	.207
BEST 123+ GAMES									
1912	154	618	176	96	2	68	.285	.379	.269

Calculation of Domination Points, MTP/MVP

	AB	PAB	MVP	MTP
CLASS I	0	0	0	0
CLASS II	0	0	0	
CLASS III	618	.269	166	
CLASS IV	1025	.220	226	
TOTAL	1643		392	
CLASS V	2858		0	
PERIOD	4501		392	

Eddie Foster played for 13 years (1910–23) in the AL with New York, Washington, Boston and St. Louis. He spent eight seasons in Washington. He was 36 when he retired.

Foster played 77 percent of his games at third base — he was an erratic glove man (career FA .930).

Per at Bat (PAB) 1901–19 — Infielders

	AT BAT	R PAB	HR PAB	RBI PAB	TOTAL PAB
Foster	4501	.128	.001	.079	.208
Sample avg.	4832	.129	.005	.107	.241

Foster, as an offensive player, was a fair contact hitter with little power. He failed to live up to his early reputation (1912, 1914) as a contact hitter.

Hobe Ferris

Born 1877; Height 5.10; Weight 170; T-R; B-R

= Net of home runs

	G	AB	H	R*	HR	RBI*	BA	SA	PAB
CLASS I **PAB .301+** None									
CLASS II **PAB .271–.300** None									
CLASS III **PAB .241–.270**									
1901	138	523	131	66	2	61	.250	.350	.247
CLASS IV **PAB .211–.240**									
1902	134	499	122	49	8	55	.244	.381	.224
1903	141	525	132	60	9	57	.251	.366	.240
1908	148	555	150	52	2	72	.270	.353	.227
Total	423	1579	404	161	19	184	.256	.366	.231

	G	AB	H	R*	HR	RBI*	BA	SA	PAB
CLASS V									
PAB .210									
1904	156	563	120	47	3	60	.213	.306	.195
1905	141	523	115	45	6	53	.220	.361	.199
1906	130	495	121	45	2	42	.244	.360	.180
1907	150	561	135	37	4	56	.241	.314	.173
1909	148	556	120	33	3	55	.216	.282	.164
Total	725	2698	611	207	18	266	.226	.323	.182
Period	1286	4800	1146	434	39	511	.239	.340	.205
Career	1286	4800	1146	434	39	511	.239	.340	.205
BEST 123+ GAMES									
1901	138	523	131	66	2	61	.250	.350	.247

CALCULATION OF DOMINATION POINTS, MTP/MVP

	AB	PAB	MVP	MTP
CLASS I	0	0	0	0
CLASS II	0	0	0	
CLASS III	523	.247	129	
CLASS IV	1579	.231	365	
TOTAL	2102		494	
CLASS V	2698		0	
PERIOD	4800		494	

Hobe Ferris had a nine-year career, all of which fell into the subject period. A second baseman, he walked right into a starting position with the Red Sox in 1901 and continued to be a regular throughout his career. During his last two seasons with the Browns, he operated mostly at third base. He retired in 1909 at 32 years of age.

Ferris was a solid second baseman and, in general, a good defensive infielder (FA .954 — led the league once).

PER AT BAT (PAB) 1901–19—INFIELDERS

	AT BAT	R PAB	HR PAB	RBI PAB	TOTAL PAB
Ferris	4800	.090	.008	.107	.205
Sample avg.	4832	.129	.005	.107	.241

Defensive ability plus above-average power kept Ferris on the field.

WID CONROY

Born 1877; Height 5.09; Weight 158; T-R; B-R

* = Net of home runs

	G	AB	H	R*	HR	RBI*	BA	SA	PAB
CLASS I									
PAB .301+									
None									
CLASS II									
PAB .271–.300									
1902	99	365	89	54	1	46	.244	.312	.277

	G	AB	H	R*	HR	RBI*	BA	SA	PAB
CLASS III									
PAB .241–.270									
1901	131	503	129	69	5	59	.256	.350	.264
CLASS IV									
PAB .211–.240									
1903	126	503	137	73	1	44	.272	.372	.235
1904	140	489	119	57	1	51	.243	.335	.223
Total	266	992	256	130	2	95	.258	.354	.229
CLASS V									
PAB .210–									
1905	102	385	105	53	2	23	.273	.395	.203
1906	148	567	139	63	4	50	.245	.332	.206
1907	140	530	124	55	3	48	.234	.315	.200
1908	141	531	126	43	1	38	.237	.296	.154
1909	139	488	119	43	1	19	.244	.293	.129
1910	105	351	89	35	1	26	.254	.311	.177
1911	104	346	80	38	2	26	.231	.304	.189
Total	879	3198	782	330	14	230	.245	.319	.179
Period	1375	5058	1256	583	22	430	.248	.329	.205
Career	1375	5058	1256	583	22	430	.248	.329	.205
BEST 123+ GAMES									
1901	131	503	129	69	5	59	.256	.350	.264

Calculation of Domination Points, MTP/MVP

	AB	PAB	MVP	MTP
CLASS I	0	0	0	101
CLASS II	365	.277	101	
CLASS III	503	.264	133	
CLASS IV	992	.229	227	
TOTAL	1860		461	
CLASS V	3198		0	
PERIOD	5058		461	

Conroy had an 11-year career starting with Milwaukee in 1901 and ending in Washington in 1911. He spent one season in the NL with the Pirates. Then he went to the Yankees in 1903, where he spent six years. In 1909, 34, he retired in Washington.

A career utility man, Conroy was apparently an adequate fielder (career FA .936).

Per at Bat (PAB) 1901–19—Infielders

	AT BAT	R PAB	HR PAB	RBI PAB	TOTAL PAB
Conroy	5058	.115	.004	.086	.205
Sample avg.	4832	.129	.005	.107	.241

Speed and flexibility kept Conroy in lineups—he stole 262 bases in 11 seasons.

Bobby Byrne

Born 1884: Height 5.08; Weight 145; T-R; B-R; Led National League: 1910-H, 2B

* = Net of home runs

	G	AB	H	R*	HR	RBI*	BA	SA	PAB
CLASS I									
PAB .301+									
None									
CLASS II									
PAB .271–.300									
None									
CLASS III									
PAB .241–.270									
1910	148	602	178	99	2	50	.296	.417	.251
1911	153	598	155	94	2	50	.259	.366	.244
1912	130	528	152	96	3	32	.288	.405	.248
Total	431	1728	485	289	7	132	.281	.396	.248
CLASS IV									
PAB .211–.240									
1909	151	589	133	91	1	39	.226	.290	.222
1913	132	506	134	61	2	49	.265	.322	.221
1916	48	141	33	22	0	9	.234	.319	.220
Total	331	1236	300	174	3	97	.243	.306	.222
CLASS V									
PAB .210-									
1907	148	558	143	55	0	29	.256	.294	.151
1908	127	439	84	27	0	14	.191	.212	.093
1914	126	467	127	61	0	26	.272	.302	.186
1915	105	387	81	50	0	21	.209	.245	.183
1917	14	15	5	1	0	0	.333	.333	.067
Total	520	1866	440	194	0	90	.236	.267	.152
Period	1282	4830	1225	657	10	319	.254	.323	.204
Career	1282	4830	1225	657	10	319	.254	.323	.204
BEST 123+ GAMES									
1910	148	602	178	99	2	50	.296	.417	.252

Calculation of Domination Points, MTP/MVP

	AB	PAB	MVP	MTP
CLASS I	0	0	0	0
CLASS II	0	0	0	
CLASS III	1728	.248	429	
CLASS IV	1236	.222	274	
TOTAL	2964		703	
CLASS V	1866		0	
PERIOD	4830		703	

Bobby Byrne had an 11-year career that began in 1907 with the Cardinals and ended in 1917 with the White Sox. In between, he played for the Pirates and Phillies.

Byrne played 90 percent of his games at third base. His overall FA (.932) was below average for the time — but he led the league twice.

Per at Bat (PAB) 1901–19 — Infielders

	AT BAT	R PAB	HR PAB	RBI PAB	TOTAL PAB
Byrne	4830	.136	.002	.066	.204
Sample avg.	4832	.129	.005	.107	.241

As a producer, Byrne was not formidable.

Buck Weaver

Born 1890; Height 5.11; Weight 170; T-R; B-B

* = Net of home runs

	G	AB	H	R*	HR	RBI*	BA	SA	PAB
CLASS I PAB .301 None									
CLASS II PAB .271–.300									
1919	140	571	169	86	3	72	.296	.401	.282
CLASS III PAB .241–.270 None									
CLASS IV PAB .211–.240									
1915	148	563	151	80	3	46	.268	.355	.229
CLASS V PAB .210-									
1912	147	533	117	54	1	42	.224	.300	.185
1913	151	523	145	47	4	48	.272	.356	.186
1914	136	541	133	62	2	26	.246	.327	.166
1916	151	582	132	75	3	35	.227	.309	.194
1917	118	447	127	61	3	29	.284	.362	.208
1918	112	420	126	37	0	29	.300	.352	.157
Total	815	3046	780	336	13	209	.256	.333	.183
Period	1103	4180	1100	502	19	327	.263	.345	.203
Other	151	630	210	102	2	73	.333	.429	.281
Career	1254	4810	1310	604	21	400	.272	.356	.213
BEST 123+ GAMES									
1919	140	571	169	86	3	72	.296	.401	.282

Calculation of Domination Points, MTP/MVP

	AB	PAB	MVP	MTP
CLASS I	0	0	0	161
CLASS II	571	.282	161	
CLASS III	0	0	0	
CLASS IV	563	.229	129	
TOTAL	1134		290	
CLASS V	3046		0	
PERIOD	4180		290	

Buck Weaver spent nine years (1912–20) with the White Sox. Most of the time he played shortstop (66 percent), but he primarily functioned for the team as a utility infielder.

Per at Bat (PAB) 1901–19—Infielders

	AT BAT	R PAB	HR PAB	RBI PAB	TOTAL PAB
Weaver	4180	.120	.005	.078	.203
Sample avg.	4832	.129	.005	.107	.241

Weaver, a fair contact hitter with above average power, was useful defensively (FA .935) and offensively, the profile of a good utility man. He was aggressive on the bases—172 steals in nine years.

John Hummel

Born 1883; Height 5.11; Weight 160; T-R; B-R

* = Net of home runs

	G	AB	H	R*	HR	RBI*	BA	SA	PAB
CLASS I PAB .301+ None									
CLASS II PAB .271–.300 None									
CLASS III PAB .241–.270									
1912	122	411	116	50	5	49	.282	.404	.253
CLASS IV PAB .211–.240									
1905	30	109	29	19	0	7	.266	.367	.239
1910	153	578	141	62	5	69	.244	.351	.235
1911	137	477	129	49	5	53	.270	.392	.224
1913	67	198	48	18	2	22	.242	.379	.212
1914	73	208	55	25	0	20	.264	.389	.216
1918	22	61	18	9	0	4	.295	.377	.213
Total	482	1631	420	182	12	175	.258	.366	.226
CLASS V PAB .210–									
1906	97	286	57	19	1	20	.199	.259	.140
1907	107	342	80	38	3	28	.234	.313	.202
1908	154	594	143	47	4	37	.241	.320	.148
1909	146	542	152	50	4	48	.280	.363	.188
1915	53	100	23	6	0	8	.230	.310	.140
Total	557	1864	455	160	12	141	.244	.339	.168
Period	1161	3906	991	392	29	365	.254	.352	.201
Career	1161	3906	991	392	29	365	.254	.352	.201
BEST 123+ GAMES									
1910	153	578	141	62	5	69	.244	.351	.235

Calculation of Domination Points, MTP/MVP

	AB	PAB	MVP	MTP
CLASS I	0	0	0	
CLASS II	0	0		
CLASS III	411	.253	104	
CLASS IV	1631	.226	369	

	AB	PAB	MVP	MTP
TOTAL	2042		473	
CLASS V	1864		0	
PERIOD	3906		473	

John Hummel spent all but one of his 11 career years with the Brooklyn Dodgers, a rare example of mutual fidelity. It all began in 1905, and Hummel retired for the first time in 1915. Three years later he reappeared in a Yankee uniform for a few games, then retired for a second time.

Hummel played more at second base than anywhere else, but he was a utility man throughout his career. He was a good glove man (FA .963; led the league twice), but he never came close to nailing down a defensive position.

Per at Bat (PAB) 1901–19—Infielders

	AT BAT	R PAB	HR PAB	RBI PAB	TOTAL PAB
Hummel	3906	.101	.007	.093	.201
Sample avg.	4832	.129	.005	.107	.241

Except for occasional pop with his bat, Hummel was not an offensive threat. His fielding and athletic ability kept his career alive.

Al Bridwell

Born 1884; Height 5.09; Weight 170; T-R; B-L

* = Net of home runs

	G	AB	H	R*	HR	RBI*	BA	SA	PAB
CLASS I PAB .301+ None									
CLASS II PAB .271–.300 None									
CLASS III PAB .241–.270									
1910	142	492	136	74	0	48	.276	.335	.248
CLASS IV PAB .211–.240									
1908	147	467	133	53	0	46	.285	.319	.212
1909	145	476	140	59	0	55	.294	.338	.239
1911	127	445	124	57	0	41	.279	.317	.220
Total	479	1388	397	169	0	142	.286	.325	.224
CLASS V PAB .210-									
1905	82	254	64	17	0	17	.252	.272	.134
1906	120	459	104	41	0	22	.227	.251	.137
1907	140	509	111	49	0	26	.218	.242	.147
1912	31	106	25	6	0	14	.236	.302	.189
1913	135	405	97	34	1	36	.240	.291	.175
1914	117	381	90	45	1	32	.236	.286	.205
1915	65	175	40	20	0	9	.229	.269	.166
Total	690	2289	531	212	2	156	.232	.268	.162

	G	AB	H	R*	HR	RBI*	BA	SA	PAB
Period	1251	4169	1064	455	2	346	.255	.295	.193
Career	1251	4169	1064	455	2	346	.255	.295	.193
BEST 123+ GAMES									
1910	142	492	136	74	0	48	.276	.335	.248

CALCULATION OF DOMINATION POINTS, MTP/MVP

	AB	PAB	MVP	MTP
CLASS I	0	0	0	0
CLASS II	0	0	0	
CLASS III	492	.248	122	
CLASS IV	1388	.224	311	
TOTAL	1880		433	
CLASS V	2289		0	
PERIOD	4169		433	

Al Bridwell spent 11 years in the majors with Cincinnati, Boston, New York and Chicago of the NL and, for his last two seasons, St. Louis of the Federal League. He retired in 1915 at 31 years of age.

Bridwell was primarily a shortstop and played 87 percent of his games at that position. Defensively, he was as busy as most and had good hands (FA .939).

PER AT BAT (PAB) 1901–19—INFIELDERS

	AT BAT	R PAB	HR PAB	RBI PAB	TOTAL PAB
Bridwell	4169	.109	.000	.084	.193
Sample avg.	4832	.129	.005	.107	.241

Patience at the plate and fair foot speed were Bridwewll's only offensive credentials.

IVY OLSON

Born 1885; Height 5.11; Weight 175; T-RR B-R; Led National League: 1919-AB, H

* = Net of home runs

	G	AB	H	R*	HR	RBI*	BA	SA	PAB
CLASS I PAB .301									
None									
CLASS II PAB .271–.300									
None									
CLASS III PAB .241–.270									
1911	140	545	142	88	1	49	.262	.332	.253
CLASS IV PAB .211–.240									
1912	123	467	118	68	0	33	.253	.285	.216
1913	104	370	92	47	0	32	.249	.300	.214
Total	227	837	210	115	0	65	.251	.292	.215

	G	AB	H	R*	HR	RBI*	BA	SA	PAB
CLASS V								
PAB .210-								
1914	89	310	75	21	1	19	.242	.284	.132
1915	81	233	50	20	0	17	.215	.278	.159
1916	108	351	89	28	1	37	.254	.322	.188
1917	139	580	156	62	2	36	.269	.328	.172
1918	126	506	121	62	1	16	.239	.292	.156
1919	140	590	164	72	1	37	.278	.337	.186
Total	683	2570	655	265	6	162	.255	.312	.168
Period	1050	3952	1007	468	7	276	.255	.311	.190
Other	522	2159	568	249	6	157	.263	.331	.191
Career	1572	6111	1575	717	13	433	.258	.318	.190
BEST 123+ GAMES								
1911	140	545	142	88	1	49	.262	.332	.253

Calculation of Domination Points, MTP/MVP

	AB	PAB	MVP	MTP
CLASS I	0	0	0	0
CLASS II	0	0	0	
CLASS III	545	.253	138	
CLASS IV	837	.215	180	
TOTAL	1383		318	
CLASS V	2570		0	
PERIOD	3952		318	

Ivy Olson had a relatively long career, a large piece of which extended beyond the subject period. Of his 14 years of play (1911–24), five are excluded from this survey.

During the subject period, Olson spent four years with Cleveland, a partial season with the Reds and over nine years with the Dodgers. He was 39 when in 1924 he retired.

For Cleveland, Olson was a utility man. For Brooklyn, he played mostly at shortstop — his FA of .932 is not impressive.

Per at Bat (PAB) 1901–19 — Infielders

	AT BAT	R PAB	HR PAB	RBI PAB	TOTAL PAB
Olson	3952	.118	.002	.070	.190
Sample avg.	4832	.129	.005	.107	.241

Olson's record on both sides of the ball makes one wonder why he lasted so long.

Infielders — Summary in Domination Point (DP) Sequence

* Net of home runs
** HOF

Player	AB	R*	PAB HR	RBI*	Total PAB	BA	SA	MTP	MVP
Avg. player	4832	.129	.005	.107	.241	.275	.360		
SUPERSTAR									
DP 1839+									
Wagner H**	8518	.157	.009	**.152**	.318	.325	**.462**	2232	2476
Lajoie N**	7501	.137	.007	.146	.290	**.336**	.451	1556	1921
Collins E**	6096	**.182**	.004	.124	.310	.325	.419	1590	1886
STAR									
DP 1377–1838									
Baker F**	5421	.135	**.015**	**.152**	.302	.309	.442	1150	1637
Doyle L	6038	.139	.012	.112	.263	.290	.411	814	1554
ABOVE AVG.									
DP 915–1376									
Zimmerman H	5304	.120	.011	.140	.271	.295	.419	805	1365
Tinker J**	6441	.115	.005	.117	.237	.263	.354	290	1360
Murphy D	5403	.121	.008	.122	.251	.288	.404	348	1335
Evers J**	6131	.148	.002	.086	.236	.270	.334	383	1257
Bush D	6058	.178	.001	.059	.238	.247	.298	451	1241
Steinfeldt H	4692	.121	.005	.125	.251	.270	.362	435	1165
Wallace B**	6211	.108	.002	.111	.221	.260	.337	292	1137
Gardner L	4902	.121	.004	.121	.246	.285	.378	328	1090
Williams J	4448	.123	.008	.129	.260	.265	.378	635	991
Fletcher A	4595	.122	.005	.117	.244	.276	.357	229	983
Lobert H	4563	.133	.007	.099	.239	.274	.366	157	972
Pratt D	4398	.112	.006	.123	.241	.282	.391	162	968
Devlin A	4412	.134	.002	.113	.249	.269	.338	421	964
Elberfeld K	4389	.140	.002	.113	.255	.272	.340	440	945
Huggins M	5557	.168	.002	.056	.226	.265	.314	154	942
BELOW AVG.									
DP 453–914									
Delahanty J	4091	.123	.004	.115	.242	.283	.373	359	852
LaPorte F	4212	.116	.003	.130	.249	.281	.376	355	844
Dahlen B	4218	.118	.005	.120	.243	.247	.322	570	820
Davis G	3545	.127	.004	.121	.252	.266	.346	309	817
Smith R	3907	.115	.007	.125	.247	.278	.377	265	811
Collins J**	3770	.131	.007	.113	.251	.284	.395	477	785
Bradley B	4858	.132	.005	.095	.232	.269	.367	659	773
Byrne B	4830	.136	.002	.066	.204	.254	.323	0	703
Herzog B	4979	.130	.004	.081	.215	.263	.341	200	687
Parent F	4976	.123	.004	.091	.218	.262	.340	305	611
Ritchey C	4019	.112	.002	.108	.222	.269	.338	0	608
Isbell F	4060	.116	.003	.107	.226	.221	.329	258	582
Cutshaw G	4141	.104	.006	.110	.220	.261	.345	0	539
Groh H	3582	.144	.005	.083	.232	.294	.391	137	511

Player	AB	R*	PAB HR	RBI*	Total PAB	BA	SA	MTP	MVP
Ferris H	4800	.090	.008	.107	.205	.239	.340	0	494
Mowrey M	4290	.111	.002	.106	.219	.256	.329	147	491
Hummel J	3906	.101	.007	.093	.201	.254	.352	0	473
Conroy W	5058	.115	.004	.086	.205	.248	.329	101	461
POOR DP 452–									
Bridwell A	4169	.109	.000	.084	.193	.255	.295	0	433
Lord H	3689	.133	.004	.076	.213	.278	.356	161	407
Foster E	4501	.128	.001	.079	.208	.264	.327	0	392
Schaefer G	3783	.129	.002	.079	.210	.257	.320	10	372
Olson I	3952	.118	.002	.070	.190	.255	.311	0	318
Weaver B	4180	.120	.005	.078	.203	.263	.345	161	290
Average	915								
SD	461								
10 BEST PAB SEASONS									
Lajoie N**-1901	543	.241	.026	.204	.471	.422	.635		
Baker F**-1912	577	.184	.017	**.213**	.414	.347	.541		
Williams J-1901	501	.212	.014	.177	.403	.317	.495		
Wagner H**-1901	556	.169	.011	**.216**	.396	.353	.491		
Collins E**-1914	526	**.228**	.004	.158	.390	.344	.452		
LaPorte F-1914	505	.162	.008	.204	.374	.311	.436		
Collins J**-1901	**564**	.183	.010	.156	.349	.332	.495		
Zimmerman H-1913	447	.134	**.020**	.193	.347	.313	.490		
Davis G-1902	485	.151	.006	.185	.342	.299	.402		
Gardner L-1912	517	.168	.005	.158	.331	.315	.449		

The prevalence of 1901 in the "10 Best PAB" listing suggests that the first year of this survey should be looked at with great suspicion. Record-keeping was poor in those days and performance numbers could to be distorted. Lajoie, for example, hit more than twice as many home runs as he did thereafter. His full-season PAB thereafter never again approached the 1901 mark. Jimmy Williams' PAB after 1901 never again exceeded .317 in a full season; the same is generally true of Jimmy Collins and George Davis (1902). The only exception is Honus Wagner. His 1901 numbers may have been as distorted as the others, but he came close to matching them in later years.

Because of the above, the second-best years in each category have also been shown in bold as being more representative of legitimate performance, and the temptation is powerful to say that nobody had a better season than Frank Baker did in 1912.

The Best of the Best

Sample size	44
NL	20
AL	24
Most durable-top 5	Wagner, Tinker, Wallace, Evers, Lajoie
Top five BA	Lajoie, Wagner, Collins E., Baker, Zimmerman
Top five SA	Wagner, Lajoie, Baker, Collins E., Zimmerman
Top five scorers (R)	Collins E., Bush, Huggins, Wagner, Evers
Top five power hitters (HR)	Baker, Doyle, Zimmerman, Wagner, Murphy
Top five clutch hitters (RBI)	Wagner, Baker, Lajoie, Zimmerman, LaPorte
Top five seasons	Lajoie, Baker, Williams, Wagner, Collins E.
Most talented producer (MTP)-top 5	Wagner, Collins E., Lajoie, Baker, Doyle
Most valuable producer (MVP)-top 5	Wagner, Lajoie, Collins E., Baker, Doyle

Infielders — Summary in Domination Point (DP) Sequence

This era featured the talents of eight HOF members: Wagner (SS), Collins, E. (2B), Baker (3B), Lajoie (2B), Collins, J. (3B), Tinker (SS), Evers (2B) and Wallace (SS).

The comparative records of these players, plus those of the neglected Doyle and Zimmerman during the subject period, follow:

Player	PAB Rank	AB	BA	SA	PAB	FA
2nd base						
Collins, E. (2)	3	6096	.325	.419	.310	.969
Lajoie (1)	2	7501	.336	.451	.290	.967
Evers (2)	9	6131	.270	.334	.236	.953
Doyle	5	6038	.290	.411	.263	.949
SS						
Wagner	1	8518	.325	.462	.318	.947
Tinker	7	6441	.263	.354	.237	.938
Wallace (1)	13	6211	.260	.337	.221	.938
3rd base						
Baker (2)	4	5421	.309	.442	.302	.943
Collins, J. (1)	27	3770	.284	.395	.251	.928
Zimmerman	6	5304	.295	.419	.271	.933

1) Career began in 1890s
2) Career extended into 1920s

It is the function of this analysis to identify the great producers of the era. On that basis, the selection of Eddie Collins, Lajoie, Wagner and Baker can be easily justified. The others, Evers, Tinker, Wallace and Jimmy Collins, cannot. Offensively, they were ranked much lower than the others; defensively they were well regarded. It must be left to others to defend these choices.

The fact that some HOF selections from this era are problematical does not suggest that the talents displayed by those players during these nineteen years were not impressive. Perhaps, for example, Tinkers to Evers to Chance (the famed double play combination) did not produce three HOF ballplayers, but these were outstanding athletes, as were Doyle and Zimmerman — who may have been more deserving than some of those who were selected for Cooperstown. This was a good crop of players, most of whom deserved the major league status that they enjoyed.

In the catcher section of this analysis, the selection of Roger Bresnahan to the HOF was questioned because he oftentimes played other positions and did not undergo the same physical conditions that drained the full-time catchers against whom he was being compared. In that comparison he was clearly superior. But the question was raised: How would his record compare with players from other positions, say, infielders, a group that contained many utility players, which in truth is what Bresnahan was?

Per at Bat (PAB) 1901–19 — Infielders

	at BAT	R PAB	HR PAB	RBI PAB	Total PAB
Bresnahan	4460	.147	.006	.112	.265
Sample avg.	4832	.128	.003	.106	.237

In this comparison, Bresnahan was more productive than the average infielder, and on the scale used to measure infielders, he would have fit into the above average classification — which is not where one normally finds HOF players.

Bresnahan was competent, but not outstanding. His choice as a HOF player was, it appears, based upon an invalid comparison of his record with legitimate catchers, a record that is otherwise commendable but not great.

Outfielders — Analysis, 1901–1919

Most great producers of any baseball era are typically found in the outfield, but in the 1901–19 period — the final days of deadball baseball — productivity between positional groups was, with the exception of catchers, quite similar.

A total of 48 outfielders qualified for the study and generated a PAB of .252, about the same as first basemen and only marginally higher than infielders. The elements for all positions are summarized below:

PAB Element	FB	C	INF	OF
Runs	.123	.091	.129	.141
Home runs	.007	.003	.005	.007
RBI	.116	.197	.107	.104
Total	.246	.191	.241	.252

Qualified outfielders during the 1901–19 period are shown on the following chart:

DOMINANT OUTFIELDERS, 1901–19 RECORD

* HOF
** Net of home runs

PLAYER	LG	AB	H	R**	HR	RBI**	BA	SA	PAB
CLASS I									
PAB .318+									
Cobb T*	A	7296	2715	1347	68	1171	.372	.517	.354
CLASS II									
PAB .285–.317									
Jackson J	A	4411	1556	726	42	622	.353	.509	.315
Speaker T*	A	5981	2019	1006	45	792	.338	.476	.308
Cravath G	N	3905	1121	455	118	590	.287	.478	.298
Magee S	N	7441	2169	1029	83	1099	.291	.427	.297
Veach B	A	3847	1169	495	21	615	.304	.424	.294
Clarke F*	N	5075	1531	902	30	560	.302	.420	.294
Crawford S*	N	9064	2821	1211	89	1357	.311	.453	.293
CLASS III									
PAB .252.284									
Beaumont G	N	4659	1448	730	31	498	.311	.392	.270
Seybold S	A	3604	1065	417	51	497	.296	.426	.268
Flick E*	A	4118	1252	635	27	440	.304	.433	.268
Seymour C	A	5013	1537	605	44	689	.307	.412	.267
Leach T	N	7381	1992	1204	56	681	.270	.372	.263
Sheckard J	N	6343	1720	1010	45	576	.271	.373	.257
Lewis D	A	4884	1400	533	34	684	.287	.391	.256
Titus J	N	4960	1401	700	38	523	.282	.385	.254
Murray R	N	4334	1170	518	37	542	.270	.379	.253
Hofman S	N	4072	1095	535	19	476	.269	.352	.253
Anderson J	A	3978	1136	449	21	536	.286	.380	.253

PLAYER	LG	AB	H	R**	HR	RBI**	BA	SA	PAB
CLASS IV									
PAB .219–.252									
Schulte W	N	6531	1766	813	93	730	.270	.395	.250
Jones F	A	4308	1156	686	10	366	.268	.326	.247
Bates J	N	3921	1088	547	25	392	.277	.376	.246
Jones D	A	3772	1020	634	9	280	.270	.325	.245
Mitchell M	N	4094	1137	487	27	487	.278	.380	.245
Burns G	N	4075	1179	627	24	327	.289	.388	.240
Wheat Z*	N	5166	1547	584	51	602	.299	.419	.239
Dougherty P	A	4558	1294	662	17	396	.284	.360	.236
Strunk A	A	3800	1067	513	11	372	.281	.374	.236
Hartsel T	N	4633	1273	770	27	293	.275	.370	.235
Bescher B	N	4536	1171	721	28	317	.258	.351	.235
Paskert D	N	5438	1461	766	37	465	.269	.360	.233
Graney J	A	4388	1092	634	16	371	.249	.342	.233
Hooper H*	A	5734	1540	874	23	421	.269	.358	.230
Carey M*	N	4696	1284	697	30	338	.273	.366	.227
Thomas R	N	4218	1191	735	7	212	.282	.329	.226
Oldring R	A	4690	1268	589	27	444	.270	.364	.226
Collins S	A	4292	1104	486	16	462	.257	.361	.225
Oakes R	N	3617	1009	412	15	382	.279	.346	.224
Wilson O	N	4624	1246	461	59	512	.269	.391	.223
McIntyre M	A	3958	1066	558	4	315	.269	.343	.222
CLASS V									
PAB .218–									
Milan C	A	6373	1803	858	13	518	.283	.347	.218
Keeler W*	N	4471	1378	684	12	275	.308	.362	.217
Slagle J	N	3823	1012	570	2	256	.265	.311	.217
Hemphill C	A	4302	1165	534	19	376	.271	.340	.216
Barry S	N	3511	935	437	8	312	.266	.325	.216
Browne G	N	4300	1176	596	18	285	.273	.339	.209
Shotton B	A	4691	1279	697	7	262	.273	.336	.206
Magee L	N	3739	1029	455	12	265	.275	.349	.196
AVG		4796	1374	679	32	499	.285	.382	.252
SD		1178						.032	

Classifications

	Class (PAB)	Durability (AB)
CLASS I	.318+	7154+
CLASS II	.285–.317	5975–7153
CLASS III	.252–.284	4796–5974
CLASS IV	.219–.251	3617–4795
CLASS V	.218–	3616–

The importance of separating production performance by position is once again validated as the new classifications of quality are added to those already shown:

	FIRST	CATCH	INFIELD	OUTFIELD
Class I	.302+	.263+	.301+	.318+
Class II	.274–.301	.227–.262	.271–.300	.285–.317
Class III	.246–.273	.191–.226	.241–.270	.252–.284
Class IV	.218–.245	.155–.190	.211–.240	.219–.251
Class V	.217–	.154	.210	.218–

Each position has unique demands; each has its own peculiarities. And the application of the incorrect yardstick to a player can result in distorted ratings.

Roger Bresnahan is the perfect example of this in the subject sample. His PAB of .265 makes him look heroic because he is measured against catchers, and it is as a catcher that he was elected to the HOF. Actually, he was a utility player who operated as a catcher only 68 percent of the time. Otherwise, he functioned mostly as an outfielder, and when measured against that standard, be was a below-average producer. This study concludes that selecting him was a mistake.

Player Analysis

Class I, PAB .318+

Only one player was so designated: Ty Cobb. He qualified dramatically with a PAB of .354. He led all other players in runs scored, and in the three averages, batting, slugging and production. Cobb, one of the few men in baseball history to totally dominate the baseball world, was, fittingly, among the first five players to be elected to the HOF in 1936.

Class II, PAB .285-.317

Seven men—15 percent of the sample—fell into this classification: Jackson, Speaker, Cravath, Magee, Veach, Clarke, and Crawford. From a pure production point of view, all should have been serious HOF candidates. Speaker, Clarke and Crawford were chosen. Had it not been for the gambling scandal of 1919, Jackson probably would have been chosen. The upcoming analysis should indicate whether the oversight of Cravath, Magee and Veach was or was not justified.

Class III, PAB .252-.284

Eleven players—23 percent of the sample—were rated above average as producers: Beaumont, Seybold, Flick, Seymour, Leach, Sheckard, Lewis, Titus, Murray, Hofman, and Anderson. Players of this quality deserve close scrutiny from HOF electors but, if chosen, should have some highly valued characteristic other than productivity to justify selection. Flick was chosen; the others were not.

On the surface, nothing in the production record of Flick justifies his selection—perhaps the upcoming player analysis will make the decision to appoint him clearer. Seybold and Leach have interesting numbers. The others had admirable gifts, but it is doubtful that the final evaluation of their records will uncover missed HOF players.

Class IV, PAB .219-.251

This classification contains 21 players—44 percent of the sample—led by Schulte, second to Cravath as a home run hitter.

Three surprises are contained in this group—Wheat, Hooper and Carey. One does not expect to find below-average producers in the HOF. Perhaps analysis will reveal the reasons for their selection; they must be powerful ones.

Several others in this group had noteworthy characteristics, for example: Paskert and Wilson were notable power hitters; Burns was a better-than-average batsman. The remaining players were important parts of the grease that keeps the baseball wheel turning.

Class V, PAB .218-

Eight players filled the lowest rung on the production ladder. And the group contains a major surprise—HOF player Willie Keeler. Keeler scored more runs than most and his BA was above average. But his selection to the HOF must have been justified by something other than production — something that should be revealed in the upcoming player analysis. Milan is the only other player with characteristics that could lift him in the final ratings after all factors have been considered.

Ty Cobb

Born 1886; Height 6.01; Weight 175; T-R; B-L; Led American League: 1907-BA, SA, H, RBI, SB; 1908-BA, SA, H, 2B, 3B, RBI; 1909-BA, SA, H, HR, R, RBI, SB; 1910-BA, SA, R; 1911-BA, SA, H, 2B, 3B, R, RBI, SB; 1912-BA, SA, H; 1913-BA; 1914-BA, SA; 1915-BA, H, R, SB; 1916-R, SB; 1917-BA, SA, AB, H, 2B, 3B, SB; 1918-BA, 3B; 1919-BA, H; MVP-AL, 1911; HOF 1936

* = Net of home runs

	G	AB	H	R*	HR	RBI*	BA	SA	PAB
CLASS I PAB .318+									
1907	150	605	212	92	5	111	.350	.473	.344
1908	150	581	188	84	4	104	.324	.475	.330
1909	156	573	216	107	9	98	.377	.517	.373
1910	140	509	196	98	8	83	.385	.554	.371
1911	146	591	238	139	8	136	.420	.621	.479
1912	140	553	227	112	7	83	.410	.586	.365
1914	97	345	127	67	2	55	.368	.513	.359
1915	156	563	208	141	3	96	.369	.487	.426
1916	145	542	201	108	5	63	.371	.493	.325
1917	152	588	225	100	7	95	.383	.571	.344
1918	111	421	161	80	3	61	.382	.515	.342
1919	124	497	191	91	1	69	.384	.515	.324
Total	1667	6368	2400	1219	62	1054	.377	.527	.367
CLASS II PAB .285-.317									
1913	122	428	167	66	4	63	.390	.535	.311
CLASS III PAB .252-.284 None									
CLASS IV PAB .219-.252									
1905	41	150	36	18	1	14	.240	.300	.220
1906	98	350	112	44	1	40	.320	.406	.243
Total	139	500	148	62	2	54	296	374	236
CLASS V PAB .218- None									
Period	1928	7296	2715	1347	68	1171	.372	.517	.354
Other	1106	4133	1476	780	50	672	.357	.506	.363
Career	3034	11429	4191	2127	118	1843	.367	.513	.358
BEST 123+ GAMES									
1911	146	591	238	139	8	136	.420	.621	.479

Calculation of Domination Points, MTP/MVP

	AB	PAB	MVP	MTP
CLASS I	6368	.367	2337	2470
CLASS II	428	.311	133	

	AB	PAB	MVP	MTP
CLASS III	0	0	0	
CLASS IV	500	.236	118	
TOTAL	7296		2588	
CLASS V			0	
PERIOD	7296		2588	

Wow!

There can be no other reaction to the Cobb record. Wow!

He was 19 when he joined the Detroit club in 1905. Talent recognition must have been in short supply in those days because this super athlete did not play regularly until 1907. Sam Crawford moved to center field for a few seasons while the youngster learned his craft in right — in 1910 he moved back to right and Cobb became the full-time center fielder.

He spent 22 years with Detroit including six (1921–26) as playing manager. He went to the Athletics for his final two seasons where he retired in 1928 at 42 years of age. In his final season his BA in 95 games was .323.

With respect to defensive ability, Cobb's FA was above .980 once; Speaker's, four times; Cobb's final FA was .961; Speaker's, .970. In short, Cobb was a good center fielder; Speaker was a great one.

Glove skills didn't put Ty Cobb in the HOF. Hitting and speed were his calling cards and they amply justified his election to the Hall in 1936 with four other titans, thusly opening the grand museum with five unforgettable records (Wagner, Cobb, Ruth, Johnson, Mathewson) that would stand the test of time.

During the subject period, Cobb was a regular for 13 years. His battle ribbons are summarized below:

Event	Frequency
BA above .400	2
BA above .350	12
SA above .600	1
SA above .500	9
Led the league:	
Batting average	12
Slugging average	8
Stolen bases	6

Did these extraordinary skills pay off in production terms?

Per at Bat (PAB) 1901–19—Outfielders

	AT BAT	R PAB	HR PAB	RBI PAB	TOTAL PAB
Cobb	7296	.185	.009	.160	.354
Sample average	4796	.141	.007	.104	.252

During the subject period, which embraced only 13 years of a 24-season career, Cobb was 52 percent more durable and 40 percent more productive than the average of this elite group of outfielders. He was the top scorer, a reflection of his BA and speed, one of the top ten home run hitters and, most importantly, the RBI leader. His PAB was 12 percent higher than that of his closest competitor (Joe Jackson, PAB .315), and 32 percent more efficient than the number ten producer in the sample (Socks Seybold, PAB .268). In the year 2007, Cobb was still listed among the top five men in baseball history in such lifetime categories as BA, 2B, 3B, RBI, R and SB. He was one of a kind.

Cobb led the Tigers in the three-year period 1907–09 to three pennants. In years that followed until the end of the subject period, his team finished second twice, but otherwise, despite the brilliance of Cobb, was not a formidable competitor.

Cobb was 34 when the 1920s began — the opening of the live-ball era — and the undisputed king of the baseball world. He didn't miss a step. For nine more seasons he continued to sparkle.

JOE JACKSON

Born 1887; Height 6.01; Weight 200; T-R; B-L; Led American League: 1912–3B; 1913–SA, H, 2B; 1916–3B

* = Net of home runs

	G	AB	H	R*	HR	RBI*	BA	SA	PAB
CLASS I									
PAB .318+									
1909	5	17	5	3	0	3	.294	.294	.353
1910	20	75	29	14	1	10	.387	.587	.333
1911	147	571	233	119	7	76	.408	.590	.354
1912	152	572	226	118	3	87	.395	.579	.364
1913	148	528	197	102	7	64	.373	.551	.328
1918	17	65	23	8	1	19	.354	.492	.431
1919	139	516	181	72	7	89	.351	.506	.326
Total	628	2344	894	436	26	348	.381	.555	.346
CLASS II									
PAB .285–.317									
1915	128	461	142	58	5	76	.308	.445	.302
1917	146	538	162	86	5	70	.301	.429	.299
Total	274	999	304	144	10	146	.304	.436	.300
CLASS III									
PAB .252–.284									
1916	155	592	202	88	3	75	.341	.495	.280
CLASS IV									
PAB .219–.251									
1914	122	453	153	58	3	50	.338	.464	.245
CLASS V									
PAB .218–									
1908	5	23	3	0	0	3	.130	.130	.130
Period	1184	4411	1556	726	42	622	.353	.509	.315
Other	146	570	218	93	12	109	.382	.588	.375
Career	1330	4981	1774	819	54	731	.356	.518	.322
BEST 123+ GAMES									
1912	152	572	226	118	3	87	.395	.579	.364

CALCULATION OF DOMINATION POINTS, MTP/MVP

	AB	PAB	MVP	MTP
CLASS I	2344	.346	811	1111
CLASS II	999	.300	300	
CLASS III	592	.280	166	
CLASS IV	453	.245	111	
TOTAL	4388		1388	
CLASS V	23		0	
PERIOD	4411		1388	

Shoeless Joe Jackson. The name stirs up memories, dramatic, controversial and sad. Jackson was one of the eight players accused of accepting bribes from gamblers intent on fixing the 1919 World Series between the White Sox (Jackson's team) and the Cincinnati Reds. The Reds won the series (5–3). Defenders of Jackson (there are many) point to his quality of play during the contest (BA .375; FA 1.000) as de facto proof of his innocence. But in 1920 Jackson and seven of his teammates were banished from baseball by the new commissioner, Kenesaw Landis.

Jackson, 19 years old, joined Connie Mack's Philadelphia club in 1908. Mack completely missed the potential of his young recruit, hardly played him and, in 1910, traded him to Cleveland for Bris Lord, a journeyman outfielder. When Jackson hit .408 in 1911, Mack must have wept. Cleveland traded Jackson during the 1915 season to the White Sox for three players and cash — he spent his final five seasons in Chicago. He was 33 when he was banished in 1920.

Jackson was not a one-dimensional player. He carried his weight in the field too. For example, Harry Hooper, a HOF corner outfielder, generated a lifetime FA of .966; Jackson at .961 was close behind.

But Jackson is best remembered for offensive prowess and his .408 BA in 1911 (Cobb hit .420 in the same year.) Next to Cobb, he was the most efficient producer in the sample group.

Per at Bat (PAB) 1901–19 — Outfielders

	AT BAT	R PAB	HR PAB	RBI PAB	TOTAL PAB
Jackson	4411	.165	.010	.140	.315
Sample average	4796	.141	.007	.104	.252

Durability was the weakness in the Jackson record. He had a short career (4,981 ABs—13 seasons) because of the before-mentioned scandal. He was permanently sidelined when he was 33, with many more possible active years before him. He was a superb offensive baseball player who had the misfortune to be active at the same time as Cobb. Not many players can say they lost the batting title with a BA of .408. But Jackson did, and Cobb was the reason.

Tris Speaker

Born 1888; Height 6.00; Weight 193; T-L; B-L; Led American League: 1912-2B, HR; 1914-H, 2B; 1916-BA, SA, H, 2B; 1918-2B; MVP-AL 1912; HOF 1937

* = Net of home runs

	G	AB	H	R*	HR	RBI*	BA	SA	PAB
CLASS I									
PAB .318+									
1912	153	580	222	126	10	88	.383	.567	.386
1913	141	520	190	91	3	78	.365	.535	.331
1914	158	571	193	96	4	86	.338	.503	.326
1915	150	547	176	108	0	69	.322	.411	.324
1916	151	546	211	100	2	81	.386	.502	.335
Total	753	2764	992	521	19	402	.359	.504	.341
CLASS II									
PAB .285-.317									
1911	141	510	167	80	8	72	.327	.492	.314
1918	127	471	150	73	0	61	.318	.435	.285
1919	134	494	146	81	2	61	.296	.433	.291
Total	402	1475	463	234	10	194	.314	.454	.297

	G	AB	H	R*	HR	RBI*	BA	SA	PAB
CLASS III									
PAB .252–.284									
1917	142	523	184	88	2	58	.352	.486	.283
1909	143	544	168	66	7	70	.309	.443	.263
1910	141	538	183	85	7	58	.340	.468	.279
Total	426	1605	535	239	16	186	.333	.465	.275
CLASS IV									
PAB .219–.251									
None									
CLASS V									
PAB .218–									
1907	7	19	3	0	0	1	.158	.158	.053
1908	31	118	26	12	0	9	.220	.288	.178
Total	38	137	29	12	0	10	.212	.270	.161
Period	1619	5981	2019	1006	45	792	.338	.476	.308
Other	1170	4227	1496	758	72	650	.354	.534	.350
Career	2789	10208	3515	1764	117	1442	.344	.500	.326
BEST 123+ GAMES									
1912	153	580	222	126	10	88	.383	.567	.386

Calculation of Domination Points, MTP/MVP

	AB	PAB	MVP	MTP
CLASS I	2764	.341	943	1381
CLASS II	1475	.297	438	
CLASS III	1605	.275	441	
CLASS IV	0	0	0	
TOTAL	5844		1822	
CLASS V	137		0	
PERIOD	5981		1822	

Tris Speaker was another of the 19-year-old wonders of that time to sign with a major league team. He played little in his first two years with the Red Sox, but in 1909 he took over the center field position and locked it up with a BA of .309.

Harry Hooper and Duffy Lewis joined him in 1910 to form one of the most famous outfield trios in the history of the Boston franchise. It was broken up when, in the spring of 1916 (after Speaker refused to accept a deep pay cut), Boston traded one of the best outfielders in history to Cleveland for pitcher Sad Sam Jones, third baseman Fred Thomas and cash.

In six seasons with Boston, Jones posted a 64–59 record; Thomas played a total of 44 games for the Red Sox, and Speaker continued to sparkle until his retirement in 1928 — yet another of the horrid deals of historical significance to the Red Sox.

After an eight-year stint as playing manager for Cleveland, Speaker moved to Washington for a season then, in 1928, finished up with the Athletics. He was 40 years old.

Speaker, with a career FA of .970 (Ty Cobb FA .961), set the standard for other center fielders of the era to meet. His FA was .980 or better in five different seasons, and he led the league twice. He had more than 20 assists in 10 different seasons — in 1909 and again in 1912 he had 35, a seasonal record.

Speaker's offensive profile was no less impressive.

Per at Bat (PAB) 1901–19 — Outfielders

	AT BAT	R PAB	HR PAB	RBI PAB	TOTAL PAB
Speaker	5981	.168	.008	.132	.308
Sample average	4796	.142	.006	.104	.252

The third highest BA, the fourth highest SA and speed enough to steal 25–50 bases a year until he was in his thirties were the tools Speaker used to generate a scoring factor of .168, the fourth highest in the group. He was far superior to the average outfielder as an RBI man — the product of his BA.

Speaker's offensive talents came to full flower in 1912 when, with a BA of .383, he generated a .386 PAB, an astounding number during the deadball era, and one that modern players would envy.

As it is with other prominent players, Speaker's full career will not be evaluated because he had one leg in the deadball era and the other in the first live-ball decade. And it was his bad luck to have played in the Cobb era. As much as he was admired, accolades would have been even more frequent and thunderous had the marvelous Georgian not been around to diminish his luster.

Speaker in 1919 became manager of the Cleveland club. He took it to a second-place finish.

The first HOF appointments (1936) were Ruth, Cobb, Wagner, Mathewson, and Johnson. Wagner and Mathewson were strictly deadball era players. The others also played in the next decade. The next batch of HOF selections (1937) were Speaker, Lajoie and pitcher Cy Young. Lajoie and Young came from the deadball era; Speaker continued to sparkle into the 1920s.

Gavvy Cravath

Born 1881; Height 5.11; Weight 186; T-R; B-R; Led National League: 1913-SA, H, HR, RBI; 1914-HR; 1915-SA, HR, R, RBI, BB; 1916-SO; 1917/18/19-HR

* = Net of home runs

	G	AB	H	R*	HR	RBI*	BA	SA	PAB
CLASS I									
PAB .318+									
1913	147	525	179	59	19	109	.341	.568	.356
1915	150	522	149	65	24	91	.285	.510	.345
Total	297	1047	328	124	43	200	.313	.539	.351
CLASS II									
PAB .285–.317									
1914	149	499	149	57	19	81	.299	.499	.315
1916	137	448	127	59	11	59	.283	.440	.288
1919	83	214	73	22	12	33	.341	.640	.313
Total	369	1161	349	138	42	173	.301	.502	.304
CLASS III									
PAB .252–.284									
1908	94	277	71	42	1	33	.256	.383	.274
1909	22	55	9	6	1	8	.164	.218	.273
1912	130	436	124	52	11	59	.284	.470	.280
1917	140	503	141	58	12	71	.280	.473	.280
Total	386	1271	345	158	25	171	.271	.441	.279
CLASS IV									
PAB .219–.251									
None									

	G	AB	H	R*	HR	RBI*	BA	SA	PAB
CLASS V									
PAB .218-									
1918	121	426	99	35	8	46	.232	.376	.209
Period	1173	3905	1121	455	118	590	.287	.478	.298
Other	46	45	13	1	1	10	.289	.478	.267
Career	1219	3950	1134	456	119	600	.287	.478	.297
BEST 123+ GAMES									
1913	147	525	179	59	19	109	.341	.568	.356

Calculation of Domination Points, MTP/MVP

	AB	PAB	MVP	MTP
CLASS I	1047	.351	367	720
CLASS II	1161	.304	353	
CLASS III	1271	.279	355	
CLASS IV	0	0	0	
TOTAL	3479		1075	
CLASS V	426		0	
PERIOD	3905		1075	

Gavvy Cravath spent his first two seasons (1908, 1909) in the AL with Boston, Chicago and Washington, none of whom could find space for the best home run hitter in the outfielder group. He disappeared from the major league scene for two years then reappeared in 1912, 31 years old, as the regular right fielder for the Phillies. He spent the balance of his career with that club. In 1918, he ceased being a regular. In 1919 and 1920 he operated as player-manager, then retired. He was 39 when he quit.

Cravath's early inability to crack the major leagues had to do with his defensive ability (FA .944). Finally, the Phillies decided his bat was worth the fielding flaws that went with it and gave him the right field position.

Over his short career, Clifford Carlton (Gavvy) Cravath earned his pay at the plate.

Per at Bat (PAB) 1901-19—Outfielders

	AT BAT	R PAB	HR PAB	RBI PAB	TOTAL PAB
Cravath	3905	.117	.030	.151	.298
Sample average	4796	.141	.007	.104	.252

Except for Cobb, Jackson and Speaker, Cravath could compete with any outfielder in the sample offensively. As a long-ball hitter, he was literally unique. In a time when a half-dozen home runs were rare, Cravath was in double figures in seven of the nine years that he wore a Philadelphia uniform. He didn't have HOF durability and he couldn't field. But Gavvy Cravath could hit a baseball. Yes indeed.

Sherry Magee

Born 1884; Height 5.11; Weight 179; T-R; B-R; Led National League: 1907-RBI; 1910-BA, SA, R, RBI; 1914-SA, H, 2B, RBI; 1918-RBI

* = Net of home runs

	G	AB	H	R*	HR	RBI*	BA	SA	PAB
CLASS I									
PAB .318+									
1905	155	603	180	95	5	93	.299	.420	.320

	G	AB	H	R*	HR	RBI*	BA	SA	PAB
1910	154	519	172	104	6	117	.331	.507	.437
1911	121	445	128	64	15	79	.288	.483	.355
1913	138	470	144	81	11	59	.306	.479	.321
1914	146	544	171	81	15	88	.314	.509	.338
Total	714	2581	795	425	52	436	.308	.478	.354
CLASS II									
PAB .285-.317									
1904	95	364	101	48	3	54	.277	.409	.288
1907	140	503	165	71	4	81	.328	.455	.310
1912	132	464	142	73	6	66	.306	.438	.313
1918	115	400	119	44	2	74	.298	.415	.300
Total	482	1731	527	236	15	275	.304	.432	.304
CLASS III									
PAB .252-.284									
1908	143	508	144	77	2	55	.283	.417	.264
1915	156	571	160	70	2	85	.280	.392	.275
Total	299	1079	304	147	4	140	.282	.404	.270
CLASS IV									
PAB .219-.251									
1906	154	563	159	71	6	61	.282	.407	.245
1909	143	522	141	58	2	64	.270	.398	.238
1916	120	419	101	41	3	51	.241	.327	.227
1917	117	383	107	40	1	51	.279	.371	.240
Total	534	1887	508	210	12	227	.269	.379	.238
CLASS V									
PAB .218-									
1919	56	163	35	11	0	21	.215	.264	.196
Period	2085	7441	2169	1029	83	1099	.291	.427	.297
Career	2085	7441	2169	1029	83	1099	.291	.427	.297
BEST 123+ GAMES									
1910	154	519	172	104	6	117	.331	.507	.437

Calculation of Domination Points, MTP/MVP

	AB	PAB	MVP	MTP
CLASS I	2581	.354	914	1440
CLASS II	1731	.304	526	
CLASS III	1079	.270	291	
CLASS IV	1887	.238	449	
TOTAL	7278		2180	
CLASS V	163		0	
PERIOD	7441		2180	

Sherwood Magee, with the unlikely nickname Sherry, was 20 when he signed with the Phillies in 1904; he played over half the scheduled games in right field. Hugh Duffy gave him the left field job in 1905, a position he held for seven years. Magee became more of a utility man and less of an outfielder during his last three seasons with Philadelphia.

Magee was sold at the end of the 1914 season to the Boston Braves, where his defensive assignments continued to be mixed. Cincinnati in 1917 picked him up for the waiver price. He finished his career there and, at the age of 35, he retired (1919).

In a 16-year career, Magee had only seven seasons as a pure left fielder. During the five-year period 1905–09, he compiled a FA of .973 versus a FA of .979 for HOF left fielder Fred Clarke. This and other comparisons of his defensive activities show no indication that he was a poor defensive player.

Managers shuffled Magee around as a defensive player, but they made sure he was in the lineup somewhere. Only Sam Crawford had more ABs during the period. The reason? His bat and his legs—he could hit and he could run (440 SBs in 16 seasons).

PER AT BAT (PAB) 1901–19—OUTFIELDERS

	AT BAT	R PAB	HR PAB	RBI PAB	TOTAL PAB
Magee	7441	.138	.011	.148	.297
Sample average	4796	.141	.007	.104	.252

Magee did it all offensively. At one time or another he led the league at least once in most offensive categories. Only the peerless Ty Cobb had a better season than Magee delivered in 1910.

Should he be in the HOF? Was he overlooked? Is he rated too high as an offensive performer? There is no better way to answer such questions than to compare his career numbers with those who played during the same era and were later elected to the HOF.

PER AT BAT (PAB) 1901–19—OUTFIELDERS

	AT BAT	R PAB	HR PAB	RBI PAB	TOTAL PAB
Magee	7441	.138	.011	.148	.297
Cobb*	11429	.185	.009	.160	.354
Crawford	9580	.136	.010	.149	.295
Speaker*	10208	.168	.008	.132	.308
Clarke	8570	.181	.008	.111	.300
Wheat*	9106	.113	.010	.116	.239
Hooper*	8785	152	004	074	230
Flick	5601	.161	.009	.126	.296
Carey*	9363	.148	.006	.073	.227
Keeler	8585	.197	.004	.091	.292

*Career ABs are shown in the above schedule because total durability is an important factor to electors. On the other hand, only PAB elements developed in 1901–19 are reflected in the schedule because it would be unfair to Magee to do otherwise when such a comparison of skills is being made.

Except for Flick, Magee was less durable than those chosen for the HOF. He was a more prolific scorer than Crawford and Wheat; a more prominent home run hitter than any in the group. As an RBI man, only Cobb and Crawford performed better.

Overall, Magee was more productive than six of the HOF appointees. As a producer, he was a HOF talent. It was no accident when, in 1910, he turned in a PAB second only to Cobb's 1911 display of offensive genius.

Except for Cobb, Crawford and Speaker, Magee was the most talented producer in the outfield sample. But HOF electors look at more than offensive records. They apparently saw in Magee weaknesses which, in their judgment, offset the value of his production talents sufficiently to deny him the vote.

From this distance one can only guess that factors such as the following were among those that weakened Magee's case:

- His durability was not unduly impressive. Superiority to Flick in this respect carries no weight since the choice of Flick is, at the least, controversial.

  Magee's defensive record is cluttered. Those chosen for the HOF commanded a defensive position for most or all of a career. Magee spent much of his defensive time shuttling from position to position.

Magee's status as a utility defensive player may have sunk his HOF chances. Fairly or not, electors do not usually favor those with ambiguous defensive records. But the Magee case raises an interesting question: Is an offensive star with a spotty defensive record of less value than a defensive star with a relatively weak production record?

BOBBY VEACH

Born 1888; Height 5.11; Weight 160; T-R; B-L; Led American League: 1915-2B, RBI; 1917/18-RBI; 1919-H, 2B, 3B

* = Net of home runs

	G	AB	H	R*	HR	RBI*	BA	SA	PAB
CLASS I PAB .318+									
1915	152	569	178	78	3	109	.313	.434	.334
1916	150	566	173	89	3	88	.306	.433	.318
1919	139	538	191	84	3	98	.355	.519	.344
Total	441	1673	542	251	9	295	.324	.461	.332
CLASS II PAB .285-.317									
1912	23	79	27	8	0	15	.342	.430	.291
1917	154	571	182	71	8	95	.319	.457	.305
Total	177	650	209	79	8	110	.322	.454	.303
CLASS III PAB .252-.284									
1918	127	499	139	56	3	75	.279	.391	.269
CLASSS IV PAB .219-.251									
1913	138	494	133	54	0	64	.269	.354	.239
1914	149	531	146	55	1	71	.275	.369	.239
Total	287	1025	279	109	1	135	.272	.362	.239
CLASS V PAB .218- None									
Period	1032	3847	1169	495	21	615	.304	.424	.294
Other	790	2812	895	394	43	487	.318	.467	.329
Career	1822	6659	2064	889	64	1102	.310	.442	.309
BEST 123+ GAMES									
1919	139	538	191	84	3	98	.355	.519	.344

CALCULATION OF DOMINATION POINTS, MTP/MVP

	AB	PAB	MVP	MTP
CLASS I	1673	.332	555	752
CLASS II	650	.303	197	
CLASS III	499	.269	134	
CLASS IV	1025	.239	245	
TOTAL	3847		1131	
CLASS V	0		0	
PERIOD	3847		1131	

Bobby Veach was 24 when in 1912 he joined the Detroit Tigers. He gave that club a dozen years, then spent his final two seasons with three AL teams, Boston, New York and Washington. When he retired in 1925, he was 37 years old.

Except for two games, Bobby Veach was a full-time left fielder. His teammates were among the best: Ty Cobb, center field; Sam Crawford or Harry Heilmann in right. It's fair to compare his career FA (.964) with that of Zack Wheat (.966). There's more to good fielding than a good glove, but the easy comparison of FAs certifies that Veach was, at the least, a dependable outfielder.

To appear in this survey a player had to have at least 3,500 ABs. Veach just made it. Over 40 percent of his career fell into the next decade, yet he managed to make his mark on this era as well as the next. He was very talented player.

Veach was a formidable offensive player, a worthy companion of the great athletes who shared the outer gardens with him.

Per at Bat (PAB) 1901-19—Outfielders

	AT BAT	R PAB	HR PAB	RBI PAB	TOTAL PAB
Veach	3847	.129	.005	.160	.294
Sample average	4796	.141	.007	.104	.252

Because of his brief exposure during the subject period it is not objectively possible to fully appraise Veach as a talent. Three factors can be noted, however. He had the defensive profile of a Hall of Fame player. And as a production man he competed head to head with several HOF outfielders. But, on the negative side, Veach's durability (career ABs 6,659) did not compare well with the great HOF outfielders, except for Flick—if Flick belongs in Cooperstown, it's difficult to see why Veach was excluded. Such comparisons are always invited when electors choose a marginal player like Flick.

Fred Clarke

Born 1872; Height 5.11; Weight 165; T-R; B-L; Led National League: 1903-SA, 2B; 1906-3B; 1909-BB; HOF 1945

* = Net of home runs

	G	AB	H	R*	HR	RBI*	BA	SA	PAB
CLASS I									
PAB .318+									
1901	129	527	171	112	6	54	.324	.461	.326
1902	114	461	148	102	2	51	.321	.453	.336
1903	104	427	150	83	5	65	.351	.532	.358
Total	347	1415	469	297	13	170	.331	.480	.339
CLASS II									
PAB .285-.317									
1907	148	501	145	95	2	57	.289	.389	.307
1909	152	550	158	94	3	65	.287	.373	.295
1911	110	392	127	68	5	44	.324	.492	.298
Total	410	1443	430	257	10	166	.298	.411	.300
CLASS III									
PAB .252-.284									
1904	72	278	85	51	0	25	.306	.410	.273
1905	141	525	157	93	2	49	.299	.402	.274
1906	118	417	129	68	1	38	.309	.412	.257
1910	123	429	113	55	2	61	.263	.373	.275
Total	454	1649	484	267	5	173	.294	.398	.270
CLASS IV									
PAB .219-.251									
1908	151	551	146	81	2	51	.265	.363	.243

	G	AB	H	R*	HR	RBI*	BA	SA	PAB
CLASS V									
PAB .218-									
1913	9	13	1	0	0	0	.077	.154	.0
1914	2	2	0	0	0	0	.000	.000	.0
1915	1	2	1	0	0	0	.500	.500	.0
Total	12	17	2	0	0	0	.118	.177	.0
Period	1374	5075	1531	902	30	560	.302	.420	.294
Other	8701	3495	1144	652	37	388	.327	.442	.308
Career	2244	8570	2675	1554	67	948	.312	.429	.300
BEST 123+ GAMES									
1901	129	527	171	112	6	54	.324	.461	.326

Calculation of Domination Points, MTP/MVP

	AB	PAB	MVP	MTP
CLASS I	1415	.339	480	913
CLASS II	1443	.300	433	
CLASS III	1649	.270	445	
CLASS IV	551	.243	134	
TOTAL	5058		1492	
CLASS V	17		0	
PERIOD	5075		1492	

The career of Fred Clarke goes back to 1894, the year the 22-year-old outfielder joined Louisville, which in 1900 became the Pittsburgh Pirates. By 1901 Clarke was a veteran with seven years of playing time and four years of managerial experience behind him (in 1897 he became playing manager).

Clarke stayed with Pittsburgh for his entire 21-year career. In 1915, manager Clarke retired. He was 43 years old.

Defensive records of players whose careers started back in the 1800s are skewed by the unreliable records of those days. Clarke was 29 when the subject period began. Prior to that he functioned as a full-time left fielder. His career FA (.952) was competitive and he led the league twice in that respect during the subject period, all of which suggests that he was an acceptable defensive player.

Clarke was one of the top ten contact hitters in the sample that, when combined with the patience to wait for his pitch, put him on base almost 40 percent of the time.

Per At Bat (PAB) 1901-19—Outfielders

	AT BAT	R PAB	HR PAB	RBI PAB	TOTAL PAB
Clarke	5075	.178	.006	.110	.294
Sample average	4796	.141	.007	.104	.252

In addition to his skills as a batsman, Clarke averaged 24 steals a season. In short, he had the characteristics of a great scorer. A well-rounded offensive performer, he had only one comparative weakness during the subject period: he didn't play enough. A good slice of his career was over by 1901.

Because of this, his durability during the subject period was only slightly above average. It was his sixth highest PAB that made his record competitive.

Clarke's durability relative to his HOF status is also of interest. He averaged only 107 games per year during his 21-year career; in five seasons he appeared in fewer than 100 games; in ten, fewer than 120 games. In other words, he was not as durable as his 21 years on the job might lead one to believe—he acquired his ABs piecemeal.

It took 30 years to vote Clarke into the HOF. Perhaps his appearance record explains why contemporaries passed him by. His selection was avoidable.

SAM CRAWFORD

Born 1880; Height 6.00; Weight 190; T-L; B-L; Led National League: 1901-HR; 1902–3B; Led American League: 1903–3B; 1907-R; 1908-AB; 1909–2B; 1910–3B, RBI; 1913-AB, 3B; 1914/15–3B, RBI; HOF 1957

* = Net of home runs

	G	AB	H	R*	HR	RBI*	BA	SA	PAB
CLASS I									
PAB .318+									
1901	131	515	170	75	16	88	.330	.528	.348
1910	154	588	170	78	5	115	.289	.423	.337
1911	146	574	217	102	7	108	.378	.526	.378
1912	149	581	189	77	4	105	.325	.470	.320
Total	580	2258	746	332	32	416	.330	.485	.345
CLASS II									
PAB .285-.317									
1902	140	555	185	91	3	75	.333	.461	.305
1903	137	550	184	84	4	85	.335	.489	.315
1907	144	582	188	98	4	77	.323	.460	.308
1908	152	591	184	95	7	73	.311	.457	.296
1909	156	589	185	77	6	91	.314	.452	.295
1914	157	582	183	66	8	96	.314	.483	.292
1915	156	612	183	77	4	108	.299	.431	.309
Total	1042	4061	1292	588	36	605	.318	.461	.303
CLASS III									
PAB .252-.284									
1916	100	322	92	41	0	42	.286	.401	.258
CLASS IV									
PAB .219-.251									
1905	154	575	171	67	6	69	.297	.433	.247
1906	145	563	166	63	2	70	.295	.407	.240
1913	153	610	193	69	9	74	.316	.489	.249
Total	452	1748	530	199	17	213	.303	.444	.245
CLASS V									
PAB .218-									
1904	150	571	143	47	2	71	.250	.357	.210
1917	61	104	18	4	2	10	.173	.269	.154
Total	211	675	161	51	4	81	.239	.343	.201
Period	2385	9064	2821	1211	89	1357	.311	.453	.293
Other	132	516	143	85	8	71	.277	.453	.318
Career	2517	9580	2964	1296	97	1428	.309	.453	.294
BEST 123+ GAMES									
1911	146	574	217	102	7	108	.378	.526	.378

CALCULATION OF DOMINATION POINTS, MTP/MVP

	AB	PAB	MVP	MTP
CLASS I	2258	.345	779	2009
CLASS II	4061	.303	1230	

	AB	PAB	MVP	MTP
CLASS III	322	.258	83	
CLASS IV	1748	.245	428	
TOTAL	8389		2520	
CLASS V	675		0	
PERIOD	9064		2520	

Sam Crawford signed with Cincinnati in the final year of the nineteenth century. The Reds didn't use the 19-year-old much in his first season, but in 1900 he became the regular right fielder of the club.

In 1901, the AL moved into the baseball world and the NL didn't like it. While the two leagues argued, Crawford hedged his bets and signed with both the Reds and the Detroit Tigers. When peace was declared, he was awarded to Detroit and became the right fielder for that club.

A youngster by the name of Ty Cobb was ready to break into the lineup in 1907, according to the judgment of manager Hughie Jennings, who had groomed the young man for two seasons. To make room for Cobb in a less stressful atmosphere, veteran Sam Crawford moved to center field and Ty handled the less-demanding right corner. Then in 1910 a seasoned Cobb shifted to center field and Crawford returned to his original position, which he filled until the end of his 19-year career in 1917. Crawford was 37 when he retired.

Willie Keeler (HOF), with a lifetime FA of .960, was a contemporary of Crawford, who had a career FA of .965. This is an indication that Crawford was a major league player on both sides of the ball.

From a production standpoint, Crawford was one of the best in the era.

PER AT BAT (PAB) 1901–19—OUTFIELDERS

	AT BAT	R PAB	HR PAB	RBI PAB	TOTAL PAB
Crawford	9064	.133	.010	.150	.293
Sample average	4796	.141	.007	.104	.252

From a durability point of view, he was the top man. More durable than Cobb? In the subject period, yes. And that's what's being measured.

An adequate scorer, Crawford relied more on power and RBI action to build his production record. He was the sixth-ranked home run hitter within the sample group and only three men topped his RBI factor (Cobb, Cravath, and Veach). It was the strength and will to apply his level of expertise over a long time, however, that was Crawford's main strength. Although not as talented as Cobb, Crawford's combination of class plus durability was almost enough to make him the most valuable producer of the era.

GINGER BEAUMONT

Born 1876; Height 5.08; Weight 190; T-R; B-L; Led National League: 1902-BA, H; 1903-AB, H, R; 1904-AB, H; 1907-H

* = Net of home runs

	G	AB	H	R*	HR	RBI*	BA	SA	PAB
CLASS I PAB .318+									
1901	133	558	185	112	8	64	.332	.418	.330
1903	141	613	209	130	7	61	.341	.444	.323
Total	274	1171	394	242	15	125	.336	.432	.326

	G	AB	H	R*	HR	RBI*	BA	SA	PAB
CLASS II									
PAB .285–.317									
1902	131	544	194	101	0	67	.357	.417	.309
1910	56	172	46	28	2	20	.267	.343	.291
Total	187	716	240	129	2	87	.335	.399	.304
CLASS III									
PAB .252–.284									
1905	103	384	126	57	3	37	.328	.424	.253
1906	80	310	82	46	2	30	.265	.332	.252
Total	183	694	208	103	5	67	.300	.383	.266
CLASS IV									
PAB .219–.251									
1904	153	615	185	94	3	51	.301	.374	.241
1907	150	580	187	63	4	58	.322	.424	.216
1908	125	476	127	64	2	50	.267	.347	.244
1909	123	407	107	35	0	60	.263	.310	.233
Total	551	2078	606	256	9	219	.292	.369	.233
CLASS V									
PAB .218–									
None									
Period	1195	4659	1448	730	31	498	.311	.392	.270
Other	249	1004	312	190	7	81	.311	.392	.277
Career	1444	5663	1760	920	38	579	.311	.392	.271
BEST 123+ GAMES									
1901	133	558	185	112	8	64	.332	.421	.330

Calculation of Domination Points, MTP/MVP

	AB	PAB	MVP	MTP
CLASS I	1171	.326	382	600
CLASS II	716	.304	218	
CLASS III	694	.266	185	
CLASS IV	2078	.233	484	
TOTAL	4659		1269	
CLASS V	0		0	
PERIOD	4659		1269	

When Ginger Beaumont, 23 years old, joined Pittsburgh in 1899, he took the center field job and held it for eight seasons. He was traded to the Boston Braves in 1906 and stayed with them for three years. A final trade in 1910 to the Cubs led to his final season in Chicago. Beaumont was 34 when he retired.

He was one of those relatively rare individuals who played from beginning to end in a single position. Except for two games at first base during his first major league season, he was a center fielder. How good? His career FA of .956, compared with Speaker's .971, suggests he was adequate, but not brilliant.

Beaumont had good speed and he was the fifth-best contact hitter (in a short career) in the sample group—he led the league in hits during four of his 12 seasons.

Per at Bat (PAB) 1901–19—Outfielders

	AT BAT	R PAB	HR PAB	RBI PAB	TOTAL PAB
Beaumont	4659	.157	.007	.106	.270
Sample average	4796	.141	.007	.104	.252

The ability to get on base, and to run the bases well when he got there, served him well as a scorer. Unfortunately, whatever his gifts, he ran out of gas in his early 30s, a problem he shared with many players down through the decades.

Socks Seybold

Born 1870; Height 5.11; Weight 175; T-R; B-R; Led American League: 1902–HR; 1903–2B

* = Net of home runs

	G	AB	H	R*	HR	RBI*	BA	SA	PAB
CLASS I PAB .318+									
1901	114	457	152	66	8	82	.333	.499	.341
1902	137	522	165	75	16	81	.316	.506	.330
Total	251	979	317	141	24	163	.324	.503	.335
CLASS II PAB .285–.317									
1903	137	522	156	70	8	76	.299	.462	.295
CLASS III PAB .252–.284									
1907	147	564	153	53	5	87	.271	.362	.257
CLASS IV PAB .219–.251									
1904	143	510	149	53	3	61	.292	.396	.229
1905	132	488	132	59	6	53	.270	.400	.242
1906	116	411	130	36	5	54	.316	.418	.231
Total	391	1409	411	148	14	168	.292	.404	.234
CLASS V PAB .218–									
1908	48	130	28	5	0	3	.215	.231	.062
Period	974	3604	1065	417	51	497	.296	.426	.268
Other	22	85	19	13	0	8	.224	.296	.247
Career	996	3689	1084	430	51	505	.294	.423	.267
BEST 123+ GAMES									
1902	137	522	165	75	16	81	.316	.506	.330

Calculation of Domination Points, MTP/MVP

	AB	PAB	MVP	MTP
CLASS I	979	.335	328	482
CLASS II	522	.295	154	
CLASS III	564	.257	145	
CLASS IV	1409	.234	330	
TOTAL	3474		957	
CLASS V	130		0	
PERIOD	3604		957	

Ralph Orlando (Socks) Seybold started with the Reds in 1899. He left no major league trail in 1900, but in 1901 he turned up as a right fielder for the Athletics, and there he stayed for the balance of his career. Socks retired in 1908. He was 38 years old.

Seybold played enough first base to muddy up his defensive records. The estimate is that he wasn't a strong defensive player either in terms of coverage or stability. It was his productivity that kept him on the field.

Per at Bat (PAB) 1901-19—Outfielders

	AT BAT	R PAB	HR PAB	RBI PAB	TOTAL PAB
Seybold	3604	.116	.014	.138	.268
Sample average	4796	.141	.007	.104	.252

Seybold only played for nine years, not long enough to make a deep impression on the game, but long enough to demonstrate that he was a natural power hitter, and a reliable clutch hitter.

Elmer Flick

Born 1876; Height 5.09; Weight 168; T-R; B-L; Led American League: 1904-SB; 1905-BA, SA, 3B; 1906-AB, 3B, R, SB; 1907-3B; HOF 1963

* = Net of home runs

	G	AB	H	R*	HR	RBI*	BA	SA	PAB
CLASS I PAB .318+									
1901	138	542	182	104	8	80	.336	.500	.354
1902	121	461	137	83	2	62	.297	.410	.319
Total	259	1003	319	187	10	142	.318	.459	.338
CLASS II PAB .285-.317 None									
CLASS III PAB .252-.284									
1904	150	579	177	91	6	50	.306	.453	.254
1905	131	496	152	67	4	60	.306	.466	.264
1906	157	624	194	97	1	61	.311	.439	.255
Total	438	1699	523	255	11	171	.308	.452	.257
CLASS IV PAB .219-.251									
1903	142	529	158	82	2	49	.299	.414	.251
1907	147	549	166	75	3	55	.302	.412	.242
Total	289	1078	324	157	5	104	.301	.413	.247
CLASS V PAB .218-									
1908	9	35	8	4	0	2	.229	.314	.171
1909	66	235	60	28	0	15	.255	.315	.183
1910	24	68	18	4	1	6	.265	.368	.162
Total	99	338	66	36	1	23	.254	.326	.178
Period	1085	4118	1252	635	27	440	.304	.433	.268
Other	399	1483	503	267	21	268	.339	.482	.375
Career	1484	5601	1755	902	48	708	.313	.446	.296
BEST 123+ GAMES									
1901	138	542	182	104	8	80	.336	.500	.354

Calculation of Domination Points, MTP/MVP

	AB	PAB	MVP	MTP
CLASS I	1003	.338	339	339
CLASS II	0	0	0	
CLASS III	1699	.257	437	
CLASS IV	1078	.247	266	

	AB	PAB	MVP	MTP
TOTAL	3780		1042	
CLASS V	338		0	
PERIOD	4118		1042	

As the 1901 season began, 25-year-old Elmer Flick could look back on three seasons as a right fielder with the Phillies. The two leagues fought each other in 1902 and Flick tried to jump to the Athletics. But he ended up in Cleveland and spent the rest of his career there. Because of a stomach ailment which seriously weakened him, Flick retired in 1910 at 34 years of age.

Except for 1906, when he played center field, Flick was predominantly a right fielder. He also played enough second base to clutter his defensive record for three seasons. His mixed record and his career FA of .947 suggest that defense was not his strength as a player. His bat was his most impressive credential.

PER AT BAT (PAB) 1901–19 — OUTFIELDERS

	AT BAT	R PAB	HR PAB	RBI PAB	TOTAL PAB
Flick	4118	.154	.007	.107	.268
Sample average	4796	.141	.007	.104	.252

During a relatively short career (5601 career ABs), Flick posted good BA, SA and PAB numbers, and he was fast on his feet — 20–40 steals a year. He was elected to the HOF in 1963 — 53 years after his retirement.

There is no explanation for the election of Elmer Flick. His career durability wasn't impressive; his overall record wasn't as good as others who were ignored, notably Magee.

CY SEYMOUR

Born 1872; Height 6.00; Weight 200; T-L; B-L; Led National League: 1905-BA, SA, H, 2B, 3B

* = Net of home runs

	G	AB	H	R*	HR	RBI*	BA	SA	PAB
CLASS I PAB .318+									
1905	149	581	219	87	8	113	.377	.559	.358
CLASS II PAB .285-.317									
1901	134	547	166	83	1	76	.303	.373	.293
CLASS III PAB .252-.284									
1902	134	515	157	61	5	73	.305	.404	.270
1903	135	558	191	78	7	65	.342	.471	.269
Total	269	1073	348	139	12	138	.324	.439	.269
CLASS IV PAB .219-.251									
1904	131	531	166	66	5	53	.313	.446	.234
1906	151	576	165	62	8	72	.286	.378	.247
1907	131	473	139	43	3	72	.294	.400	.249
1908	156	587	157	55	5	87	.267	.339	.250
1909	80	280	87	36	1	29	.311	.400	.236
1910	79	287	76	31	1	39	.265	.334	.247

	G	AB	H	R*	HR	RBI*	BA	SA	PAB
Total	728	2734	790	293	23	352	.289	.384	.244
CLASS V									
PAB .218-									
1913	39	73	13	2	0	10	.178	.205	.164
Period	1322	5013	1537	605	44	689	.307	.412	.267
Other	209	665	186	82	8	58	.280	.352	.223
Career	1531	5678	1723	687	52	747	.303	.405	.262
BEST 123+ GAMES									
1905	149	581	219	87	8	113	.377	.559	.358

Calculation of Domination Points, MTP/MVP

	AB	PAB	MVP	MTP
CLASS I	581	.358	208	368
CLASS II	547	.293	160	
CLASS III	1073	.269	289	
CLASS IV	2734	.244	667	
TOTAL	4935		1324	
CLASS V	73		0	
PERIOD	5008		1324	

By the time 1901 rolled around, Cy Seymour was 29 years old with five seasons behind him as a frustrated pitcher (63–57, ERA 3.70, wild as a hawk). John McGraw made an outfielder out of him in 1901 (BA .303). Seymour signed up with the Reds in 1902, where he stayed until sold back to the Giants (and his old boss, McGraw) in 1906 — by this time, 34 years old. Seymour was an experienced center fielder. He remained with the Giants until 1910, when he apparently retired. Then in 1913 he reappeared with the Boston Braves for 39 games. Seymour was 41 when he finally quit.

He had two good defensive seasons (1906, 1907), but overall his career FA (.933) is a fair indicator of his erratic fielding ability. It was his offensive potential that kept him on the field.

Per at Bat (PAB) 1901–19 — Outfielders

	AT BAT	R PAB	HR PAB	RBI PAB	TOTAL PAB
Seymour	5013	.121	.009	.137	.267
Sample average	4796	.141	.007	.104	.252

McGraw's decision to convert Seymour into an outfielder was immediately justified by his BA — he was one of nine outfielders to post a BA above .300 during the period. Indeed, in 1905 (BA .377), it appeared he was headed for a long and productive career. But after that year (he was 33), he faded quickly. His general impact on the game was fleeting.

Tommy Leach

Born 1877; Height 5.07; Weight 150; T-R; B-R; Led National League: 1902-HR; 1909/13-R

= Net of home runs

	G	AB	H	R*	HR	RBI*	BA	SA	PAB
CLASS I									
PAB .318+									
1902	135	514	144	91	6	79	.280	.442	.342
1903	127	507	151	90	7	80	.298	.438	.349

	G	AB	H	R*	HR	RBI*	BA	SA	PAB
1912	110	362	93	72	2	49	.257	.340	.340
Total	372	1383	388	253	15	208	.281	.414	.344
CLASS II									
PAB .285-.317									
1901	98	374	114	63	1	43	.305	.414	.286
CLASS III									
PAB .252-.284									
1904	146	579	149	90	2	54	.257	.335	.252
1907	149	547	166	98	4	39	.303	.404	.258
1909	151	587	153	120	6	37	.261	.368	.278
1910	135	529	143	79	4	48	.270	.357	.248
1911	108	386	92	57	3	40	.238	.324	.259
1913	130	454	131	93	6	26	.289	.423	.275
1918	30	72	14	14	0	5	.194	.306	.264
Total	849	3154	848	551	25	249	.269	.367	.262
CLASS IV									
PAB .219-.251									
1905	131	499	128	69	2	51	.257	.345	.244
1908	152	583	151	88	5	36	.259	.381	.221
Total	283	1082	279	157	7	87	.258	.364	.232
CLASS V									
PAB .218-									
1906	133	476	136	65	1	38	.286	.342	.218
1914	153	577	152	73	7	39	.263	.373	.206
1915	107	335	75	42	0	17	.224	.275	.176
Total	393	1388	363	180	8	94	.262	.339	.203
Period	1995	7381	1992	1204	56	681	.270	.372	.263
Other	160	576	154	89	6	67	.267	.344	.281
Career	2155	7957	2146	1293	62	748	.270	.370	.264
BEST 123+ GAMES									
1903	127	507	151	90	7	80	.298	.438	.349

Calculation of Domination Points, MTP/MVP

	AB	PAB	MVP	MTP
CLASS I	1383	.344	476	583
CLASS II	374	.286	107	
CLASS III	3154	.262	826	
CLASS IV	1082	.232	251	
TOTAL	5993		1660	
CLASS V	1388		0	
PERIOD	7381		1660	

Tommy Leach, 21, joined the Louisville organization in 1898 as a third baseman. When 1901 rolled around, he was starting his fourth season in major league baseball as a utility infielder with the Pirates. Playing manager Fred Clarke (a left fielder) in 1902 assigned Leach to the hot corner job, which gave the youngster a chance to play beside Honus Wagner for a short time.

In 1905, Leach's good bat at the plate and his weak glove at third provoked manager Clarke to move Leach to the outfield. Thereafter, he mostly played in the outer gardens.

Leach was traded to the Cubs in 1912. He gave them two seasons, then caught on with Cincinnati for one more. He retired for the first time in 1915, then, in 1918, returned to play 30 more games for the Pirates. He was 41 when he hung them up for the last time.

Leach spent about half his time in the outfield and the other half in various infield positions. A poor third baseman, he didn't fare much better in the outfield; he never found a defensive home during his 19-year career. But he was an above-average producer, a skill that always catches a manager's eye.

PER AT BAT (PAB) 1901-19—OUTFIELDERS

	AT BAT	R PAB	HR PAB	RBI PAB	TOTAL PAB
Leach	7381	.163	.008	.092	.263
Sample average	4796	.141	.007	.104	.252

Leach was a fair contact hitter (BA .270) with an OBP of .340. This combination plus fair speed (an average of 19 steals per year) partly explains his scoring ability. For the rest of it, it didn't hurt his numbers that he was on the same team as Honus Wagner during most of his career. The Dutchman was building records for himself and everyone near him.

The Leach record probably overstates his ability. His personal skills were not great. He was not HOF material. But he was a good general-purpose athlete who was handy to have around.

JIMMY SHECKARD

Born 1878; Height 5.09; Weight 175; T-R; B-L; Led National League: 1901-SA, 3B; 1903-HR, SB; 1911-R, BB; 1912-BB

* = Net of home runs

	G	AB	H	R*	HR	RBI*	BA	SA	PAB
CLASS I PAB .318+									
1901	133	558	197	105	11	93	.353	.536	.375
1903	139	515	171	90	9	66	.332	.476	.320
Total	272	1073	368	195	20	159	.343	.507	.349
CLASS II PAB .285-.317									
1911	156	539	149	117	4	46	.276	.388	.310
CLASS III PAB .252-.284									
1910	144	507	130	77	5	46	.256	.363	.252
CLASS IV PAB .219-.251									
1902	127	501	135	85	4	33	.269	.375	.244
1904	143	507	121	69	1	45	.239	.314	.227
1906	149	549	144	89	1	44	.262	.353	.244
1907	142	484	129	75	1	35	.267	.324	.229
1909	148	525	134	80	1	42	.255	.335	.234
1912	146	523	128	82	3	44	.245	.342	.247
1913	99	252	49	34	0	24	.194	.238	.230
Total	954	3341	840	514	11	267	.251	.333	.237
CLASS V PAB .218-									
1905	130	480	140	55	3	38	.292	.398	.200
1908	115	403	93	52	2	20	.231	.305	.184
Total	245	883	233	107	5	58	.264	.356	.193
Period	1771	6343	1720	1010	45	576	.271	.373	.257
Other	350	1266	365	230	11	181	.288	.409	.333

	G	AB	H	R*	HR	RBI*	BA	SA	PAB
Career	2121	7609	2085	1240	56	757	.274	.379	.270
BEST 123+ GAMES									
1901	133	558	197	105	11	93	.353	.536	.375

Calculation of Domination Points, MTP/MVP

	AB	PAB	MVP	MTP
CLASS I	1073	.349	374	541
CLASS II	539	.310	167	
CLASS III	507	.252	128	
CLASS IV	3341	.237	792	
TOTAL	5460		1461	
CLASS V	883		0	
PERIOD	6343		1461	

Jimmy Sheckard, 19 years of age, joined the Brooklyn Dodgers in 1897. He was still in Brooklyn when the 1901 season began after a quick side trip in 1899 to Baltimore. The two teams in 1902 again shared his services.

Sheckard settled down in left field for the Dodgers for the next three seasons. Then it was moving time for him again. The Cubs offered four players and a cash sweetener for Sheckard at the end of the 1905 season. The Dodgers took the deal and Sheckard spent the next seven years as the left fielder for the Cubs of Frank Chance.

Sheckard was sold to St. Louis in 1913 and, in the same year, he finished up in Cincinnati. He was 35 years old.

After an erratic five-year beginning during which he moved from position to position, Sheckard settled into left field and seldom left it thereafter. He was a competent outfielder; for example, during the 1905–09 period his FA was .970, as compared with .979 for Fred Clarke, a right fielder who was elected to the HOF.

Sheckard was also an above-average producer who stole an average of 27 bases a season.

Per at Bat (PAB) 1901–19—Outfielders

	AT BAT	R PAB	HR PAB	RBI PAB	TOTAL PAB
Sheckard	6343	.159	.007	.091	.257
Sample average	4796	.141	.007	.104	.252

He led the NL in SB in 1903; he was a constant base-stealing threat. This and a good on-base average (.375) were the principal offensive tools he used to good advantage and which were sufficiently admired by managers to allow him to accumulate the third highest durability rating of this elite group of outfielders. He was not an outstanding player, but he was a valuable one.

Duffy Lewis

Born 1888; Height 5.11; Weight 165; T-R; B-R

* = Net of home runs

	G	AB	H	R*	HR	RBI*	BA	SA	PAB
CLASS I									
PAB .318+									
1912	154	581	165	79	6	103	.284	.408	.324

	G	AB	H	R*	HR	RBI*	BA	SA	PAB
CLASS II									
PAB .285–.314									
1911	130	469	144	57	7	79	.307	.437	.305
CLASS III									
PAB .252–.284									
1913	149	551	164	54	0	90	.298	.397	.261
1914	146	510	142	51	2	77	.278	.398	.255
1915	152	557	162	67	2	74	.291	.382	.257
1919	141	559	152	60	7	82	.272	.365	.267
Total	588	2177	620	232	11	323	.285	.385	.260
CLASS IV									
PAB .219–.251									
1910	151	541	153	56	8	60	.283	.407	.229
CLASS V									
PAB .218–									
1916	152	563	151	55	1	55	.268	.343	.197
1917	150	553	167	54	1	64	.302	.392	.215
Total	302	1116	318	109	2	119	.285	.367	.206
Period	1325	4884	1400	533	34	684	.287	.391	.256
Other	134	467	118	41	4	71	.253	.311	.248
Career	1459	5351	1518	574	38	755	.284	.384	.255
BEST 123+ GAMES									
1912	154	581	165	79	6	103	.284	.408	.324

Calculation of Domination Points, MTP/MVP

	AB	PAB	MVP	MTP
CLASS I	581	.324	188	331
CLASS II	469	.305	143	
CLASS III	2177	.260	566	
CLASS IV	541	.229	124	
TOTAL	3768		1021	
CLASS V	1116		0	
PERIOD	4884		1021	

Duffy Lewis came to the Red Sox in 1910 when he was 22 to complete the formation of the Lewis/Speaker/Hooper outfield of Fenway Park fame. After sitting out the 1918 season, he was part of a seven-man deal that took him to the Yankees. A final trade sent him to Washington in 1921, where he ended his career at 33 years of age.

Zack Wheat, a HOF player and a contemporary of Duffy Lewis, also played left field. Lewis's career FA of .959, compared with Wheat's .966, indicates he was a competent, but not an outstanding defensive player.

Lewis had a short career—11 years—during which he was an above average producer.

Per at Bat (PAB) 1901–19—Outfielders

	AT BAT	R PAB	HR PAB	RBI PAB	TOTAL PAB
Lewis	4884	.109	.007	.140	.256
Sample average	4796	.141	.007	.104	.252

Put a man on base, and Lewis came alive. That was his primary offensive profile. A good contact hitter (BA .284), and a minor base-stealing threat with good middle-distance power,

Lewis was an asset to the lineup. He is the only member of the Lewis/Speaker/Hooper outfield to miss the HOF. It is appropriate that he was overlooked. He didn't play long enough or well enough to earn that high honor — some think Speaker is the only one who did.

JOHN TITUS

Born 1876; Height 5.09; Weight 156; T-L; B-L

* = Net of home runs

	G	AB	H	R*	HR	RBI*	BA	SA	PAB
CLASS I									
PAB .318+									
1905	147	548	169	97	2	87	.308	.436	.339
1912	141	502	155	94	5	65	.309	.446	.327
Total	288	1050	324	191	7	152	.309	.441	.333
CLASS II									
PAB .285-.317									
None									
CLASS III									
PAB .252-.284									
1906	145	484	129	66	1	56	.267	.339	.254
1907	145	523	144	69	3	60	.275	.382	.252
	290	1007	273	135	4	116	.271	.361	.253
CLASS IV									
PAB .219–251									
1903	72	280	80	36	2	32	.286	.404	.250
1908	149	539	154	73	2	46	.286	.360	.224
1913	87	269	80	28	5	33	.297	.420	.245
1910	143	535	129	88	3	32	.241	.325	.230
1911	76	236	67	27	8	18	.284	.453	.225
1904	146	504	148	56	4	51	.294	.387	.220
Total	673	2363	658	308	24	212	.278	.379	.230
CLASS V									
PAB .218-									
1909	151	540	146	66	3	43	.270	.350	.207
Period	1402	4960	1401	700	38	523	.282	.385	.254
Career	1402	4960	1401	700	38	523	.282	.385	.254
BEST 123+ GAMES									
1905	147	548	169	97	2	87	.308	.436	.339

CALCULATION OF DOMINATION POINTS, MTP/MVP

	AB	PAB	MVP	MTP
CLASS I	1050	.333	350	350
CLASS II	0	0	0	
CLASS III	1007	.253	255	
CLASS IV	2363	.230	543	
TOTAL	4420		1148	
CLASS V	540		0	
PERIOD	4960		1148	

Titus was a 27-year-old rookie when he joined the Phillies in 1903, and he stayed with that club into the 1912 season, during which he was traded to the Braves of Boston. He finished his career there — he was 35 when he retired.

He functioned exclusively as an outfielder throughout his 11-year career, and his FA of .959 suggests he was not a very good one.

Per at Bat (PAB) 1901–19—Outfielders

	AT BAT	R PAB	HR PAB	RBI PAB	TOTAL PAB
Titus	4960	.141	.008	.105	.254
Sample average	4796	.141	.007	.104	.252

Titus showed flashes of brilliance, but he couldn't sustain it. He swung a fair bat and was a consistent, if not brilliant base runner.

Red Murray

Born 1884; Height 5.11; Weight 190; T-R; B-R; Led National League: 1909-HR

* = Net of home runs

	G	AB	H	R*	HR	RBI*	BA	SA	PAB
CLASS I									
PAB .318+									
None									
CLASS II									
PAB .285-.317									
1910	149	553	153	74	4	83	.299	.476	.291
1911	140	488	142	67	3	75	.291	.426	.297
1912	143	549	152	80	3	89	.277	.413	.313
1914	86	139	31	19	0	23	.223	.309	.302
Total	518	1729	478	240	10	270	.276	.428	.301
CLASS III									
PAB .252-.284									
1909	149	570	150	67	7	84	.263	.368	.277
CLASS IV									
PAB .219-.251									
1906	46	144	37	17	1	15	.257	.438	.229
1913	147	520	139	68	2	57	.267	.331	.244
Total	193	664	176	85	3	72	.265	.354	.241
CLASS V									
PAB .218-									
1907	132	485	127	39	7	39	.262	.367	.175
1908	154	593	167	57	7	55	.282	.400	.201
1915	96	271	71	29	3	19	.262	.343	.188
1917	22	22	1	1	0	3	.045	.091	.182
Total	404	1371	366	126	17	116	.267	.372	.189
Period	1264	4334	1170	518	37	542	.270	.379	.253
Career	1264	4334	1170	518	37	542	.270	.379	.253
BEST 123+ GAMES									
1912	143	549	152	80	3	89	.277	.413	.313

Calculation of Domination Points, MTP/MVP

	AB	PAB	MVP	MTP
CLASS I	0	0	0	520
CLASS II	1729	.301	520	
CLASS III	570	.277	158	
CLASS IV	664	.241	160	
TOTAL	2963		838	
CLASS V	1371		0	
PERIOD	4334		838	

John Joseph (Red) Murray joined the Cardinals in 1906 when he was 22 years old. In 1909, as part of the trade that moved Roger Bresnahan to St. Louis, Murray found himself in the outer gardens of the New York Giants. He left them in mid-season 1915 and appeared in 51 games for the Cubs.

Murray did not play in the major leagues in 1916, but returned to the Giants in 1917 for his final 22 games. He was 33 when he retired.

Red Murray was a right fielder for most of his career — his career FA of .950 suggests that he was a competent, but not an outstanding, outfielder. His bat, more than his glove, kept his career alive.

PER AT BAT (PAB) 1901–19—OUTFIELDERS

	AT BAT	R PAB	HR PAB	RBI PAB	TOTAL PAB
Murray	4334	.119	.009	.125	.253
Sample average	4796	.141	.007	.104	.252

Murray stole over 35 bases per year for six seasons, which explains why he lasted as long as he did. Apart from speed, he was a journeyman outfielder who was fortunate to have an 11-year career.

SOLLY HOFMAN

Born 1882; Height 6.00; Weight 160; T-R; B-R

* = Net of home runs

	G	AB	H	R*	HR	RBI*	BA	SA	PAB
CLASS I PAB .318+									
1904	7	26	7	6	1	3	.269	.385	.385
1910	136	477	155	80	3	83	.325	.459	.348
Total	143	503	162	86	4	86	.322	.455	.350
CLASS II PAB .285–.317									
1912	53	178	49	35	0	20	.275	.371	.309
CLASS III PAB .252–.284									
1905	86	287	68	42	1	37	.237	.324	.279
1911	143	512	129	64	2	68	.252	.305	.262
1914	147	515	148	60	5	78	.287	.412	.278
Total	376	1314	345	166	8	183	.263	.351	.272
CLASS IV PAB .219–.251									
1906	64	195	50	28	2	18	.256	.328	.246
1908	120	411	100	53	2	40	.243	.319	.231
1909	153	527	150	58	2	56	.285	.351	.220
Total	337	1133	300	139	6	114	.265	.335	.229
CLASS V PAB .218–									
1903	3	2	0	1	0	0	.000	.000	.000
1907	134	470	126	66	1	35	.268	.311	.217
1913	28	83	19	11	0	7	.229	.337	.217
1915	109	346	81	29	0	27	.234	.298	.162
1916	11	43	13	2	0	4	.302	.465	.140

	G	AB	H	R*	HR	RBI*	BA	SA	PAB
Total	285	944	239	109	1	73	.253	.315	.194
Period	1194	4072	1095	535	19	476	.269	.352	.253
Career	1194	4072	1095	535	19	476	.269	.352	.253
BEST 123+ GAMES									
1910	136	477	155	80	3	834	.325	.461	.348

Calculation of Domination Points, MTP/MVP

	AB	PAB	MVP	MTP
CLASS I	505	.350	177	232
CLASS II	178	.309	55	
CLASS III	1314	.272	357	
CLASS IV	1133	.229	259	
TOTAL	3130		848	
CLASS V	942		0	
PERIOD	4072		848	

Arthur Frederick (Solly) Hofman entered major league baseball with Pittsburgh in 1903 at 21 years of age. Next he went to the Cubs and in 1907 played a full season with them as a utility man, thus establishing the defensive role he would fill for the balance of his career.

Hofman was traded back to the Pirates in 1912; he jumped to the Federal League in 1914, and when it folded he finished his career with the Yankees and Cubs. He was 34 when he retired in 1916.

Hofman played more outfield than anything else but was in reality a little bit of everything. Defensively, one can only say that he handled a glove well enough to put a 14-year career together.

Per at Bat (PAB) 1901–19 — Outfielders

	AT BAT	R PAB	HR PAB	RBI PAB	TOTAL PAB
Hofman	4072	.131	.005	.117	.253
Sample average	4796	.141	.007	.104	.252

Hofman had at least 500 AB in only three seasons. His career was made up of a number of part-time seasons.

John Anderson

Born 1873; Height 6.02; Weight 180; T-x; B-B; Led American League: 1906-SB

* = Net of home runs

	G	AB	H	R*	HR	RBI*	BA	SA	PAB
CLASS I PAB .318+									
None									
CLASS II PAB .285-.317									
1901	138	576	190	82	8	91	.330	.476	.314
CLASS III PAB .252-.284									
1902	126	524	149	56	4	81	.284	.385	.269

	G	AB	H	R*	HR	RBI*	BA	SA	PAB
1903	138	550	156	63	2	76	.284	.385	.256
1904	143	558	155	59	3	79	.278	.385	.253
Total	407	1632	460	178	9	236	.282	.385	.259
CLASS IV									
PAB .219-.251									
1905	125	499	139	61	1	51	.279	.361	.226
1906	151	583	158	59	3	67	.271	.343	.221
1907	87	333	96	33	0	44	.288	.348	.231
1908	123	355	93	36	0	47	.262	.315	.234
Total	486	1770	486	189	4	209	.275	.343	.227
CLASS V									
PAB .218-									
None									
Period	1031	3978	1136	449	21	536	.286	.380	.253
Other	596	2363	705	373	27	392	.298	.444	.335
Career	1627	6341	1841	822	48	928	.290	.404	.284
BEST 123+ GAMES									
1901	138	576	190	82	8	91	.330	.476	.314

Calculation of Domination Points, MTP/MVP

	AB	PAB	MVP	MTP
CLASS I	0	0	0	181
CLASS II	576	.314	181	
CLASS III	1632	.259	423	
CLASS IV	1770	.227	402	
TOTAL	3978		1006	
CLASS V	0		0	
PERIOD	3978		1006	

John Anderson was 28 in 1901, a veteran of six big league seasons, mostly as an outfielder with Brooklyn. Like so many other players of the time, he jumped to the newly-formed AL and over the next seven seasons played for Milwaukee, the Browns, Yankees, Senators and White Sox. He was 35 when he retired in 1908.

Anderson started as an outfielder, moved to first base, then came back to the outfield again, always playing some of each, depending on need. His defensive record, as a consequence, is muddled, but he was apparently capable enough to justify a 14-year career, most of it as a regular.

Anderson's bat, more than his glove, was his signature talent.

Per at Bat (PAB) 1901–19—Outfielders

	AT BAT	R PAB	HR PAB	RBI PAB	TOTAL PAB
Anderson	3978	.113	.005	.135	.253
Sample average	4796	.141	.007	.104	.252

He spent six years of his 14-year career in the deadball era, which means that his full career is not fully evaluated in a 1901–19 analysis. He was a timely and skilled contact hitter during the subject period, and a useful all-round athlete at the plate, on the bases and in the field.

WILDFIRE SCHULTE

Born 1882; Height 5.11; Weight 170; T-R; B-L; Led National League: 1910-HR; 1911-SA, HR, RBI; MVP-NL, 1911

* = Net of home runs

	G	AB	H	R*	HR	RBI*	BA	SA	PAB
CLASS I									
PAB .318+									
1904	20	84	24	14	2	11	.286	.476	.321
1911	154	577	173	84	21	100	.300	.534	.355
Total	174	661	197	98	23	111	.298	.527	.351
CLASS II									
PAB .285-.317									
1913	132	495	138	76	9	63	.279	.414	.299
1918	93	267	77	35	0	44	.288	.363	.296
Total	225	762	215	111	9	107	.282	.396	.298
CLASS III									
PAB .252-.284									
1910	151	559	168	83	10	58	.301	.460	.270
1912	139	553	146	77	13	57	.264	.423	.266
Total	290	1112	314	160	23	115	.282	.442	.268
CLASS IV									
PAB .219-.251									
1905	123	493	135	66	1	46	.274	.267	.229
1906	146	563	158	70	7	53	.281	.396	.231
1914	137	465	112	49	5	56	.241	.351	.237
1915	151	550	137	54	12	57	.249	.373	.224
Total	557	2071	542	239	25	212	.262	.349	.230
CLASS V									
PAB .218-									
1907	97	342	98	42	2	30	.287	.386	.216
1908	102	386	91	41	1	42	.236	.306	.218
1909	140	538	142	53	4	56	.264	.357	.210
1916	127	407	113	38	5	36	.278	.373	.194
1917	94	252	54	31	1	21	.214	.294	.210
Total	560	1925	498	205	13	185	.259	.347	.209
Period	1806	6531	1766	813	93	730	.270	.395	.250
Career	1806	6531	1766	813	93	730	.270	.395	.250
BEST 123+ GAMES									
1911	154	577	173	84	21	100	.300	.534	.355

CALCULATION OF DOMINATION POINTS, MTP/MVP

	AB	PAB	MVP	MTP
CLASS I	661	.351	232	459
CLASS II	762	.298	227	
CLASS III	1112	.268	298	
CLASS IV	2071	.230	476	
TOTAL	4606		1233	
CLASS V	1925		0	
PERIOD	6531		1233	

Frank Selee, manager of the 1904 Cubs, greeted 22-year-old Wildfire Schulte when he made his first appearance in a major league uniform. Schulte played his first season as a regular in left field. Selee's successor, Frank Chance, moved Schulte to right field in 1906 where he played until, in 1914, manager Hank O'Day moved him back to left.

Schulte, 34 in 1916, and no longer part of Chicago's plans, was traded to Pittsburgh. Then, in 1917, he went to the Phillies for the waiver price. He was sold in 1918 to Washington, where he retired at 36 years of age.

Schulte played all of his defensive innings in the outfield. His career FA of .966 was in the top ten of those men in the sample who spent 90 percent or more of their time in an outfield position. The evidence suggests that he was at the least an adequate defensive player.

He was slightly above average as a producer.

PER AT BAT (PAB) 1901-19—OUTFIELDERS

	AT BAT	R PAB	HR PAB	RBI PAB	TOTAL PAB
Schulte	6531	.124	.014	.112	.250
Sample average	4796	.141	.007	.104	.252

Power! The long ball was Schulte's specialty. He led the league in slugging average and triples once and in home runs twice. Only one outfielder, Cravath, hit more home runs during the subject period—and he only weighed 170 pounds. Schulte had a very useful 15-year career.

FIELDER JONES

Born 1871; Height 5.11; Weight 180; T-R; B-L

* = Net of home runs

	G	AB	H	R*	HR	RBI*	BA	SA	PAB
CLASS I PAB .318+									
1901	133	521	162	118	2	63	.311	.365	.351
CLASS II PAB .285-.317									
1902	135	532	171	98	0	54	.321	.370	.286
CLASS III PAB .252-.284									
1908	149	529	134	91	1	49	.253	.306	.267
CLASS IV PAB .219-.251									
1903	136	530	152	71	0	45	.287	.340	.219
1905	153	568	139	89	2	36	.245	.327	.224
1906	144	496	114	75	2	32	.230	.302	.220
Total	433	1594	405	235	4	113	.254	.324	.221
CLASS V PAB .218-									
1904	154	564	137	71	3	40	.243	.305	.202
1907	154	559	146	72	0	47	.261	.297	.213
1914	5	3	1	0	0	0	.333	.333	.0
1915	7	6	0	1	0	0	.0	.0	.167
Total	320	1132	284	144	3	87	.251	.300	.207
Period	1170	4308	1156	686	10	366	.268	.326	.247
Other	623	2456	768	476	10	246	.313	.381	.298
Career	1793	6764	1924	1162	20	612	.284	.346	.265
BEST 123+ GAMES									
1901	133	521	162	118	2	63	.322	.365	.351

Calculation of Domination Points, MTP/MVP

	AB	PAB	MVP	MTP
CLASS I	521	.351	183	335
CLASS II	532	.286	152	
CLASS III	529	.267	141	
CLASS IV	1594	.221	352	
TOTAL	3176		828	
CLASS V	1132		0	
PERIOD	4308		828	

Fielder Allison Jones joined the Brooklyn Dodgers in 1896 when he was 25 years old. He jumped to Chicago in the AL in 1901 and became its manager in 1904. He stayed with the team until his first retirement in 1908 — he was 37 years old. Jones appeared again when the Federal League got underway in 1914 as player manager and in 1915 he retired again — he was 44 years old.

Jones was a right fielder for Brooklyn during his first three seasons, but he was moved to center in 1899 when Willie Keeler joined the club. Except for his first year with the White Sox (1901), when he returned to right field, Jones finished his career as a middle gardener. And he was a good one (FA .962). He was also a fair offensive player:

Per at Bat (PAB) 1901–19 — Outfielders

	AT BAT	R PAB	HR PAB	RBI PAB	TOTAL PAB
Jones	4308	.159	.002	.086	.247
Sample average	4796	.141	.007	.104	.252

Jones was one of the top ten scorers in the group. A good bat, an impressive OBP (.368) and speed (359 SBs in 15 years) were his primary weapons.

Johnny Bates

Born 1882; Height 5.07; Weight 168; T-L; B-L

* = Net of home runs

	G	AB	H	R*	HR	RBI*	BA	SA	PAB
CLASS I PAB .318+ None									
CLASS II PAB .285-.317									
1910	135	498	152	88	3	58	.305	.420	.299
1911	148	518	151	88	1	60	.292	.394	.288
1912	81	239	69	44	1	28	.289	.410	.305
1914	135	361	99	59	3	42	.274	.380	.288
Total	499	1616	471	279	8	188	.291	.401	.294
CLASS III PAB .252-.284									
1913	131	407	113	57	6	45	.278	.388	.265
CLASS IV PAB .219-.251									
1907	126	447	116	50	2	47	.260	.367	.221
CLASS V PAB .218-									
1906	140	504	127	46	6	48	.252	.349	.198

	G	AB	H	R*	HR	RBI*	BA	SA	PAB
1908	127	445	115	47	1	28	.258	.324	.171
1909	140	502	146	68	2	36	.291	.371	.211
Total	407	1451	388	161	9	112	.267	.349	.194
Period	1163	3921	1088	547	25	392	.277	.376	.246
Career	1163	3921	1088	547	25	392	.277	.376	.246
BEST 123+ GAMES									
1910	135	498	152	88	3	58	.305	.420	.299

Calculation of Domination Points, MTP/MVP

	AB	PAB	MVP	MTP
CLASS I	0	0	0	475
CLASS II	1616	.294	475	
CLASS III	407	.265	108	
CLASS IV	447	.221	99	
TOTAL	2470		682	
CLASS V	1451		0	
PERIOD	3921		682	

Johnny Bates came to the Braves in 1906 when he was 24 years old. His NL career lasted nine years. He left Boston in 1909 for the Phillies. In 1911, Cincinnati was his next baseball home, followed in 1914 by the Cubs. Then in 1914 he jumped to Baltimore of the Federal League and finished up with them. He was 32 when he retired.

Bates eventually played all outfield positions (career FA, .955). He stole 21–37 times per season. Speed plus a fair bat kept him in the lineup.

Per at Bat (PAB) 1901–19—Outfielders

	AT BAT	R PAB	HR PAB	RBI PAB	TOTAL PAB
Bates	3921	.140	.006	.100	.246
Sample average	4796	.141	.007	.104	.252

He was a short-careered player with adequate defensive skills.

Davy Jones

Born 1880; Height 5.10; Weight 165; T-R; B-L

* = Net of home runs

	G	AB	H	R*	HR	RBI*	BA	SA	PAB
CLASS I									
PAB .318+									
None									
CLASS II									
PAB .285-.317									
None									
CLASS III									
PAB .252-.284									
1901	14	52	9	9	3	2	.173	.346	.269
1903	130	497	140	63	1	61	.282	.336	.252
1907	126	491	134	101	0	27	.273	.318	.261
1909	69	204	57	44	0	10	.279	.309	.265

	G	AB	H	R*	HR	RBI*	BA	SA	PAB
1910	113	377	100	77	0	24	.265	.313	.268
1911	98	341	93	78	0	19	.273	.302	.284
Total	550	1962	553	372	4	143	.272	.319	.265
CLASS IV									
PAB .219-.251									
1904	98	336	82	41	3	36	.244	.333	.238
1908	56	121	25	17	0	10	.207	.240	.223
1912	97	316	93	54	0	24	294	323	247
1914	97	352	96	56	2	22	.273	.361	.227
Total	348	1125	296	168	5	92	.263	.329	.236
CLASS V									
PAB .218-									
1902	79	292	85	45	0	17	.291	.363	.212
1906	84	323	84	41	0	24	.260	.310	.201
1913	10	21	6	2	0	0	.286	.286	.095
1915	14	49	16	6	0	4	.327	.367	.204
Total	187	685	191	94	0	45	.279	.336	.203
Period	1085	3772	1020	634	9	280	.270	.325	.245
Career	1085	3772	1020	634	9	280	.270	.325	.245
BEST 123+ GAMES									
1907	126	491	134	101	0	27	.273	.318	.261

CALCULATION OF DOMINATION POINTS, MTP/MVP

	AB	PAB	MVP	MTP
CLASS I	0	0	0	0
CLASS II	0	0	0	
CLASS III	1962	.265	520	
CLASS IV	1125	.236	266	
TOTAL	3087		786	
CLASS V	685		0	
PERIOD	3772		786	

Davy (Kangaroo) Jones in 1901 joined the new AL franchise in Milwaukee. In 1902, he started with the Browns and ended up with the Cubs in the NL. It was back to the AL again in 1906 with the Tigers, for whom he played until 1913. He spent that year with the White Sox, then jumped to the Federal League for his final two seasons. The much-traveled Jones was 35 years old when he retired in 1915.

PER AT BAT (PAB) 1901–19—OUTFIELDERS

	AT BAT	R PAB	HR PAB	RBI PAB	TOTAL PAB
Jones	3772	.168	.002	.075	.245
Sample average	4796	.141	.007	.104	.252

Jones played in over 100 games only three times in 14 years. He was a career-long substitute who just barely qualified for inclusion in this survey, and further details of his actions are of no particular interest.

MIKE MITCHELL

Born 1879; Height 6.01; Weight 185; T-R; B-R; Led National League: 1909/10–3B

* = Net of home runs

	G	AB	H	R*	HR	RBI*	BA	SA	PAB
CLASS I									
PAB .318+									
None									
CLASS II									
PAB .285–.317									
1909	145	523	162	79	4	82	.310	.430	.315
1911	142	529	154	72	2	82	.291	.427	.295
Total	287	1052	316	151	6	164	.300	.428	.305
CLASS III									
PAB .252–.284									
1910	156	583	167	74	5	83	.286	.401	.278
CLASS IV									
PAB .219–.251									
1912	157	552	156	56	4	74	.283	.377	.243
1913	135	477	126	57	5	46	.264	.369	.226
Total	292	1029	282	113	9	120	.274	.373	.235
CLASS V									
PAB .218–									
1907	148	558	163	61	3	44	.292	.382	.194
1908	119	406	90	40	1	36	.222	.281	.190
1914	131	466	119	48	3	40	.255	.343	.195
Total	398	1430	372	149	7	120	.260	.341	.193
Period	1133	4094	1137	487	27	487	.278	.380	.245
Career	1133	4094	1137	487	27	487	.278	.380	.245
BEST 123+ GAMES									
1909	145	523	162	79	4	82	.310	.430	.315

CALCULATION OF DOMINATION POINTS, MTP/MVP

	AB	PAB	MVP	MTP
CLASS I	0	0	0	321
CLASS II	1052	.305	321	
CLASS III	583	.278	162	
CLASS IV	1029	.235	242	
TOTAL	2664		725	
CLASS V	1430		0	
PERIOD	4094		725	

Mike Mitchell had a late start—he was 28 in 1907 when he joined the Cincinnati Reds. He spent six seasons as a regular with that club; then he played for the Cubs, Pirates and Senators during the final two years of his short career. He was 35 in 1914 when he retired.

PER AT BAT (PAB) 1901–19—OUTFIELDERS

	AT BAT	R PAB	HR PAB	RBI PAB	TOTAL PAB
Mitchell	4094	.119	.007	.119	.245
Sample average	4796	.141	.007	.104	.252

Mitchell ran the bases well and was a timely hitter—a sound journeyman ballplayer.

George Burns

Born 1889; Height 5.07; Weight 160; T-R; B-R; Led National League: 1913-SO; 1914-R, SB; 1915-AB; 1916-AB, R; 1917-R, BB; 1919-R, BB, SB

* = Net of home runs

	G	AB	H	R*	HR	RBI*	BA	SA	PAB
CLASS I PAB .318+ None									
CLASS II PAB .285-.317 None									
CLASS III PAB .252-.284									
1912	29	51	15	11	0	3	.294	.373	.275
1914	154	561	170	97	3	57	.303	.417	.280
1918	119	465	135	76	4	47	.290	.389	.273
Total	302	1077	320	184	7	107	.297	.403	.277
CLASS IV PAB .219-.251									
1913	150	605	173	79	2	52	.286	.370	.220
1916	155	623	174	100	5	36	.279	.368	.226
1917	152	597	180	98	5	40	.302	.412	.240
1919	139	534	162	84	2	44	.303	.404	.243
Total	596	2359	689	361	14	172	.292	.388	.232
CLASS V PAB .218-									
1911	6	17	1	2	0	0	.059	.059	.118
1915	155	622	169	80	3	48	.272	.375	.211
Total	161	639	170	82	3	48	.266	.367	.208
Period	1059	4075	1179	627	24	327	.289	.388	.240
Other	794	3166	898	520	17	243	.284	.379	.246
Career	1853	7241	2077	1147	41	570	.287	.384	.243
BEST 123+ GAMES									
1914	154	561	170	97	3	57	.303	.417	.280

Calculation of Domination Points, MTP/MVP

	AB	PAB	MVP	MTP
CLASS I	0	0	0	0
CLASS II	0	0	0	
CLASS III	1077	.277	298	
CLASS IV	2359	.232	547	
TOTAL	3436		845	
CLASS V	639		0	
PERIOD	4075		845	

George Burns, 22, joined in 1911 the Giants of McGraw. He diddled for two seasons, then, in 1913, took over the left field position, which he held for the balance of the subject period (later he moved to center and right).

Burns moved on to Cincinnati in 1922 for three seasons; then he finished his 15-year career with the Phillies in 1925. He was 36 when he quit.

George Burns was a top-of-the line left fielder. His career FA (.986) was third highest in the 48-man sample. But his production record was modest.

PER AT BAT (PAB) 1901–19 — OUTFIELDERS

	AT BAT	R PAB	HR PAB	RBI PAB	TOTAL PAB
Burns	4075	.154	.006	.080	.240
Sample average	4796	.141	.007	.104	.252

The full career of Burns (7,241 ABs) fell into the 1910–29 period — only 56 percent of it was spent in the subject period. Durability for him was not the problem that the above graphic suggests. He was a good contact hitter (BA .289) but, more importantly, he was on base about 37 percent of the time. These skills, plus speed (383 SBs in 15 years), made him the league's top scorer five times. Burns was a full cut above the journeymen of the day who had the misfortune to play in both the deadball and live-ball eras, which obscured his comparative abilities.

ZACK WHEAT

Born 1888; Height 5.10; Weight 170; T-R; B-L; Led National League: 1916-SA; 1918-BA; HOF 1959

* = Net of home runs

	G	AB	H	R*	HR	RBI*	BA	SA	PAB
CLASS I PAB .318+ None									
CLASS II PAB .285–.317 None									
CLASS III PAB .252–.284									
1912	123	453	138	62	8	57	.305	.450	.280
1914	145	533	170	57	9	80	.319	.452	.274
Total	268	986	308	119	17	137	.312	.451	.277
CLASS IV PAB .219–.251									
1910	156	606	172	76	2	53	.284	.403	.216
1911	140	534	153	50	5	71	.287	.412	.236
1913	138	535	161	57	7	64	.301	.430	.239
1915	146	528	136	59	5	61	.258	.360	.237
1916	149	568	177	67	9	64	.312	.461	.246
1918	105	409	137	39	0	51	.335	.386	.220
1919	137	536	159	65	5	57	.297	.409	.237
Total	971	3716	1095	413	33	421	.295	.410	.233
CLASS V PAB .218–									
1909	26	102	31	15	0	4	.304	.431	.186
1917	109	362	113	37	1	40	.312	.423	.215
Total	135	464	144	52	1	44	.310	.425	.209
Period	1374	5166	1547	584	51	602	.299	.419	.239
Other	1036	3940	1337	573	81	527	.339	.491	.300
Career	2410	9106	2884	1157	132	1129	.317	.450	.266
BEST 123+ GAMES									
1912	123	453	138	62	8	57	.305	.450	.280

CALCULATION OF DOMINATION POINTS, MTP/MVP

	AB	PAB	MVP	MTP
CLASS I	0	0	0	0
CLASS II	0	0	0	
CLASS III	986	.277	273	
CLASS IV	3716	.233	866	
TOTAL	4702		1139	
CLASS V	464		0	
PERIOD	5166		1139	

Zack Wheat was 21 in 1909 when he became a Dodger. He stayed with them for 18 years. Then Brooklyn sold him in 1927 to the Phillies, where he played his final season at 41 years of age.

Wheat played left field for almost his entire career and compiled a career FA of .965. Since Fred Clarke, a Hall of Fame outfielder from the same era, had an FA of .950, one must conclude that Wheat was a better than average fly-chaser.

Wheat was a good contact hitter with fair power during subject period. He was not unusually fast on his feet — 18–20 steals a year when he was young.

PER AT BAT (PAB) 1901–19 — OUTFIELDERS

	AT BAT	R PAB	HR PAB	RBI PAB	TOTAL PAB
Wheat	5166	.113	.010	.116	.239
Sample average	4796	.141	.007	.104	.252

Wheat's election to the HOF in 1959 was certainly not based upon the 11 seasons that fell into this analytical period. His full career fell into the 1910–29 period, the era that mixed dead-ball and live-ball baseball, and it must have been his career BA of .318, and his final eight years, that drew the attention of HOF electors, plus the sheer longevity of his career (ABs 9,106).

The 1910–29 period is not analyzed because answers would be meaningless, and Wheat's career is a perfect example of this. He was 21 when he entered major league baseball and 31 when the 1919 season ended. His early years should have been his best ones, and during them his BA was .300 or better in four relatively full seasons — .319 was his highest mark. In the 1920s, which should have been Wheat's declining years, his BA was consistently in the .300s, and once reached .375. This lifted his career BA from .299 in 1919, to .317 in 1927. He was a completely different player during the live-ball era.

Wheat's election to the HOF is statistically understandable, but analytically questionable.

PATSY DOUGHERTY

Born 1876; Height 6.02; Weight 190; T-R; B-L; Led American League: 1903-AB, H, R; 1904-AB, R; 1908-SB

* = Net of home runs

	G	AB	H	R*	HR	RBI*	BA	SA	PAB
CLASS I PAB .318+									
1911	76	211	61	39	0	32	.289	.422	.336
CLASS II PAB .285–.317									
None									

	G	AB	H	R*	HR	RBI*	BA	SA	PAB
CLASS III									
PAB .252–.284									
1902	108	438	150	77	0	34	.342	.397	.253
1903	139	590	195	104	4	55	.331	.424	.276
1909	139	491	140	70	1	54	.285	.391	.255
Total	386	1519	485	251	5	143	.319	.406	.263
CLASS IV									
PAB .219–.251									
1907	148	533	144	68	1	58	.270	.315	.238
1908	138	482	134	68	0	45	.278	.326	.234
Total	286	1015	278	136	1	103	.274	.320	.236
CLASS V									
PAB .218–									
1904	155	647	181	107	6	20	.280	.379	.206
1905	116	418	110	53	3	26	.263	.335	.196
1906	87	305	69	32	1	30	.226	.298	.207
1910	127	443	110	44	1	42	.248	.300	.196
Total	485	1813	470	236	11	118	.259	.336	.201
Period	1233	4558	1294	662	17	396	.284	.360	.236
Career	1233	4558	1294	662	17	396	.284	.360	.236
BEST 123+ GAMES									
1903	139	590	195	104	4	55	.331	.424	.276

Calculation of Domination Points, MTP/MVP

	AB	PAB	MVP	MTP
CLASS I	211	.336	71	71
CLASS II	0	0	0	
CLASS III	1519	.263	399	
CLASS IV	1015	.236	240	
TOTAL	2745		710	
CLASS V	1813		0	
PERIOD	4558		710	

Patrick Henry (Patsy) Dougherty started his AL career at the age of 26 in 1902, and finished it in 1911 when he was 35. Boston and New York shared the first half of his 10-year career. He spent the last half in Chicago.

Dougherty, a left fielder from beginning to end, also played a few games at third base. He was a poor fielder (FA .931)—one of the worst in the sample. But he hit well and was quick on the bases (19–47 steals per year).

Per at Bat (PAB) 1901–19—Outfielders

	AT BAT	R PAB	HR PAB	RBI PAB	TOTAL PAB
Dougherty	4558	.145	.004	.087	.236
Sample average	4796	.141	.007	.104	.252

Speed and a good bat kept Patsy going for a decade.

Amos Strunk

Born 1889; Height 6.00; Weight 175; T-L; B-L

* = Net of home runs

	G	AB	H	R*	HR	RBI*	BA	SA	PAB
CLASS I PAB .318+ None									
CLASS II PAB .285-.317									
1911	74	215	55	41	1	20	.256	.321	.288
1912	120	412	119	55	3	60	.289	.400	.286
Total	194	627	174	96	4	80	.278	.373	.287
CLASS III PAB .252-.284									
1913	93	292	89	30	0	46	.305	.425	.260
CLASS IV PAB .219-.251									
1910	16	48	16	9	0	2	.333	.375	.229
1914	122	404	111	56	2	43	.275	.342	.250
1915	132	485	144	75	1	44	.297	.427	.247
1917	148	540	152	82	1	44	.281	.361	.235
Total	418	1477	423	222	4	133	.286	.378	.243
CLASS V PAB .218-									
1908	12	34	8	4	0	0	.235	.265	.118
1909	11	35	4	1	0	2	.114	.114	.086
1916	150	544	172	68	3	46	.316	.421	.215
1918	114	413	106	50	0	35	.257	.344	.206
1919	108	378	91	42	0	30	.241	.323	.190
Total	395	1404	381	165	3	113	.271	.361	.200
Period	1100	3800	1067	513	11	372	.281	.374	.236
Other	407	1194	348	167	4	141	.291	.370	.261
Career	1507	4994	1415	680	15	513	.283	.373	.242
BEST 123+ GAMES									
1915	132	485	144	75	1	44	.297	.427	.247

Calculation of Domination Points, MTP/MVP

	AB	PAB	MVP	MTP
CLASS I	0	0	0	180
CLASS II	627	.287	180	
CLASS III	292	.260	76	
CLASS IV	1477	.243	359	
TOTAL	2396		615	
CLASS V	1404		0	
PERIOD	3800		615	

Amos Strunk joined the Athletics in 1908 when he was 19 years old. He finished the era with the same team after a brief stay with the Red Sox. In the 1920s he mostly played with the White Sox. He returned to the Athletics in 1924 and, at 35, retired.

Per at Bat (PAB) 1901–19—Outfielders

	AT BAT	R PAB	HR PAB	RBI PAB	TOTAL PAB
Strunk	3800	.135	.003	.098	.236
Sample average	4796	.141	.007	.104	.252

Strunk was mostly a center fielder — and a good one (FA .980). Offensively, speed (50+ SBs in his prime) and an adequate bat kept him in the majors. In his later years he was an active and efficient pinch hitter.

Topsy Hartsel

Born 1874; Height 5.05; Weight 155; T-L; B-L; Led American League: 1902-R, BB, SB; 1905/06/07/08-BB

* = Net of home runs

	G	AB	H	R*	HR	RBI*	BA	SA	PAB
CLASS I PAB .328+									
None									
CLASS II PAB .285–.327									
1902	137	545	154	104	5	53	.283	.391	.297
CLASS III PAB .252–.284									
1901	140	558	187	104	7	47	.335	.475	.283
CLASS IV PAB .219–.251									
1903	98	373	116	60	5	21	.311	.477	.231
1906	144	533	136	95	1	29	.255	.334	.235
1907	143	507	142	90	3	26	.280	.367	.235
1910	90	285	63	45	0	22	.221	.277	.235
1911	25	38	9	8	0	1	.237	.289	.237
Total	500	1736	466	298	9	99	.268	.364	.234
CLASS V PAB .218–									
1904	147	534	135	77	2	23	.253	.341	.191
1905	148	533	147	88	0	28	.276	.347	.218
1908	129	460	112	69	4	25	.243	.330	.213
1909	83	267	72	30	0	18	.270	.322	.180
Total	507	1794	466	264	6	94	.260	.337	.203
Period	1284	4633	1273	770	27	293	.275	.370	.235
Other	70	210	62	26	3	18	.295	.370	.224
Career	1354	4843	1335	796	30	311	.276	.370	.235
BEST 123+ GAMES									
1902	137	545	154	104	5	53	.283	.391	.297

Calculation of Domination Points, MTP/MVP

	AB	PAB	MVP	MTP
CLASS I	0	0	0	162
CLASS II	545	.297	162	
CLASS III	558	.283	158	
CLASS IV	1736	.234	406	

	AB	PAB	MVP	MTP
TOTAL	2839	726		
CLASS V	1794	0		
PERIOD	4633	726		

Tully Frederick (Topsy) Hartsel started in the NL in 1898 at the age of 24 but, like so many of his contemporaries, moved to the AL during its early formative years. He was the left fielder for the Athletics in 1902, and he held that position as a regular through the 1908 season. Then he spent his final seasons with the same club as a part-time outfielder. He ended his 14-year career in 1911 when he was 37 years old.

There was nothing defensively special about Hartsel as an outfielder (FA .956). Offensively, he was primarily a scorer who capitalized on speed and his ability to get on base; he led the league five times on base-on-balls and his OBP was .384.

PER AT BAT (PAB) 1901–19 — OUTFIELDERS

	AT BAT	R PAB	HR PAB	RBI PAB	TOTAL PAB
Hartsel	4633	.166	.006	.063	.235
Sample average	4796	.141	.007	.104	.252

Foot speed was highly valued in this period, and Hartsel had plenty of it. Without Hartsel-like players in the baseball world there would be no great RBI men.

BOB BESCHER

Born 1884; Height 6.01; Weight 200; T-L; B-B; Led National League: 1909/10-SB; 1911-SO, SB; 1912-R-SB; 1913-BB

* = Net of home runs

	G	AB	H	R*	HR	RBI*	BA	SA	PAB
CLASS I									
PAB .318+									
None									
CLASS II									
PAB .285-.317									
1908	32	114	31	16	0	17	.272	.404	.289
1918	25	60	20	12	0	6	.333	.400	.300
Total	57	174	51	28	0	23	.293	.403	.293
CLASS III									
PAB .252-.284									
1912	145	548	154	116	4	34	.281	.396	.281
CLASS IV									
PAB .219-.251									
1909	124	446	107	72	1	33	.240	.312	.238
1910	150	589	147	91	4	44	.250	.338	.236
1911	153	599	165	105	1	44	.275	.367	.250
1913	141	511	132	85	1	36	.258	.350	.239
Total	568	2145	551	353	7	157	.257	.344	.241
CLASS 5									
PAB .218-									
1914	135	512	138	76	6	29	.270	.365	.217
1915	130	486	128	67	4	30	.263	.348	.208
1916	151	561	132	72	6	37	.235	.339	.205

	G	AB	H	R*	HR	RBI*	BA	SA	PAB
1917	42	110	17	9	1	7	.155	.209	.155
Total	458	1669	415	224	17	103	.249	.341	.206
Period	1228	4536	1171	721	28	317	.258	.351	.235
Career	1228	4536	1171	721	28	317	.258	.351	.235
BEST 123+ GAMES									
1912	145	548	154	116	4	34	.281	.396	.281

Calculation of Domination Points, MTP/MVP

	AB	PAB	MVP	MTP
CLASS I	0	0	0	51
CLASS II	174	.293	51	
CLASS III	548	.281	154	
CLASS IV	2145	.241	517	
TOTAL	2867		722	
CLASS V	1669		0	
PERIOD	4536		722	

Bob Bescher came to Cincinnati in 1908 when he was 24 years old. He played left field for that club until a 1914 trade moved him to the center field of the New York Giants. He spent the final season of his 11-year career with the Indians. He was 34 when he retired in 1918.

Bescher covered left field well — his career FA of .960 was adequate.

Bescher's BA was low (.258) but he was constantly on base (OBP .353) because of his discriminating batting eye. This amplified his abilities as a runner. In his eight seasons as a regular, he never stole fewer than 27 bases. He led the league four times in his specialty.

Per at Bat (PAB) 1901–19 — Outfielders

	AT BAT	R PAB	HR PAB	RBI PAB	TOTAL PAB
Bescher	4536	.159	.006	.070	.235
Sample average	4796	.141	.007	.104	.252

Bescher's usefulness declined with his foot speed.

Dode Paskert

Born 1881; Height 5.11; Weight 165; T-R; B-R

*= Net of home runs

	G	AB	H	R*	HR	RBI*	BA	SA	PAB
CLASS I									
PAB .318+									
1907	16	50	14	9	1	7	.280	.420	.340
CLASS II									
PAB .285–.317									
None									
CLASS III									
PAB .252–.284									
1909	104	322	81	49	0	33	.252	.298	.255
1912	145	540	170	100	2	41	.315	.413	.265
1915	109	328	80	48	3	36	.244	.348	.265
1918	127	461	132	66	3	56	.286	.371	.271
Total	485	1651	463	263	8	166	.280	.366	.265

	G	AB	H	R*	HR	RBI*	BA	SA	PAB
CLASS IV									
PAB .219-.251									
1911	153	560	153	92	4	43	.273	.345	.248
1913	124	454	119	79	4	25	.262	.374	.238
1914	132	451	119	56	3	41	.264	.366	.222
1916	149	555	155	74	8	38	.279	.402	.216
Total	558	2020	546	301	19	147	.270	.372	.232
CLASS V									
PAB .218-									
1908	118	395	96	39	1	35	.243	.306	.190
1910	144	506	152	61	2	44	.300	.374	.211
1917	141	546	137	74	4	39	.251	.363	.214
1919	87	270	53	19	2	27	.196	.281	.178
Total	490	1717	438	193	9	145	.255	.340	.202
Period	1549	5438	1461	766	37	465	.269	.360	.233
Other	166	579	152	60	5	70	.263	.370	.233
Career	1715	6017	1613	826	42	535	.268	.361	.271
BEST 123+ GAMES									
1918	127	461	132	66	3	56	.286	.371	.271

Calculation of Domination Points, MTP/MVP

	AB	PAB	MVP	MTP
CLASS I	50	.340	17	17
CLASS II	0	0	0	
CLASS III	1651	.265	438	
CLASS IV	2020	.232	469	
TOTAL	3721		924	
CLASS V	1717		0	
PERIOD	5438		924	

George Henry (Dode) Paskert was 26 when he started with Cincinnati in 1907. After break-in seasons in left and right field, manager Clark Griffith gave Paskert the center field job in 1910, and there he played for the rest of his career. Paskert was sent to the Phillies in 1911 in an eight-man deal. He played regularly for them for seven years until, in 1918, another trade moved him to the Cubs for three years. He returned to Cincinnati for his final season. He was 40 when he retired in 1921.

Dode Paskert was a center fielder for most of his career. His career FA (.968) compares favorably with two HOF center fielders, Ty Cobb (.962) and Tris Speaker (.972), which indicates that glove work was one of his highest skills. But on the other side of the ball, he wasn't much of a producer.

Per at Bat (PAB) 1901-19—Outfielders

	AT BAT	R PAB	HR PAB	RBI PAB	TOTAL PAB
Paskert	5438	.141	.007	.085	.233
Sample average	4796	.141	.007	.104	.252

Over 30 percent of Paskert's ABs (four of his 15 seasons) fell into Class V.
Speed (he averaged almost 20 steals per season) plus a good glove kept him active.

Jack Graney

Born 1886; Height 5.09; Weight 180; T-L; B-L; Led American League: 1916–2B; 1917/19–BB

* = Net of home runs

	G	AB	H	R*	HR	RBI*	BA	SA	PAB
CLASS I PAB .318+									
None									
CLASS I PAB .285–.317									
None									
CLASS III PAB .252–.284									
1916	155	589	142	101	5	49	.241	.384	.263
CLASS IV PAB .219–.251									
1911	146	527	142	83	1	44	.269	.342	.243
1912	78	264	64	44	0	20	.242	.307	.242
1913	148	517	138	53	3	65	.267	.366	.234
1914	130	460	122	62	1	38	.265	.352	.220
1915	116	404	105	41	1	55	.260	.351	.240
1917	146	535	122	84	3	32	.228	.325	.222
1919	128	461	108	78	1	29	.234	.323	.234
Total	892	3168	801	445	10	283	.253	.340	.233
CLASS V PAB .218–									
1908	2	0	0	0	0	0	.0	.0	.0
1910	116	454	107	61	1	30	.236	.311	.203
1918	72	177	42	27	0	9	.237	.322	.203
Total	190	631	149	88	1	39	.236	.314	.203
Period	1237	4388	1092	634	16	371	.249	.342	.233
Other	167	317	86	54	2	31	.271	.342	.274
Career	1404	4705	1178	688	18	402	.250	.342	.235
BEST 123+ GAMES									
1916	155	589	142	101	5	49	.241	.384	.263

Calculation of Domination Points, MTP/MVP

	AB	PAB	MVP	MTP
CLASS I	0	0	0	0
CLASS II	0	0	0	
CLASS III	589	.263	155	
CLASS IV	3168	.233	738	
TOTAL	3757		893	
CLASS V	631		0	
PERIOD	4388		893	

Jack Graney was a 22-year-old pitcher when in 1908 he joined the Cleveland organization. He next appeared on the big league stage in 1910 as a right fielder. In the next season, he was moved to left, which thereafter became his permanent defensive home. Graney spent his full 14-year career with the Indians. He was 36 when he retired in 1922.

HOF left outfielders Fred Clarke and Zack Wheat had career FAs of .950 and .966, respectively. Based on that yardstick, Graney was a competent glove man — FA .953. But he wasn't much of a producer.

Per at Bat (PAB) 1901-19—Outfielders

	AT BAT	R PAB	HR PAB	RBI PAB	TOTAL PAB
Graney	4388	.144	.004	.085	.233
Sample average	4796	.141	.007	.104	.252

Graney wasn't an impressive hitter but his OBP was .354 — he was an expert "walker." He led the league twice in walks — in a full season he was commonly on base over 200 times. This, plus better-than-average speed, kept him in the business.

Harry Hooper

Born 1887; Height 5.10; Weight 168; T-R; B-L; HOF 1971

* = Net of home runs

	G	AB	H	R*	HR	RBI*	BA	SA	PAB
CLASS I PAB .318+ None									
CLASS II PAB .285-.317 None									
CLASS III PAB .252-.284									
1911	130	524	163	89	4	41	.311	.395	.256
1912	147	590	143	96	2	51	.242	.327	.253
1918	126	474	137	80	1	43	.289	.405	.262
Total	403	1588	443	265	7	135	.279	.373	.256
CLASS IV PAB .219-.251									
1913	148	586	169	96	4	36	.288	.399	.232
1914	141	530	137	84	1	40	.258	.364	.236
1915	149	566	133	88	2	49	.235	.327	.246
1917	151	559	143	86	3	42	.256	.349	.234
1919	128	491	131	73	3	46	.267	.360	.248
Total	717	2732	713	427	13	213	.261	.360	.239
CLASS V PAB .218-									
1909	81	255	72	29	0	12	.282	.325	.161
1910	155	584	156	79	2	25	.267	.327	.182
1916	151	575	156	74	1	36	.271	.350	.193
Total	387	1414	384	182	3	73	.272	.336	.182
Period	1507	5734	1540	874	23	421	.269	.358	.230
Other	801	3051	926	480	52	321	.304	.442	.280
Career	2308	8785	2466	1354	75	742	.281	.387	.247
BEST 123+ GAMES									
1918	126	474	137	80	1	43	.289	.405	.262

Calculation of Domination Points, MTP/MVP

	AB	PAB	MVP	MTP
CLASS I	0	0	0	0
CLASS II	0	0	0	
CLASS III	1588	.256	407	

	AB	PAB	MVP	MTP
CLASS IV	2732	.239	653	
TOTAL	4320		1060	
CLASS V	1414		0	
PERIOD	5734		1060	

Harry Hooper joined the Red Sox as a 22-year-old in 1909 and enjoyed himself playing alongside the center field marvel, Tris Speaker, until Speaker moved to Cleveland in 1916. At the end of the 1920 season Hooper, then 33 years old, had money troubles with management and was traded to the White Sox for two players. He spent five years in Chicago. Then, at 38, he retired in 1925.

Hooper was one of the better outfielders of the period. A right fielder in the famous Lewis/Speaker/Hooper trio of outer gardeners for the Red Sox, his career statistics (FA .966) are a good model to use when measuring defensive abilities of other right fielders. The "rump slide" that outfielders like Carl Yastrzemski later used to get under certain fly balls was originated by Hooper.

Hooper was not a formidable offensive player, but he had his talents. His BA wasn't impressive but his OBP of .368 allowed him to exercise his skills as a base runner — he averaged over 20 SBs per year. His BA, in other words, does not accurately profile his full value as an offensive player.

Per at Bat (PAB) 1901–19 — Outfielders

	AT BAT	R PAB	HR PAB	RBI PAB	TOTAL PAB
Hooper	5734	.152	.004	.074	.230
Sample average	4796	.141	.007	.104	.252

This is not HOF performance. In 1971, 46 years after he retired, Hooper was elected to the HOF. He spent 65 percent of his ABs in the subject period, too little to judge fully his HOF credentials, but sufficient to measure him during his best years against his contemporaries.

Those most familiar with Hooper's talents passed him by during the years when the memory of his skills was sharpest. He was without doubt a highly skilled defensive player, but he did not demonstrate HOF offensive skills during the subject period. His career BA of .281 is respectable, but during the subject period it was .269 — the live ball pulled his numbers up from nowhere to somewhere.

Assuming Hooper's play in the 1920s, compared to other outfielders of that era, was relatively the same as in the subject period, it appears he was a weak HOF choice.

Max Carey

Born 1890; Height 6.00; Weight 170; T-x; B-B; Led National League: 1913-AB, R, SB; 1914-AB; 1915/16/17-SB; 1918-BB, SB; HOF 1961

* = Net of home runs

	G	AB	H	R*	HR	RBI*	BA	SA	PAB
CLASS I PAB .318+									
1910	2	6	3	2	0	2	.500	.833	.667
CLASS II PAB .285–.317									
1912	150	587	177	109	5	61	.302	.394	.298

	G	AB	H	R*	HR	RBI*	BA	SA	PAB
CLASS III									
PAB .252-.284									
1911	129	427	110	72	5	38	.258	.375	.269
CLASS IV									
PAB .219-.251									
1913	154	620	172	94	5	44	.277	.371	.231
1917	155	588	174	81	1	50	.296	.378	.224
1918	126	468	128	67	3	45	.274	.348	.246
Total	435	1676	474	242	9	139	.283	.367	.233
CLASS V									
PAB .218-									
1914	156	593	144	75	1	30	.243	.347	.179
1915	140	564	143	73	3	24	.254	.333	.177
1916	154	599	158	83	7	35	.264	.374	.209
1919	66	244	75	41	0	9	.307	.365	.205
Total	516	2000	520	272	11	98	.260	.353	.191
Period	1232	4696	1284	697	30	338	.273	.366	.227
Other	1244	4667	1381	779	39	393	.296	.404	.259
Career	2476	9363	2665	1476	69	731	.285	.385	.243
BEST 123+ GAMES									
1912	150	587	177	109	5	61	.302	.394	.298

CALCULATION OF DOMINATION POINTS, MTP/MVP

	AB	PAB	MVP	MTP
CLASS I	6	.667	4	179
CLASS II	587	.298	175	
CLASS III	427	.269	115	
CLASS IV	1676	.233	390	
TOTAL	2696		684	
CLASS V	2000		0	
PERIOD	4696		684	

Maximilian (Max) Carnarius Carey was 20 years old when in 1910 he joined the Pittsburgh Pirates. He spent over 16 years with that club until, in 1926, he was sold to the Dodgers. He was 39 when in 1929 he retired after a final season in Brooklyn.

In 1911, his first as a starter, playing manager Fred Clarke put Carey in center field between himself and Owen Wilson. Clarke sat down in 1912 and gave Carey his job in left field, a situation that pertained for four seasons. In 1916, Nixey Callahan took the team over and moved Carey back to center field, the position he was born to fill.

Carey was one of the best defensive center fielders of his time. Two fellow HOF center fielders in the same general time period are compared with him below:

Player	FA	Chances per game
Carey	.966	2.8
Cobb	.962	2.4
Speaker	.971	2.8

In career assists per game and double plays per game, Carey ranks behind Speaker and Cobb in the record books. This fact must be accepted in the light of the playing environment in the deadball era. The ball was indeed dead, home runs were rare and outfielders played shallow. The above comparisons are valid for the era, but are invalid when compared with the records of modern players who operate in a completely different environment.

As brilliant as he was in the field, Carey was nowhere the equal of the same HOF center fielders offensively:

	CAREY			COBB			SPEAKER		
	AB	PAB	DP	AB	PAB	DP	AB	PAB	DP
Superstar	6	.667	4	6368	.367	2335	2764	.341	943
Star	587	.298	175	428	.311	133	1475	.297	438
Above avg.	427	.269	115	0		0	1605	.275	441
Below avg.	1676	.233	390	500	.236	118	0		0
Total	2696		684	7296		2586	5844		1822
Other	2000		0	0		0	137		0
1901–19	4696		684	7296		2586	5981		1822

About 43 percent of Carey's ABs were graded poor; zero percent for Cobb; two percent for Speaker—13 percents of Carey's ABs fell into the Superstar/Star categories; 93 percent for Cobb; 71 percent for Speaker.

PER AT BAT (PAB) 1901–19—OUTFIELDERS

	AT BAT	R PAB	HR PAB	RBI PAB	TOTAL PAB
Carey	4696	.148	.006	.073	.227
Sample average	4796	.141	.007	.104	.252

Max Carey was elected to the HOF in 1961, 32 years after his retirement, an act which the above figures do not justify. He was not an unusually gifted hitter during the period (BA .273), but his OBP was .363, which means that he had ample opportunity to exploit his major offensive talent—foot speed. His SBs led the league five times during the 10 years he spent in the subject period. And although his durability during the period was unimpressive, his career ABs were 9,363 over a full 20-year career.

Carey's selection to the HOF was based on the totality of a career that didn't end until 1929. His defensive mastery, his record as one of the game's best base stealers and his endurance overcame his productivity record and persuaded HOF electors to honor him. He wasn't a Cobb; he wasn't a Speaker. But he was a fine player.

The question persists: Where does one draw the line between a fine player and a HOF player? The distinction wasn't clear when Carey was chosen in 1961; it isn't clear today.

ROY THOMAS

Born 1874 Height 5.11; Weight 150; T-L; B-L; Led National League: 1901/02/03/04/06/07-BB

* = Net of home runs

	G	AB	H	R*	HR	RBI*	BA	SA	PAB
CLASS I PAB .318+									
None									
CLASS II PAB .285–.317									
None									
CLASS III PAB .253–.284									
1901	129	479	148	101	1	27	.309	.334	.269
1905	147	562	178	118	0	31	.317	.358	.265
Total	276	1041	326	219	1	58	.313	.347	.267

	G	AB	H	R*	HR	RBI*	BA	SA	PAB
CLASS IV									
PAB .219–.251									
1902	138	500	143	89	0	24	.286	.322	.226
1903	130	477	156	87	1	26	.327	.365	.239
1904	139	496	144	89	3	26	.290	.345	.238
1907	121	419	102	69	1	22	.243	.301	.220
1911	21	30	5	5	0	2	.167	.233	.233
Total	549	1922	550	339	5	100	.286	.333	.231
CLASS V									
PAB .218–									
1906	142	493	125	81	0	16	.254	.302	.197
1908	108	410	103	53	1	23	.251	.334	.188
1909	83	281	74	36	0	11	.263	.302	.167
1910	23	71	13	7	0	4	.183	.239	.155
Total	356	1255	315	177	1	54	.251	.309	.185
Period	1181	4218	1191	735	7	212	.282	.329	.226
Other	290	1078	346	268	0	80	.321	.349	.323
Career	1471	5296	1537	1003	7	292	.290	.333	.246
BEST 123+ GAMES									
1901	129	479	148	101	1	27	.309	.334	.269

Calculation of Domination Points, MTP/MVP

	AB	PAB	MVP	MTP
CLASS I	0	0	0	0
CLASS II	0	0	0	
CLASS III	1041	.267	278	
CLASS IV	1922	.231	444	
TOTAL	2963		922	
CLASS V	1255		0	
PERIOD	4218		922	

Thomas was 27 when the 1901 season opened with him in center field for the Phillies for the third straight year. He stayed with that club as a regular through the 1907 season. Then he moved to the Pirates and Braves for two years. He returned to the Phillies for his final two seasons. He was 37 when he retired in 1911.

Thomas was one of the finest defensive outfielders of his time. In four seasons he had 20+ assists. His area coverage was competitive with the best. His career FA of .972 was the best in the sample (Speaker's FA was .971), which is more than usually impressive because he was most active during the first decade of the century when FAs were characteristically low.

Thomas was also a valuable offensive player. He was always on base (OBP .413). His BA was also above average; he led the league in walks seven times. This combination, plus the ability to steal 20–40 bases a year, made him an above-average scorer.

Per at Bat (PAB) 1901–19 — Outfielders

	AT BAT	R PAB	HR PAB	RBI PAB	TOTAL PAB
Thomas	4218	.174	.002	.050	.222
Sample average	4796	.141	.007	.104	.252

Ray Thomas had a late start in his major league baseball career (25 years old). Had he started sooner, the talented center fielder may have developed more impressive numbers. And had he played for a more competitive organization, his PAB would have been richer. He was a very talented ballplayer.

Rube Oldring

Born 1884; Height 5.10; Weight 186; T-R; B-R

* = Net of home runs

	G	AB	H	R*	HR	RBI*	BA	SA	PAB
CLASS I PAB .318+ None									
CLASS II PAB .285–.317									
1913	136	538	152	96	5	66	.283	.394	.310
CLASS III PAB .252–.284									
1911	121	495	147	81	3	56	.297	.394	.283
CLASS IV PAB .219–.251									
1905	8	30	9	1	1	5	.300	.467	.233
1910	134	546	168	75	4	53	.308	.430	.242
1914	119	466	129	65	3	46	.277	.371	.245
Total	261	1042	306	141	8	104	.294	.405	.243
CLASS V PAB .218–									
1906	59	174	42	15	0	19	.241	.310	.195
1907	117	441	126	47	1	39	.286	.395	.197
1908	116	434	96	37	1	38	.221	.270	.175
1909	90	326	75	38	1	27	.230	.328	.202
1912	98	395	119	60	1	23	.301	.370	.213
1915	107	408	101	43	6	36	.248	.363	.208
1916	83	304	73	26	1	25	.240	.322	.171
1918	49	133	31	5	0	11	.233	.263	.120
Total	719	2615	663	271	11	218	.254	.336	.191
Period	1237	4690	1268	589	27	444	.270	.364	.226
Career	1237	4690	1268	589	27	444	.270	.364	.226
BEST 123+ GAMES									
1913	136	538	152	96	5	66	.283	.394	.310

Calculation of Domination Points, MTP/MVP

	AB	PAB	MVP	MTP
CLASS I	0	0	0	167
CLASS II	538	.310	167	
CLASS III	495	.283	140	
CLASS IV	1042	.243	253	
TOTAL	2075		560	
CLASS V	2615		0	
PERIOD	4690		560	

Rube Oldring was 21 when he joined the Yankees in 1905, only to be immediately sold to the Athletics. In 1916, the Athletics shared him with the Yankees. He retired in 1917 then returned in 1918 to play his final 49 games with the Athletics. He was 34 when he quit.

Rube Oldring was a utility player of no particular distinction. Mostly an outfielder, he also played every other position on the field except catcher and pitcher.

Per at Bat (PAB) 1901-19—Outfielders

	AT BAT	R PAB	HR PAB	RBI PAB	TOTAL PAB
Oldring	4690	.126	.006	.094	.226
Sample average	4796	.141	.007	.104	.252

Oldring could run and he was a useful pinch hitter and situation player.

Shano Collins

Born 1885; Height 6.00; Weight 185; T-R; B-R

* = Net of home runs

	G	AB	H	R*	HR	RBI*	BA	SA	PAB
CLASS I									
PAB .318+									
None									
CLASS II									
PAB .285-.317									
None									
CLASS III									
PAB .252-.284									
1912	153	575	168	73	2	79	.292	.397	.268
1915	153	576	148	71	2	83	.257	.368	.271
Total	306	1151	316	144	4	162	.275	.382	.269
CLASS IV									
PAB .219-.251									
1911	106	370	97	44	4	44	.262	.403	.249
1916	143	527	128	74	0	42	.243	.342	.220
1918	103	365	100	29	1	55	.274	.392	.233
Total	352	1262	325	147	5	141	.258	.374	.232
CLASS V									
PAB .218-									
1910	97	315	62	28	1	23	.197	.289	.165
1913	148	535	128	52	1	46	.239	.327	.185
1914	154	598	164	58	3	62	.274	.376	.206
1917	82	252	59	37	1	13	.234	.321	.202
1919	63	179	50	20	1	15	.279	.363	.201
Total	544	1879	463	195	7	159	.246	.339	.192
Period	1202	4292	1104	486	16	462	.257	.361	.225
Other	596	2094	583	238	6	221	.278	.373	.222
Career	1798	6386	1687	724	22	683	.264	.365	.224
BEST 123+ GAMES									
1915	153	576	148	71	2	83	.257	368	.271

Calculation of Domination Points, MTP/MVP

	AB	PAB	MVP	MTP
CLASS I	0	0	0	0
CLASS II	0	0	0	
CLASS III	1151	.269	310	
CLASS IV	1262	.232	293	
TOTAL	2413		603	
CLASS V	1879		0	
PERIOD	4292		603	

John Francis (Shano) Collins was 25 when he joined the White Sox in 1910. He stayed with that club throughout the subject period. During the 1920s, he moved to Boston and completed his 16-year career there. He was 40 when he retired in 1925.

Collins mostly played right field and occasionally appeared at the other outfield positions and at first base. He did well enough to last for 16 years.

Per at Bat (PAB) 1901–19—Outfielders

	AT BAT	R PAB	HR PAB	RBI PAB	TOTAL PAB
Collins	4292	.113	.004	.108	.225
Sample average	4796	.142	.006	.104	.252

He was a good glove man (FA .972) and a base-stealing threat, talents he skillfully used to maintain a 16-year career in the bigs.

Rebel Oakes

Born 1886; Height 5.08; Weight 170; T-R; B-L

*= Net of home runs

	G	AB	H	R*	HR	RBI*	BA	SA	PAB
CLASS I PAB .318+ None									
CLASS II PAB .285-.317 None									
CLASS III PAB .252-.284									
1914	145	571	178	75	7	68	.312	.415	.263
CLASS IV PAB .219-.251									
1911	154	551	145	67	2	57	.263	.319	.229
1912	136	495	139	54	3	55	.281	.358	.226
1915	153	580	161	55	0	82	.278	.336	.236
Total	443	1626	445	176	5	194	.274	.337	.231
CLASS V PAB .218-									
1909	120	415	112	52	3	28	.270	.340	.200
1910	131	468	118	50	0	43	.252	.308	.199
1913	146	537	156	59	0	49	.291	.335	.201
Total	397	1420	386	161	3	120	.272	.328	.200
Period	985	3617	1009	412	15	382	.279	.346	.224
Career	985	3617	1009	412	15	382	.279	.346	.224
BEST 123+ GAMES									
1914	145	571	178	75	7	68	.312	.415	.263

Calculation of Domination Points, MTP/MVP

	AB	PAB	MVP	MTP
CLASS I	0	0	0	0
CLASS II	0	0	0	
CLASS III	571	.263	150	

	AB	PAB	MVP	MTP
CLASS IV	1626	.231	376	
TOTAL	2197		526	
CLASS V	1420		0	
PERIOD	3617		526	

Ennis Telfair (Rebel) Oakes zipped in and out of major league baseball, starting when he was 23, quitting when he was 29. He started with the Reds in 1909, moved to the Cardinals for four seasons, then jumped to the Federal League for its two years of existence. That was it for Oakes. He was a regular during every season of his seven-year career.

Oakes was a center fielder. He had a fair arm, covered ground well, but was not as sure-handed as the better outfielders (FA .961).

Per at Bat (PAB) 1901–19—Outfielders

	AT BAT	R PAB	HR PAB	RBI PAB	TOTAL PAB
Oakes	3617	.114	.004	.106	.224
Sample average	4796	.141	.007	.104	.252

He was a timely contact hitter with good speed who probably spent as much time in baseball as he should have.

Owen Wilson

Born 1883; Height 6.02; Weight 185; T-R; B-L; Led National League: 1912–3B

*= Net of home runs

	G	AB	H	R*	HR	RBI*	BA	SA	PAB
CLASS I PAB .318+									
None									
CLASS II PAB .285–.317									
1911	148	544	163	60	12	95	.300	.472	.307
CLASS III PAB .252–.284									
1912	152	583	175	69	11	84	.300	.513	.281
CLASS IV PAB .219–.251									
1913	155	580	154	61	10	63	.266	.386	.231
1914	154	580	150	55	9	64	.259	.393	.221
Total	309	1160	304	116	19	127	.262	.390	.226
CLASS V PAB .218–									
1908	144	529	120	44	3	40	.227	.285	.164
1909	154	569	155	60	4	55	.272	.374	.209
1910	146	536	148	55	4	46	.276	.373	.196
1915	107	348	96	30	3	36	.276	.374	.198
1916	120	355	85	27	3	29	.239	.299	.166
Total	671	2337	604	216	17	206	.258	.342	.188
Period	1280	4624	1246	461	59	512	.269	.391	.223
Career	1280	4624	1246	461	59	512	.269	.391	.223
BEST 123+ GAMES									
1911	148	544	163	60	12	95	.300	.472	.307

Calculation of Domination Points, MTP/MVP

	AB	PAB	MVP	MTP
CLASS I	0	0	0	167
CLASS II	544	.307	167	
CLASS III	583	.281	164	
CLASS IV	1160	.226	262	
TOTAL	2287		593	
CLASS V	2337		0	
PERIOD	4624		593	

John Owen (Chief) Wilson (25) stepped right into the right field job with the Pittsburgh Pirates in 1908, his first year in the major leagues. He moved to the Cardinals in 1914, as a result of an eight-man trade. He retired in St. Louis in 1916 — 33 years old.

Wilson could play right field with anyone. He had one of the best arms in the business, covered his territory well and was sure-handed. His career FA of .968 puts him in the top ten of the sample. Chief was not a consistent contact hitter but he did hit for power.

Per at Bat (PAB) 1901–19 — Outfielders

	AT BAT	R PAB	HR PAB	RBI PAB	TOTAL PAB
Wilson	4624	.110	.013	.110	.223
Sample average	4796	.141	.007	.104	.252

Chief Wilson, a slow-of-foot power hitter, was a promising player until he turned 30 — then his talents leaked away.

Matty McIntyre

Born 1880; Height 5.11; Weight 175; T-L; B-L; Led American League: 1908-R

* = Net of home runs

	G	AB	H	R*	HR	RBI*	BA	SA	PAB
CLASS I PAB .318+ None									
CLASS II PAB .285–.317 None									
CLASS III PAB .252–.284									
1901	82	308	85	38	0	46	.276	.341	.273
1911	146	569	184	101	1	51	.323	.401	.269
Total	228	877	269	139	1	97	.307	.380	.270
CLASS IV PAB .219–.251									
1908	151	569	168	105	0	28	.295	.383	.234
1912	45	84	14	10	0	10	.167	.167	.238
Total	196	653	182	115	0	38	.279	.355	.234
CLASS V PAB .218–									
1904	152	578	146	72	2	44	.253	.317	.204
1905	131	495	130	59	0	30	.263	.325	.180

	G	AB	H	R*	HR	RBI*	BA	SA	PAB
1906	133	493	128	63	0	39	.260	.343	.207
1907	20	81	23	6	0	9	.284	.321	.185
1909	125	476	116	64	1	33	.244	.326	.206
1910	83	305	72	40	0	25	.236	.318	.213
Total	644	2428	615	304	3	180	.253	.326	.201
Period	1068	3958	1066	558	4	315	.269	.343	.222
Career	1068	3958	1066	558	4	315	.269	.343	.222
BEST 123+ GAMES									
1911	146	569	184	101	1	51	.323	.401	.269

Calculation of Domination Points, MTP/MVP

	AB	PAB	MVP	MTP
CLASS I	0	0	0	0
CLASS II	0	0	0	
CLASS III	877	.270	237	
CLASS IV	653	.234	153	
TOTAL	1530		390	
CLASS V	2428		0	
PERIOD	3958		390	

Matty McIntyre (21) appeared in 82 games for the 1901 Athletics. Then he disappeared for two years. He next played with Detroit in 1904 and stayed with that club through the 1910 season. He spent his last two years with the White Sox where, in 1912, he retired — 32 years old.

McIntyre played some right field toward the end of his career, but in Detroit, where he spent most of his time, he was a left fielder, sharing garden duty with Cobb and Crawford. As one might expect, given the company he was keeping, he was a good outfielder (FA .964).

Per at Bat (PAB) 1901-19 — Outfielders

	AT BAT	R PAB	HR PAB	RBI PAB	TOTAL PAB
McIntyre	3958	.141	.001	.080	.222
Sample average	4796	.141	.007	.104	.252

McIntyre had an inauspicious ten-year career.

Clyde (Deerfoot) Milan

Born 1887; Height 5.09; Weight 168; T-R; B-L; Led American League: 1911-AB; 1912/13-SB

* = Net of home runs

	G	AB	H	R*	HR	RBI*	BA	SA	PAB
CLASS I PAB .318+ None									
CLASS II PAB .285-.317									
1912	154	601	184	104	1	78	.306	.379	.304
CLASS III PAB .252-.284									
1915	153	573	165	81	2	64	.288	.346	.257

	G	AB	H	R*	HR	RBI*	BA	SA	PAB
CLASS IV									
PAB .219–.251									
1911	154	616	194	106	3	32	.315	.394	.229
1913	154	579	174	89	3	51	.301	.378	.247
1914	115	437	129	62	1	38	.295	.396	.231
1918	128	503	146	56	0	56	.290	.346	.223
1919	88	321	92	43	0	37	.287	.361	.249
Total	639	2456	735	356	7	214	.299	.376	.235
CLASS V									
PAB .218									
1907	48	183	51	22	0	9	.279	.328	.169
1908	130	485	116	54	1	31	.239	.315	.177
1909	130	400	80	35	1	14	.200	.258	.125
1910	142	531	148	89	0	16	.279	.333	.198
1916	150	565	154	57	1	44	.273	.313	.181
1917	155	579	170	60	0	48	.294	.333	.187
Total	755	2743	719	317	1	162	.262	.314	.176
Period	1701	6373	1803	858	13	518	.283	.347	.218
Other	280	986	297	129	4	82	.301	.392	.218
Career	1981	7359	2100	987	17	600	.285	.353	.218
BEST 123+ GAMES									
1912	154	601	184	104	1	78	.306	.379	.304

Calculation of Domination Points, MTP/MVP

	AB	PAB	MVP	MTP
CLASS I	0	0	0	183
CLASS II	601	.304	183	
CLASS III	573	.247	142	
CLASS IV	2456	.235	577	
TOTAL	3630		902	
CLASS V	2743		0	
PERIOD	6373		902	

Clyde Milan was called Deerfoot for good reason. From the time he joined the Washington organization in 1907 at the age of 20, until he left it in 1922 at the age of 35, he was a base-stealing menace — he led the league twice, and stole 40 or more bases five times — a talent that kept him in the lineup despite a less-than-impressive fielding record (FA .953).

Per at Bat (PAB) 1901–19 — Outfielders

	AT BAT	R PAB	HR PAB	RBI PAB	TOTAL PAB
Milan	6373	.135	.002	.081	.218
Sample average	4796	.141	.007	.104	.252

Speed plus the ability to get on base (OBP .353) was Milan's offensive headline. In an era that placed a high value on the ability to run, players like him were prized. He was also a good contact hitter and one of the most durable outfielders in the period.

WILLIE KEELER

Born 1872; Height 5.05; Weight 140; T-L; B-L; HOF 1939

* = Net of home runs

	G	AB	H	R*	HR	RBI*	BA	SA	PAB
CLASS I **PAB .318+**									
1910	19	10	3	5	0	0	.300	.300	.500
CLASS II **PAB .285–.317** None									
CLASS III **PAB .252–.284**									
1901	136	589	209	121	2	41	.355	.443	.278
CLASS IV **PAB .219–.251**									
1902	132	556	188	86	0	38	.338	.396	.223
1903	132	515	164	95	0	32	.318	.373	.247
Total	264	1071	352	181	0	70	.329	.385	.234
CLASS V **PAB .218–**									
1904	143	543	186	76	2	38	.343	.409	.214
1905	149	560	169	77	4	34	.302	.363	.205
1906	152	592	180	94	2	31	.304	.338	.215
1907	107	423	99	50	0	17	.234	.255	.158
1908	91	323	85	37	1	13	.263	.288	.158
1909	99	360	95	43	1	31	.264	.319	.208
Total	741	2801	814	377	10	164	.291	.336	.197
Period	1160	4471	1378	684	12	275	.308	.362	.217
Other	962	4114	1569	1009	22	501	.383	.481	.372
Career	2122	8585	2947	1693	34	776	.343	.419	.292
BEST 123+ GAMES									
1901	136	589	209	121	2	41	.355	.443	.278

CALCULATION OF DOMINATION POINTS, MTP/MVP

	AB	PAB	MVP	MTP
CLASS I	10	.500	5	5
CLASS II	0	0	0	
CLASS III	589	.278	164	
CLASS IV	1071	.234	251	
TOTAL	1670		420	
CLASS V	2801		0	
PERIOD	4471		420	

William Henry (Wee Willie) Keeler was 29 in 1901 with nine brilliant seasons behind him as a batsman. He broke in with the Giants and Dodgers before moving to his first NL baseball home with Baltimore. In 1899, along with his manager, Ned Hanlon, and a few teammates, Willie moved to Brooklyn for a four-year stint, which is where he was playing when the subject period began.

Willie jumped to the new AL in 1903 and accepted the money lures of New York, becoming in the process the first man in baseball history to get a $10,000 salary. Willie had seven years in the AL, then returned to the team of his pal, John McGraw. He finished his 19-year career with the Giants in 1910 — he was 38 when he retired.

Although a lefty all the way, Keeler broke in as an infielder and didn't give serious time to the outfield until 1894, when Baltimore manager Ned Hanlon put him in right field. But that didn't totally stop Keeler's unorthodox defensive assignments—in five later seasons he appeared in one or more infield positions. He was an acceptable defensive player (FA .955), but it was his ability to hit that drew attention—in 1901, his career BA was .383 (BA .424 in 1897).

Per at Bat (PAB) 1901–19—Outfielders

	AT BAT	R PAB	HR PAB	RBI PAB	TOTAL PAB
Keeler	4471	.153	.003	.061	.217
Sample average	4796	.141	.007	.104	.252

"Hit 'em where they ain't" is the phrase that immortalized Willie's batting philosophy. During the 1901–1919 period he aimed, chopped and bunted his way to one of the top ten BAs within the outfield group and, despite advancing age, continued to be an effective base stealer. He had seven seasons during the era of 100+ games, and in six of them his BA was over .300. He won no batting titles as he had in earlier years but, albeit at a less brilliant level, he continued to hit the ball with more regularity than most. At age 35, his batting skills declined sharply.

Keeler played about half of his career in the subject period. His performance therein did not justify his selection in 1939 to the HOF. But in the opinion of electors, his record over his total career did.

Based upon the above evidence, it seems obvious that the productivity of Keeler was not the reason for his election to the HOF, nor was extraordinary defensive ability a part of the equation. He, it seems, represents another instance of the "durability plus special skills" formula which can lead to a HOF appointment, regardless of productivity. In Keeler's case, the formula was easy to fill in. His career ABs were well above average for the era, which establishes the entry qualification.

Special abilities admired by baseball people? With Willie, it had to be contact hitting. His career BA of .343 is one of the ten highest in history. As further support for his selection, it didn't hurt that Willie's base-stealing talents were also impressive.

Jimmy Slagle

Born 1873; Height 5.07; Weight 150; T-R; B-L

* = Net of home runs

	G	AB	H	R*	HR	RBI*	BA	SA	PAB
CLASS I PAB .318+ None									
CLASS II PAB .285–.317 None									
CLASS III PAB .252–.284									
1903	139	543	162	104	0	44	.298	.357	.273
CLASS IV PAB .219–.251									
1905	155	568	153	96	0	37	.269	.317	.234
CLASS V PAB .218–									
1901	114	438	106	54	1	26	.242	.288	.185

	G	AB	H	R*	HR	RBI*	BA	SA	PAB
1902	115	454	143	64	0	28	.315	.357	.203
1904	120	481	125	72	1	30	.260	.333	.214
1906	127	498	119	71	0	33	.239	.279	.209
1907	136	489	126	71	0	32	258	.294	.211
1908	104	352	78	38	0	26	.222	.239	.182
Total	716	2712	697	370	2	175	.257	.301	.202
Period	1010	3823	1012	570	2	256	.265	.311	.217
Other	288	1173	328	207	0	86	.280	.337	.250
Career	1298	4996	1340	777	2	342	.268	.317	.224
BEST 123+ GAMES									
1903	139	543	162	104	0	44	.298	.357	.273

CALCULATION OF DOMINATION POINTS, MTP/MVP

	AB	PAB	MVP	MTP
CLASS I	0	0	0	0
CLASS II	0	0	0	
CLASS III	543	.273	148	
CLASS IV	568	.234	133	
TOTAL	1111		281	
CLASS V	2712		0	
PERIOD	3823		281	

Jimmy Slagle, 28 years old with two years of major league experience, spent the 1901 season with the Phillies and Braves. He was in Chicago in 1902 and he stayed with the Cubs until his retirement in 1908—he was 35 when he quit.

Slagle played a full season only once during his entire 10-year career. He played all the outfield positions without distinction (FA .950).

PER AT BAT (PAB) 1901–19—OUTFIELDERS

	AT BAT	R PAB	HR PAB	RBI PAB	TOTAL PAB
Slagle	3823	.149	.001	.067	.217
Sample average	4796	.141	.007	.104	.252

Like so many of his contemporaries, Slagle was a fair contact hitter who could run well—17 to 40 stolen bases in a year.

CHARLIE HEMPHILL

Born 1876; Height 5.09; Weight 160; T-L; B-L

* = Net of home runs

	G	AB	H	R*	HR	RBI*	BA	SA	PAB
CLASS I PAB .318+ None									
CLASS II PAB .285-.317 None									
CLASS III PAB .252-.284									
1902	128	510	157	75	6	63	.308	.418	.282

	G	AB	H	R*	HR	RBI*	BA	SA	PAB
1906	154	585	169	86	4	58	.289	.383	.253
Total	282	1095	326	161	10	121	.298	.399	.267
CLASS IV									
PAB .219–.251									
1901	136	545	142	68	3	59	.261	.332	.239
1911	69	201	57	31	1	14	.284	.338	.229
Total	205	746	199	99	4	73	.267	.334	.236
CLASS V									
PAB .218–									
1903	105	383	94	33	3	26	.245	.300	.162
1904	114	438	112	45	2	43	.256	.308	.205
1907	153	603	156	66	0	38	.259	.322	.172
1908	142	505	150	62	0	44	.297	.356	.210
1909	73	181	44	23	0	10	.243	.282	.182
1910	102	351	84	45	0	21	.239	.288	.188
Total	689	2461	640	274	5	182	.260	.315	.187
Period	1176	4302	1165	534	19	376	.271	.340	.216
Other	66	239	65	24	3	23	.272	.359	.209
Career	1242	4541	1230	558	22	399	.271	.341	.216
BEST 123+ GAMES									
1902	128	510	157	75	6	63	.308	.418	.282

Calculation of Domination Points, MTP/MVP

	AB	PAB	MVP	MTP
CLASS I	0	0	0	0
CLASS II	0	0	0	
CLASS III	1095	.267	292	
CLASS IV	746	.236	176	
TOTAL	1841		468	
CLASS V	2461		0	
PERIOD	4302		468	

Charlie Hemphill was 25 when he opened the 1901 season with the Red Sox. It was his second year in the major leagues. He stayed in the AL for the balance of his career, playing for Cleveland, St. Louis and New York. He was 35 when in 1911 he retired.

Hemphill opened his career as a right fielder and finished it in center field. He was no star in either position, as his career FA of .943 attests.

Per at Bat (PAB) 1901–19—Outfielders

	AT BAT	R PAB	HR PAB	RBI PAB	TOTAL PAB
Hemphill	4302	.124	.004	.088	.216
Sample average	4796	.141	.007	.104	.252

Hemphill was a fair contact hitter with good speed on the bases (42 steals in 1908).

Shad Barry

Born 1876; Height ?; Weight ?; T-R; B-R

* = Net of home runs

	G	AB	H	R*	HR	RBI*	BA	SA	PAB
CLASS I PAB .318+ None									
CLASS II PAB .285–.317 None									
CLASS III PAB .252–.284									
1905	152	598	182	99	1	65	.304	.371	.276
CLASS IV PAB .219–.251									
1901	78	292	69	37	1	27	.236	.288	.223
1902	138	543	156	62	3	54	.287	.363	.219
1903	138	550	152	74	1	59	.276	.344	.244
Total	354	1385	377	173	5	140	.272	.340	.230
CLASS V PAB .218–									
1904	108	385	94	43	1	28	.244	.286	.187
1906	135	516	139	63	1	44	.269	.335	.209
1907	81	292	72	30	0	19	.247	.277	.168
1908	111	335	71	29	0	16	.212	.251	.134
Total	435	1528	376	165	2	107	.246	.293	.179
Period	941	3511	935	437	8	312	.266	.325	.216
Other	159	501	137	69	2	68	.273	.365	.277
Career	1100	4012	1072	506	10	380	.267	.330	.223
BEST 123+ GAMES									
1905	152	598	182	99	1	65	.304	.371	.276

Calculation of Domination Points, MTP/MVP

	AB	PAB	MVP	MTP
CLASS I	0	0	0	0
CLASS II	0	0	0	
CLASS III	598	.276	165	
CLASS IV	1385	.230	319	
TOTAL	1983		484	
CLASS V	1528		0	
PERIOD	3511		484	

John (Shad) Barry's NL career started in 1899 and finished in 1908. He was 23 when he started with Washington (NL); then he played for the Braves, Phillies, Cubs, Reds, Cardinals and Giants before he retired.

Barry, a utility man, was mostly an outfielder but eventually played most positions during the course of his career. He used a glove well enough to keep himself in the majors for ten years.

Per at Bat (PAB) 1901–19 — Outfielders

	AT BAT	R PAB	HR PAB	RBI PAB	TOTAL PAB
Barry	3511	.124	.002	.090	.216
Sample average	4796	.141	.007	.104	.252

Shad Barry was athletic and useful during his short career.

George Browne

Born 1876; Height 5.11; Weight 160; T-R; B-L; Led National League: 1904-R

* = Net of home runs

	G	AB	H	R*	HR	RBI*	BA	SA	PAB
CLASS I								
PAB .318+								
None								
CLASS II								
PAB .285–.317								
None								
CLASS III								
PAB .252–.284								
None								
CLASS IV								
PAB .219–.251								
1901	8	26	5	2	0	4	.192	.231	.231
1902	123	497	142	71	0	40	.286	.342	.223
1903	141	591	185	102	3	42	.313	.372	.249
1904	150	596	169	95	4	35	.284	.347	.225
1905	127	536	157	91	4	39	.293	.397	.250
1911	8	12	4	1	0	2	.333	.333	.250
Total	557	2258	662	362	11	162	.293	.363	.237
CLASS V								
PAB .218–								
1906	122	477	126	61	0	38	.264	.302	.208
1907	127	458	119	49	5	32	.260	.360	.188
1908	138	536	122	60	1	33	.228	.274	.175
1909	115	432	115	46	1	16	.266	.336	.146
1910	37	134	31	18	0	4	.231	.276	.164
1912	6	5	1	0	0	0	.200	.200	.000
Total	545	2042	514	234	7	123	.252	.313	.178
Period	1102	4300	1176	596	18	285	.273	.339	.209
Career	1102	4300	1176	596	18	285	.273	.339	.209
BEST 123+ GAMES								
1905	127	536	157	91	4	39	.293	.397	.250

Calculation of Domination Points, MTP/MVP

	AB	PAB	MVP	MTP
CLASS I	0	0	0	0
CLASS II	0	0	0	
CLASS III	0	0	0	
CLASS IV	2258	.237	535	
TOTAL	2258		535	
CLASS V	2042		0	
PERIOD	4300		535	

Browne entered major league baseball at 25 years of age in 1901 with the Phillies, who, in 1902, sold him to the Giants. He spent five seasons with New York before an eight-man deal in 1908 sent him to the Braves. His stay in Boston was short. Over the next four years, Browne played for the Cubs, Senators, White Sox, Dodgers and Phillies. He retired in 1912 — 35 years old.

Browne was essentially a right fielder, and not a very good one — FA of .927. And he was not much more impressive with a bat in his hands.

PER AT BAT (PAB) 1901-19—OUTFIELDERS

	AT BAT	R PAB	HR PAB	RBI PAB	TOTAL PAB
Browne	4300	.139	.004	.066	.209
Sample average	4796	.141	.007	.104	.252

Browne, a fair contact hitter (BA .273), also ran well, a combination of talents that helped him as a scorer. But it wasn't enough to extend the career of the poor-fielding outfielder.

BURT SHOTTON

Born 1884; Height 5.11; Weight 175; T-R; B-L; Led American League: 1913-BB; 1916-AB, BB

* = Net of home runs

	G	AB	H	R*	HR	RBI*	BA	SA	PAB
CLASS I PAB .318+ None									
CLASS II PAB .285-.317 None									
CLASS III PAB .252-.284 None									
CLASS IV PAB .219-.251									
1913	147	549	163	104	1	27	.297	.373	.240
CLASS V PAB .219-									
1909	17	61	16	5	0	0	.262	.295	.082
1911	139	572	146	85	0	36	.255	.302	.212
1912	154	580	168	85	2	38	.290	.353	.216
1914	154	579	156	82	0	38	.269	.333	.207
1915	156	559	158	92	1	29	.283	.360	.218
1916	157	618	174	96	1	35	.282	.343	.214
1917	118	398	89	46	1	19	.224	.259	.166
1918	126	505	132	68	0	21	.261	.321	.176
1919	85	270	77	34	1	19	.285	.381	.200
Total	1106	4142	1116	593	6	235	.269	.331	.201
Period	1253	4691	1279	697	7	262	.273	.336	.206
Other	135	258	59	41	2	19	.229	.278	.240
Career	1388	4949	1338	738	9	281	.270	.333	.208
BEST 123+ GAMES									
1913	147	549	163	104	1	27	.297	.373	.240

CALCULATION OF DOMINATION POINTS, MTP/MVP

	AB	PAB	MVP	MTP
CLASS I	0	0	0	0
CLASS II	0	0	0	
CLASS III	0	0	0	
CLASS IV	549	.240	132	
TOTAL	549		132	
CLASS V	4142		0	
PERIOD	4691		132	

Burt Shotton joined the Browns in 1909 when he was 25 years old. He spent eight years with that organization. Then, in 1918, he moved to Washington for a year in transit to the St. Louis Cardinals. At the end of the subject period, he was still active with that club and later retired in St. Louis—he was 39 when in 1923 he ended his 14-year playing career.

Shotton split his time between center and left field. His career FA of .942 is unimpressive.

PER AT BAT (PAB) 1901–19—OUTFIELDERS

	AT BAT	R PAB	HR PAB	RBI PAB	TOTAL PAB
Shotton	4691	.149	.001	.056	.206
Sample average	4796	.141	.007	.104	.252

He was a fair contact hitter with a high on base average (OBP .365)—he led the league in walks once. In his prime, he stole 40 bases a year, hence his above-average scoring record.

Burt Shotton is most remembered as a manager.

LEE MAGEE

Born 1889; Height 5.11; Weight 165; T-R; B-B

* = Net of home runs

	G	AB	H	R*	HR	RBI*	BA	SA	PAB
CLASS I PAB .318+ None									
CLASS II PAB .285-.317 1915	121	452	146	83	4	45	.323	.436	.292
CLASS III PAB .252-.284 None									
CLASS IV PAB .219-.251 1911	26	69	18	9	0	8	.261	.304	.246
CLASS V PAB .218- 1912	128	458	133	60	0	40	.290	.354	.218
1913	136	529	140	51	2	29	.265	.327	.155
1914	162	529	150	57	2	38	.284	.353	.183
1916	131	510	131	54	3	42	.257	.325	.194
1917	87	285	57	28	0	12	.200	.225	.140
1918	119	459	133	62	0	28	.290	.394	.196
1919	124	448	121	51	1	23	.270	.346	.167
Total	887	3218	865	363	8	212	.269	.338	.181
Period	1034	3739	1029	455	12	265	.275	.349	.196
Career	1034	3739	1029	455	12	265	.275	.349	.196
BEST 123+ GAMES 1912	128	458	133	60	0	40	.290	.354	.218

Calculation of Domination Points, MTP/MVP

	AB	PAB	MVP	MTP
CLASS I	0	0	0	132
CLASS II	452	.292	132	
CLASS III	0	0	0	
CLASSS IV	69	.246	17	
TOTAL	521		149	
CLASS V	3218		0	
PERIOD	3739		149	

Leopold Christopher Hoernschemeyer somehow or another became Lee Magee by the time (1911) he reached the Cardinals. He had a nine-year career that ended in 1919. In the NL he played for the Cardinals, Cubs and Dodgers; in the Federal League, for Brooklyn; in the AL, for New York and St. Louis. He was 30 when he quit.

Magee was a utility man who spent most of his time in the outfield. His FA is meaningless because he moved so often from position to position. Like most journeymen of the time, he ran well when he got on base.

Per at Bat (PAB) 1901–19 — Outfielders

	AT BAT	R PAB	HR PAB	RBI PAB	TOTAL PAB
Magee	3739	.122	.003	.071	.196
Sample average	4796	.141	.007	.104	.252

Magee was the lowest-rated outfielder in the survey.

Outfielders — Summary in Domination Point (DP) Sequence

* Net of home runs
** HOF

Player	AB	R*	PAB HR	RBI*	TOTAL PAB	BA	SA	MTP	MVP
Avg. player	4796	.141	.007	.104	.252	.285	.382		
SUPERSTAR DP 2007+									
Cobb T**	7296	.185	.009	.160	.354	.372	.517	2470	2588
Crawford S**	9064	.133	.010	.150	.293	.311	.453	2009	2520
Magee S	7441	.138	.011	.148	.297	.291	.427	1440	2180
STAR DP 1484–2006									
Speaker T**	5981	.168	.008	.132	.308	.338	.476	1381	1822
Leach T	7381	.163	.008	.092	.263	.270	.372	583	1660
Clarke F**	5075	.178	.006	.110	.294	.302	.420	913	1492
ABOVE AVG. DP 961–1483									
Sheckard J	6343	.159	.007	.091	.257	.271	.373	541	1461
Jackson J	4411	.165	.010	.140	.315	.353	.509	1111	1388
Seymour C	5013	.121	.009	.137	.267	.307	.412	368	1324
Beaumont G	4659	.157	.007	.106	.270	.311	.392	600	1269
Schulte W	6531	.124	.014	.112	.250	.270	.395	459	1233
Titus J	4960	.141	.008	.105	.254	.282	.385	350	1148
Wheat Z**	5166	.113	.010	.116	.239	.299	.419	0	1139
Veach B	3847	.129	.005	.160	.294	.304	.424	752	1131
Cravath G	3905	.117	**.030**	.151	.298	.287	.478	720	1075
Hooper H**	5734	.152	.004	.074	.230	.269	.358	0	1060
Flick E**	4118	.154	.007	.107	.268	.304	.433	339	1042
Lewis D	4884	.109	.007	140	.256	.287	.391	331	1021
Anderson J	3978	.113	.005	.135	.253	.286	.380	181	1006
BELOW AVG. DP 438–960									
Seybold S	3604	.116	.014	.138	.268	.296	.426	482	957
Paskert D	5438	.141	.007	.085	.233	.269	.360	17	924
Thomas R	4218	.174	.002	.050	.226	.282	.329	0	922
Milan C	6373	.135	.002	.081	.218	.283	.347	183	902
Graney J	4388	.144	.004	.085	.233	.249	.342	0	893
Hofman S	4072	.131	.005	.117	.253	.269	.352	232	848
Burns G	4075	.154	.006	.080	.240	.289	.388	0	845
Murray R	4334	.119	.009	.125	.253	.270	.379	520	838
Jones F	4308	.159	.002	.086	.247	.268	.326	335	828
Jones D	3772	.168	.002	.075	.245	.270	.325	0	786
Hartsel T	4633	.166	.006	.063	.235	.275	.370	162	726
Mitchell M	4094	.119	.007	.119	.245	.278	.380	321	725
Bescher B	4536	.159	.006	.070	.235	.258	.351	51	722
Dougherty P	4558	.145	.004	.087	.236	.284	.360	71	710
			PAB		TOTAL				

Player	AB	R*	HR	RBI*	PAB	BA	SA	MTP	MVP
Carey M**	4696	.148	.006	.073	.227	.273	.366	179	684
Bates J	3921	.140	.006	.100	.246	.277	.376	475	682
Strunk A	3800	.135	.003	.098	.236	.281	.374	180	615
Collins S	4292	.113	.004	.108	.225	.257	.361	0	603
Wilson O	4624	.110	.013	.110	.223	.269	.391	167	593
Oldring R	4690	.126	.006	.094	.226	.270	.364	167	560
Browne G	4300	.139	.004	.066	.209	.273	.339	0	535
Oakes R	3617	.114	.004	.106	.224	.279	.346	0	526
Barry S	3511	.124	.002	.090	.216	.266	.325	0	484
Hemphill C	4302	.124	.004	.088	.216	.271	.340	0	468
POOR DP									
437-									
Keeler W**	4471	.153	.003	.061	.217	.308	.362	5	420
McIntyre M	3958	.141	.001	.080	.222	.269	.343	0	390
Slagle J	3823	.149	.001	.067	.217	.265	.311	0	281
Magee L	3739	.122	.003	.071	196	.275	349	132	149
Shotton B	4691	.149	.001	.056	.206	.273	.336	0	132
Average	961								
SD	522								
10 BEST PAB SEASONS									
Cobb T**-1911	591	.235	.014	.230	.479	.420	.621		
Magee S-1910	519	.200	.012	.225	.437	.331	.507		
Speaker T**1912	580	.217	.017	.152	.386	.383	.567		
Crawford S**1911	574	.178	.012	.188	.378	.378	.526		
Sheckard J-1901	558	.188	.020	.167	.375	.353	.536		
Jackson J-1912	572	.207	.005	.152	.364	.395	.579		
Seymour C-1905	581	.150	.014	.194	.358	.377	.559		
Cravath G-1913	525	.112	.036	.208	.356	.341	.568		
Schulte W-1911	577	.146	.036	.173	.355	.300	.534		
Flick E**-1901	542	.192	.015	.147	.354	.336	.500		

The year 1901 again produced some distorted results. Sheckard's best PAB after 1901 was .320 (1903). Thereafter, he was mostly a Class IV producer. Flick's record has a similar problem. After 1901, most of his numbers fell into the Class III and Class IV PAB classifications.

Except for the above comments, the 10-Best PAB Seasons list features the robust talents of superior players.

THE BEST OF THE BEST

Sample size	48
NL	27
AL	21
Most durable-top 5	Crawford, Magee, Leach, Cobb, Schulte
Top five BA	Cobb, Jackson, Speaker, Crawford, Beaumont
Top five SA	Cobb, Jackson, Cravath, Speaker, Crawford
Top five scorers (R)	Cobb, Clarke, Thomas, Speaker, Jones
Top five power hitters (HR)	Cravath, Schulte, Seybold, Wilson, Magee
Top five clutch hitters (RBI)	Cobb, Veach, Cravath, Crawford, Magee
Top five seasons	Cobb, Speaker, Magee, Crawford, Sheckard
Most talented producer (MTP)-top 5	Cobb, Crawford, Magee, Speaker, Jackson
Most valuable producer (MVP)-top 5	Cobb, Crawford, Magee, Speaker, Leach

Nine HOF players performed during the subject era: Cobb, Crawford, Speaker, Clarke, Wheat, Hooper, Flick, Carey and Keeler. And two dominant players were ignored by HOF electors: Magee and Leach. The comparative records of these men during the subject period appear below:

Player	DP Rank	AB	BA	SA	PAB	FA
LF						
Clarke (1)	6	5075	.302	.420	.294	.950
Wheat (2)	13	5166	.299	.419	.239	.966
Magee	3	7441	.291	.427	.297	.971
CF						
Cobb (2)	1	7296	.372	.517	.354	.962
Speaker (2)	4	5981	.338	.475	.308	.971
Carey (2)	34	4696	.273	.366	.227	.966
Leach	5	7381	.270	.372	.263	*.959
RF						
Crawford	2	9064	.311	.453	.293	.969
Hooper (2)	16	5734	.269	.358	.230	.966
Flick (1)	17	4118	.304	.433	.268	.947
Keeler (1)	43	4471	.308	.362	.217	.955

*As an outfielder
1) Career began in 1890s
2) Career extended into 1920s

    Cobb, Crawford, Speaker and Clarke were relatively easy HOF choices.

    Zack Wheat blossomed during the live-ball era, played effectively until the mid–1920s and accumulated more than nine thousand ABs. Presumably, those were the factors that took him to Cooperstown.

    Max Carey played until 1929 and also accumulated over nine thousand ABs. His durability plus his fielding skills were apparently his ticket to immortality.

    Hooper played extensively into the 1920s, and Flick and Keeler did the same in the 1890s. Keeler had a BA of .424 in 1897 and did almost as well in the next year, accomplishments that must have influenced HOF electors. But neither he, nor the other two, rated highly as producers during their careers.

    Why Magee was overlooked is a mystery. He was one of the most dominant players in the era. The same can be said for Leach, although not so intensively. He moved between infield and outfield, which may have worked against him.

Summary, 1901–1919

And so the review of 1901-19 ends. It was an interesting time. Rules were being finalized and offensive players were essentially measured on how well they controlled a bat and ran the bases. Power hitting was rare. What later became known as "little-ball" was the standard form of the game — get on base; steal, hit-and-run. It was exciting; it was the beginning.

These early years produced some mind-boggling numbers that gradually became more real as the game stabilized and as competitions became equalized. Large names appeared that are still a part of baseball lore — Honus Wagner and Ty Cobb, for example, led a small pack of highly talented performers.

First basemen and catchers were uninspiring in numbers, and produced few luminaries, but infielders and outfielders didn't disappoint.

Per at Bat (PAB) 1901–19
Sample Averages

	No.	AT BAT	R PAB	HR PAB	RBI PAB	TOTAL PAB	BA	SA
First Basemen	15	5072	.123	.007	.116	.246	.281	.376
Catchers	13	3210	.091	.003	.097	.191	.247	.316
Infielders	44	4832	.129	.005	.107	.241	.275	.360
Outfielders	48	4796	.141	.007	.104	.252	.285	.382

HOF choices for first basemen from the period were, from a production standpoint, controversial. Frank Chance, a part-time first baseman, was selected; Hal Chase and Harry Davis were not. It's difficult to believe that any manager of the era would not choose either of the latter two over Chance.

The same situation exists with catchers. Roger Bresnahan and Ray Schalk were chosen. No comment is made about the choice of Schalk (the 1901-19 era covered about half of his career) except to say he was not an impressive producer in his early years. But the selection of Bresnahan at the expense of Johnny Kling seems dead wrong.

Bresnahan was not a full-time catcher in the first place. Compared with relatively low-producing full-time catchers, he looks good. In any other comparison he doesn't. Kling, on the other hand, was clearly the production leader of the full-time catchers. It would have been understandable if no catchers from this era were chosen for the HOF. But if one man was to be selected, it should have been Kling, not Bresnahan.

Infielder choices were also controversial. Selecting Wagner, Lajoie, Eddie Collins and Frank Baker was easy. It wasn't much of a stretch to pick Evers in 1946, who played deeply into the 1920s — one suspects that his was the broad back that carried his partners in the famed double-play combination (Tinkers and Chance) into the HOF in the same year.

Wallace played for 18 years in the subject period. He was a superior shortstop and a weak producer. Is that a HOF combination? Jimmy Collins had a 14-year career, eight of which fell into this era. His supporters refer to him as a fielding wizard. Perhaps he was (he played for six years in the 1890s when equipment and playing conditions were poor), but his production numbers were poor. Is that a HOF combination?

Doyle and Zimmerman were not shoo-in choices for Cooperstown, but in 1901-19 they outproduced Jimmy Collins, Evers, Tinker and Wallace. They were two of the six best offensive players in the era and they were defensively adequate.

The Doyle case is especially troubling. He was a Star performer in 1901-19 — more durable than Frank Baker, and almost as productive. The second baseman's career covered the 1907-20 period. He compiled a FA of .949. Johnny Evers, a HOF second baseman from the same era, had a career FA of .953. This establishes the point that Doyle was a competent fielder. He was also about equal to Evers in durability. His MTP rating was 151 percent higher, and his MVP rating was 24 percent higher. Analysis clearly indicates the fifth-best offensive performer in 1901-19 should have been elected to the HOF.

Heinie Zimmerman was also a superior performer during the subject era. His career spanned the 1907-19 period. Primarily a third baseman (65 percent), he also played the other infield positions. His career FA was .933. HOF third baseman Frank Baker had a career FA of .943, which suggest that Zimmerman was not a fielding wizard (he failed to anchor a single position), but it's also apparent that, given his offensive skills, he was an acceptable defensive risk. And his durability (ABs) was about the same as Baker's. Over the years, HOF electors have shown a bias against men who moved from position to position. Perhaps that is why the sixth-highest rated infielder on offense was kept from the HOF. Others can reasonably disagree.

Controversy continues in the outfielder section. Picking Cobb, Crawford, Speaker and Clarke for the HOF was not difficult. In the light of the 1919 gambling scandal, the omission of Jackson is understandable (although, many believe, unfair). But thereafter, HOF decisions are not self–explanatory. Magee and Leach, for example, two of the six-best offensive outfielders, were ignored. On the other hand, Wheat, Hooper, Flick (above average), Carey (below average) and Keeler (poor) were selected.

Magee, an offensive Superstar, was primarily a left fielder. His career covered the 1904-19 period — only Sam Crawford was more durable. He compiled a FA of .971. Fred Clarke (FA .950, depressed due to playing seven years in the 1890s) and Zack Wheat (FA .966) were elected to the HOF. This comparison simply demonstrates that Magee was not an iron glove in the field. That being the case, it seems evident that this durable, high-producing and adequate fielding outfielder should have been sent to Cooperstown.

Tommy Leach's career spanned the 1898-1918 period (he actually retired in 1915 and returned for a cup of coffee in 1918). During his early years, Leach was a third baseman. But from 1909 on, he was primarily an outfielder — overall, he played about half of his games in the outfield. It seems apparent that his bat kept him in the lineup; he never completely nailed a defensive position. Presumably, that's why HOF electors turned away from him. Some might disagree because of his production record; others will understand. That's baseball.

Wheat and Hooper played well into the 1920s and both did well with the live ball. Wheat, for example, had a PAB of .239 during the subject period compared to one of .300 in the 1920s — an increase of 26 percent; Hooper went from a PAB of .230 to one of .280 — an increase of 22 percent. This, plus their general durability, could explain their selection. In fact, however, when compared with their peers during their younger years, these men were not HOF producers.

Elmer Flick was essentially a right fielder, 1898-1910. His career record as a producer is not impressive, but he had individual accomplishments that apparently drew the attention of HOF electors. He led the league in BA in 1906; triples in 1906-07; runs scored, 1906; and stolen bases, 1904-06. He was one of the nine men in the outfield sample with a BA above .300. These were good, but not conclusive, arguments for choosing Flick.

Max Carey wasn't offensively impressive in 1901-19, but his career extended to 1929 — 20 years and 9,363 ABs. A good on-base average (.361) plus speed on the bases (one of the best base stealers in history) and defensive excellence: all of this, combined with his durability, took

Carey to the HOF. Few would argue. But some would, on the grounds that no HOF player should be deficient in one of the most important aspects of the game — production.

Finally, the choice of Willie Keeler was primarily based on his performance in the 1890s (BA from .361–.424 in 1894–1900). His early numbers boosted his career BA to .343, a number that places him with baseball's elite. HOF electors couldn't turn their backs on that even though his offensive performance was mundane in 1901–19.

All Star Team-Position Players, 1901-19

The selection of the All-Star Team will be done objectively, according to the final ratings for each position, except when departures from that rule can be easily understood from the analysis.

Player	Position	Comment
Johnny Kling (1)	Catcher	Overlooked by HOF
Hal Chase	First base	Overlooked by HOF
Nap Lajoie	Second base	HOF 1937
Honus Wagner	Shortstop	HOF 1936
Frank Baker	Third Base	HOF 1955
Ty Cobb	Outfield	HOF 1936
Sam Crawford	Outfield	HOF 1957
Tris Speaker	Outfield	HOF 1937
Roger Bresnahan	Utility catcher	HOF 1945
Eddie Collins	Utility infielder	HOF 1939
Larry Doyle	Utility infielder	Overlooked by HOF
Sherry Magee*	Utility outfielder	Overlooked by HOF
Tommy Leach	Utility outfielder	Overlooked by HOF
Harry Davis	Pinch hit/utility first base	Overlooked by HOF

Magee actually rated higher than Speaker in the subject period, but Speaker's full career (ABs 10,208) was much longer and more impressive.

The above table gives readers the chance to compare the results of this analysis with the selections of HOF electors, and it presents food for argument among baseball fans. The reasons for differences have been presented elsewhere.

So ends the analysis of the records of the best offensive players during the final days of the dead-ball era. Leagues were smaller; the talent pool was smaller because the game as a way of life was not as financially attractive as it is today, except for the few top players.

The distribution of talent throughout the classification system demonstrated once again that in any endeavor, many may participate but few are excellent.

Position	Superstar	Star	Above Average	Below Average	Poor	Total
Catch	1	1	4	5	2	13
First base	0	2	5	6	2	15
Infield	3	2	15	18	6	44
Outfield	1	7	11	21	8	48
Total	5	12	35	50	18	120
%	4%	10%	29%	42%	15%	100%

Read on, argue and enjoy.

Bibliography

The Baseball Encyclopedia. 8th ed. New York: Macmillan, 1990.
baseball-reference.com
Baseball's Hall of Fame: Cooperstown: Where Legends Live Forever. Chesterfield, MO: *The Sporting News*, 1988.
Chronicle of the 20th Century. New York: Dorling Kindersley, 1987.
Daguerreotypes. 8th ed. Chesterfield, MO: *The Sporting News*, 1990.
Deadball Stars of the American League: The Society for American Baseball Research. Dulles, VA: Potomac Books, 2006.
Gammons, Peter, Gary Gillette, and Pete Palmer. *ESPN Baseball Encyclopedia.* 4th ed. New York: Sterling, 2007.
National Hall of Fame and Museum 2007 Yearbook. New York: Cooperstown.
New York Public Library Book of Chronologies. New York: Simon and Schuster, 1990.
New York Public Library Desk Reference. New York: Simon and Schuster, 1989.
New York Times Almanac. New York: *The Times*, 2007.

Index

Alexis 13
Allies 13
America 13
American League 15
Anderson, J. 132, 134, 161–162, 200
Archduke Ferdinand 14
Armistice 13

Baines, H. 9, 10
Baker, F. 16, 27, 64, 66, 70–72, 78, 91, 95, 117, 129, 130, 131, 203, 204, 205
Baltimore Orioles 44, 45, 79
Bancroft, D. 92
Barry, J. 27, 70, 72
Barry, S. 133, 195, 201
Bates, J. 132, 165–166, 201
Beaumont, G. 132, 134, 148–150, 200, 201
Beckley, J. 30
Bergen, B. 43, 60, 61, 62
Bescher, B. 133, 175–176, 200
Birth of a Nation 13
Bolsheviks 13
Boston Braves 15, 23, 30, 31, 38, 46, 48, 53, 77, 84, 85, 87, 89, 93, 95, 103, 109, 116, 127, 142, 149, 158, 166, 183, 193, 195, 196
Boston Red Sox 15, 19, 24, 27, 51, 54, 56, 71, 85, 86, 88, 90, 96, 115, 117, 120, 121, 139, 141, 144, 157, 172, 173, 180, 186, 194
Bottomley, J. 28
Bradley, B. 65, 72, 104–105, 117, 129
Bransfield, K. 17, 18, 34, 35, 40, 41
Bresnahan, R. 16, 42, 43, 44, 45, 47, 48, 62, 63, 67, 131, 134, 203, 205
Bridwell, A. 65, 126–127
Brooklyn Dodgers 15, 30, 32, 36, 48, 61, 80, 89, 93, 113, 126, 128, 156, 162, 165, 171, 181, 191, 196, 199
Brouthers, D. 28
Browne, G. 133, 196–197, 201
Burns, G. 133, 134, 169–170, 200
Burns, T. 14
Bush, D. 65, 98–100, 101, 111, 129, 130
Byrne, B. 65, 66, 123–124, 129

Carey, M. 16, 133, 134, 143, 180–182, 201, 202, 204
Caruso, E. 14
Chance, F. 16, 18, 19, 20, 22, 26, 28, 37, 40, 41, 76, 84, 101, 103, 203
Chadwick, H. 1
Chaplin, C. 14
Chase, H. 17, 18, 20, 25, 26, 30, 37, 40, 41, 203, 205
Chicago Coliseum 13

Chicago Cubs 15, 19, 32, 34, 35, 45, 46, 54, 59, 76, 77, 84, 90, 93, 95, 98, 101, 103, 104, 107, 116, 119, 127, 149, 154, 156, 161, 163, 166, 167, 168, 177, 193, 195, 196, 199
Chicago White Sox 15, 16, 26, 33, 49, 51, 53, 70, 71, 103, 115, 117, 123, 124, 138, 141, 162, 165, 167, 172, 173, 186, 189, 196
Churchill, W. 13
Cincinnati Reds 15, 24, 26, 36, 46, 52, 54, 57, 61, 71, 80, 84, 95, 101, 106, 108, 109, 114, 116, 127, 128, 138, 142, 148, 150, 153, 166, 168, 169, 176, 177, 187, 195
Clarke, F. 16, 132, 134, 142, 143, 145–147, 200, 202, 204
Cleveland Indians 15, 21, 33, 39, 51, 56, 74, 81, 91, 104, 119, 128, 138, 139, 140, 152, 176, 178, 194
Cohen, M. 1
Cobb, T. 16, 66, 69, 75, 99, 132, 134, 135–137, 138, 139, 140, 141, 143, 145, 148, 200, 201, 202, 203, 204, 205
Collins, E. 16, 27, 64, 66, 67, 69–71, 72, 74, 79, 83, 95, 103, 129, 130, 131, 203, 205
Collins, J. 16, 64, 66, 67, 72, 85–86, 91, 129, 131, 203, 204
Collins, S. 133, 185–186, 201
Connor, R. 28
Conroy, W. 65, 68, 121–122, 129
Cravath, G. 132, 134, 140–141, 148, 200, 201
Crawford, S. 16, 99, 132, 134, 136, 143, 145, 147–148, 200, 201, 202, 204, 205
Cutshaw, G. 65, 112–113, 129
Czar Nicholas II 13
Czolgosz, L. 13

Dahlen, B. 65, 93–94, 111, 129
Daubert, J. 17, 18, 33, 36, 37, 38, 40, 41
Davis, G. 64, 80–82, 129
Davis, H. 17, 18, 20, 22, 26, 27, 37, 40, 41, 203, 205
Delahanty, E. 95
Delahanty, F. 95
Delahanty, Jim 65, 94–95, 129
Delahanty, Joe 95
Delahanty, T. 95
Dempsey, J. 14
Detroit Tigers 15, 53, 56, 80, 95, 96, 99, 119, 136, 137, 144, 148, 167, 189
Devlin, A. 64, 86–87, 129
DiMaggio, J. 11
Donovan, P. 111

Dooin, R. 42, 43, 56, 57, 62, 63
Dougherty, P. 133, 171–172, 200
Doyle, L. 64, 66, 76–78, 129, 130, 131, 204, 205
Duffy, H. 142

Earned run defined 15
Elberfeld, K. 64, 79–80, 129
Ely, B. 68
Evers, J. 16, 20, 65, 66, 67, 74, 77, 78, 84, 91, 92, 96, 97, 100–103, 129–131, 203, 204

Fairbanks, D. 14
Father's Day 13
Federal League 15, 26, 30, 39, 83, 88, 95, 101, 104, 114, 117, 119, 127, 161, 165, 166, 167, 187, 199
Ferris, H. 65, 66, 120–121, 129
Fletcher, A. 65, 91–92, 101, 129
Flick, E. 16, 132, 134, 143, 145, 151–152, 200, 201, 202, 204
Foster, E. 65, 119–120
Foul balls as strikes 15

Gandil, C. 17, 18, 32, 33, 40, 41
Ganzel, J. 24, 25
Gardner, L. 65, 90–91, 129
Gehringer, C. 3
Germans 13
Gibson, G. 42, 43, 57, 58, 62.63
Gonzalez, M. 52
Graney, J. 133, 178–179, 200
Grebey, R. 2
Grebey Procedure 2
Greenberg, H. 28
Griffith, C. 24
Griffith, T. 36
Grimes, G. 113
Groh, H. 65, 105–106, 129

Hall of Fame 6, 28, 30, 41, 43, 45, 47, 48, 49, 50, 63, 66, 69, 72, 76, 78, 86, 91, 92, 100, 101, 103, 112, 131, 134, 136, 138, 140, 142, 145, 147, 152, 170, 179, 180, 191, 203
Hanlon, N. 191
Hart, M. 14
Hartsel, T. 133, 174–175, 200
Heilmann, H. 145
Hemphill, C. 133, 193–194, 201
Herzog, B. 65, 115–116, 129
Hoblitzel, R. 17, 18, 23, 24, 40, 41
Hofman, S. 132, 134, 160–161, 200
Hooper, H. 16, 133, 134, 138, 139, 143, 179–180, 200, 201, 202, 204
Huggins, M. 65, 107–108, 129, 130
Hummel, J. 65, 66, 125–126, 129

209

Index

Infield fly rule 15
Isbell, F. 65, 106–107, 129

Jackson, J. 132, 134, 136, 137–138, 141, 200, 201
Jeffries, J. 14
Jennings, H. 99, 148
Johnson, B. 15, 21, 45, 74
Johnson, J. 14
Johnson, W. 16, 66, 69, 136, 140
Jones, D. 133, 166–167, 200, 201
Jones, F. 133, 164–165, 200
Jones, S. 139
Joss, A. 16

Keeler, W. 16, 67, 133, 134, 143, 148, 191–192, 201, 202, 204, 205
Kelly, G. 28
Killefer, B. 43, 59, 60, 62
Kling, J. 42, 43, 46, 47, 62, 63, 203, 205
Konetchy, E. 17, 18, 26, 29, 30, 33, 40, 41

Lajoie, N. 16, 21, 64, 66, 67, 72–75, 95, 129, 130, 131, 140, 203, 205
Lake 90
Landis, K. 138
LaPorte, F. 65, 87–88, 129, 130
Leach, T. 132, 134, 153–155, 200, 201, 202, 204, 205
Lenin, V. 13
Leonard, D. 16
Levin, L. 13
Lewis, D. 132, 134, 139, 156–158, 200
Lobert, H. 65, 97–98, 129
Lord, B. 138
Lord, H. 65, 90, 117–118
Louisville 68, 109, 146, 154
Lowe, B. 103
Luderus, F. 17, 18, 26, 33, 34, 40, 41
Lusitania 13

Mack, C. 21, 27, 70–72, 138
Magee, L. 133, 141–144, 198–199, 200, 204, 205
Magee, S. 132, 134, 141, 201, 202
Maranville, R. 101
Marquard, R. 48
Mathewson, C. 16, 45, 48, 66, 69, 136, 140
McCarty, L. 32
McCormick, B. 101
McGann, D. 17, 18, 22, 23, 31, 40
McGinnity, J. 45
McGraw, J. 31, 45, 77, 87, 92, 191
McGuire 74
McInnis, S. 17, 18, 21, 26–28, 38, 40, 41, 70, 72, 90
McIntyre, M. 133, 188–189, 201
McKinley, W. 13
McLean, L. 42, 43, 54, 55, 62, 63
Merkle, F. 17, 18, 31, 32, 40, 41
Meyers, C. 42, 43, 47, 48, 62, 63
Milan, C. 133, 135, 189–190, 200
Miller, D. 17, 18, 22, 28, 29, 30, 40, 41
Milwaukee 122, 162, 167
Mitchell, M. 133, 168, 200

Mize, J. 28
Mollwitz, F. 24
Mother's Day 13
Mowrey, M. 65, 113–114, 128
Murphy, D. 64, 70, 82–83, 129, 130
Murray, R. 132, 134, 159–161, 200

New England League 74
New York Giants 15, 23, 26, 31, 45, 48, 49, 54, 57, 58, 76, 77, 83, 87, 92, 93, 95, 98, 105, 116, 127, 153, 160, 169, 176, 191, 195, 196
New York Yankees 15, 19, 25, 32, 56, 79, 80, 81, 88, 96, 119, 120, 122, 126, 144, 161, 162, 191, 194, 199

Oakes, R. 133, 157, 172, 184, 186–187, 201
O'Connor, J. 111
Oldring, R. 133, 184–185, 201
Olson, I. 65, 127–128
O'Neil, S. 42, 43, 55, 56, 62

Panama Canal 3
Parent, F. 65, 114–115, 129
Paskert, D. 133, 134, 176–177, 200
Pekinpaugh, R. 19
Philadelphia Athletics 15, 21, 27, 51, 56, 70–72, 74, 83, 85, 90, 136, 138, 139, 173, 175, 184, 189
Philadelphia Phillies 15, 27, 28, 30, 34, 35, 57, 59, 74, 80, 92, 98, 103, 123, 141, 142, 152, 158, 164, 166, 169, 171, 177, 183, 193, 195, 196
Pickford, M. 14
Pitcher's mound 15
Pittsburgh Pirates 15, 28, 30, 35, 58, 68, 79, 86, 98, 105, 109, 113, 114, 122, 123, 146, 149, 154, 161, 164, 168, 181, 183, 188
Plank, E. 16, 96
Pratt, D. 65, 77, 95–97, 129

Ritchey, C. 65, 109–110, 129
Romanov Dynasty 13
Roosevelt, T. 13
Russia 13
Ruth, B. 1, 6, 66, 69, 108, 136, 140

Sacrifice fly rule 15
St. Louis Browns 15, 39, 56, 59, 79, 88, 96, 111, 112, 120, 121, 162, 194, 198, 199
St. Louis Cardinals 15, 23, 28, 30, 45, 52, 54, 95, 108, 111, 114, 123, 156, 160, 187, 188, 195, 198, 199
Schaefer, G. 65, 99, 103, 118–119
Schalk, R. 7, 16, 42, 43, 45, 48–50, 56, 62, 63, 70, 203
Schreckengost, O. 42, 43, 50, 51, 62, 63
Schulte, W. 133, 134, 163–164, 200, 201
Selective Service, 1917 16
Selee, F. 101, 103
Sennett, M. 14
Seybold, A. 132, 134, 136, 150–151, 200, 201
Seymour, C. 132, 152–53, 200, 201

Sheckard, J. 132, 134, 155–156, 200, 201
Shotton, B. 133, 197–198
Siberia 13
Slagle, J. 133, 192–193, 201
Smith, R. 65, 88–89, 122
Society for American Baseball Research (SABR) 2
Soviet Union 13
Spalding, A.G. 1
Spalding Guide 1
Speaker, T. 16, 67, 132, 134, 136, 138–140, 141, 143, 200, 201, 202, 204, 205
Stalin, J. 13
Steinfeldt, H. 64, 76, 83–84, 129
Stengel, C. 113
Stovall, G. 17, 18, 38, 39, 40, 111
Strunk, A. 133, 173–174, 201
Sullivan, B. 42, 43, 52, 53, 62, 63

Taft, W. 13
Tenney, F. 17, 18, 31, 37–38, 40
Terry, B. 28
Third-strike bunt rule 15
Thomas, F. 139, 200, 201
Thomas, R. 133, 182–184
Tinker, J. 16, 20, 65, 66, 67, 68, 78, 84, 91, 92, 99, 100–103, 129, 130, 131, 203, 204
Titus, J. 132, 134, 158–159, 200
Trotsky, L. 13

United States 13

Veach, B. 132, 134, 144–145, 148, 200

Waddell, R. 16
Wagner, H. 15, 16, 64, 66, 67–69, 70, 72, 95, 103, 109, 111, 129, 130, 131, 136, 140, 203, 205
Wallace, B. 16, 65, 66, 67, 68, 78, 91, 92, 100, 110–112, 129, 130, 131, 203, 204
Walsh, E. 15, 16
Washington Senators 15, 33, 44, 88, 95, 99, 119, 120, 122, 139, 141, 144, 157, 162, 164, 168, 190, 195, 196, 198
Weaver, B. 65, 124–125
Western League 15
Wheat, Z. 132, 134, 143, 145, 170–171, 200, 204
White Sox scandal 16
Willard, J. 14
Williams, J. 64, 78–79, 129, 130
Williams, T. 11
Wilson, O. 133, 134, 187–188, 201
Wilson, W. 13
Wingo, I. 42, 43, 51, 52, 62, 63
Wolverton, H. 19
World Series 15, 70, 71, 86, 138
World War I 3, 13

Young, C. 15, 140

Zimmerman, H. 64, 66, 75–77, 129, 130, 131

www.ingramcontent.com/pod-product-compliance
Lightning Source LLC
Chambersburg PA
CBHW081555300426
44116CB00015B/2890